THE UNKNOWN CITY

THE
UNKNOWN CITY

*Lives of Poor
and Working-Class
Young Adults*

Michelle Fine and
Lois Weis

Beacon Press   Boston

Beacon Press
25 Beacon Street
Boston, Massachusetts 02108-2892
www.beacon.org

Beacon Press books
are published under the auspices of
the Unitarian Universalist Association of Congregations.

03 02 01 00 99   8 7 6 5 4 3 2

This book is printed on recycled acid-free paper that contains at least
20 percent postconsumer waste and meets the uncoated paper ANSI/NISO
specifications for permanence as revised in 1992.

Text design by Lucinda L. Hitchcock
Composition by Wilsted & Taylor Publishing Services

Chapter 2 was published in a somewhat different form in the *Anthropology and
Education Review*. A version of the Epilogue was previously published in *Qualitative
Inquiry,* and a more theoretically based version of chapter 3 was published in *Off White*
(Routledge, 1997).

"nuyorican" by Tato Laviera is reprinted with permission from the publisher of
AmeRícan (Houston: Arte Público Press—University of Houston, 1985).

LIBRARY OF CONGRESS CATALOGING-IN-PUBLICATION DATA
The unknown city : lives of poor and working-class young adults / [compiled by]
Michelle Fine and Lois Weis.
     p.   cm.
   Includes bibliographical references and index.
   ISBN 0-8070-4112-2 (cloth)
   ISBN 0-8070-4113-0 (paper)
     1. Young adults – New York (State) – Buffalo – Social conditions.   2. Young
adults – New Jersey – Jersey City – Social conditions.   3. Working class – New York
(State) – Buffalo.   4. Working class – New Jersey – Jersey City.   5. Urban poor – New
York (State) – Buffalo.   6. Urban poor – New Jersey – Jersey City.   7. Buffalo (N.Y.) –
Social conditions.   8. Buffalo (N.Y.) – Economic conditions.   9. Jersey City (N.J.) –
Social conditions.   I. Fine, Michelle.   II. Weis, Lois.
HQ799.73.B83U55   1998
305.235'0973 – dc21   97-37193

It's been a busy year — lots of graduations [referring to her daughter's and nephew's graduation from high school]. But I tell you, I'm so happy for these kids. I just hope they do the right thing and go to college. 'Cause there's nothing out here . . . nothing, I tell you. I just hate to turn on the news, 'cause every time you turn around, somebody out here is getting killed.

DIANE, AN AFRICAN AMERICAN
WOMAN IN BUFFALO

Contents

THIS PROJECT COULD NOT HAVE BEEN COMPLETED WITHOUT THE HELP OF OUR
STUDENTS. THEIR NAMES FOLLOW THE CHAPTERS TO WHICH THEY CONTRIBUTED.

Acknowledgments

This volume could not have happened without the intellectual and personal support offered by so many. The Spencer Foundation has been and continues to be very generous in funding our work and exhibits deep commitment to both scholarship on and justice in the American mosaic. Thanks especially to Rebecca Barr, senior program officer, and Pat Graham, president, who are enormously supportive of our work.

Many colleagues and friends have contributed to our thinking both before and over the duration of this project. While too numerous to mention here, we would like to thank, in particular, Phil Altbach, Michael Apple, Rina Benmayor, Ellen Grant Bishop, Kathy Borman, Kathy Boudin, Linda Brodkey, Hank Bromley, Arthur Brown, Steve Brown, Dennis Carlson, Cathie Cornbleth, Linda Croglia, Joe Doria, Catherine Emihovich, Henry Giroux, Marilyn Gittell, Maxine Greene, Liz Huckabone, Lourdes Iglesias, Michael Katz, Liz Kennedy, Carolyn Korsmeyer, Demie Kurz, Marki LeCompte, Isabel Marcus, Cameron McCarthy, Peter McClaren, Suzanne Ouellette, David Perry, Dolores Perry, Robert Perry, Hugh Petrie, LeAdelle Phelps, Linda Powell, Maxine Seller, Mwalimu Shujaa, Sheila Slaughter, Barbara Williams, Scott Williams, and William Julius Wilson.

We are indeed fortunate to have had talented graduate assistants working with us, helping to conceptualize the project, doing much of the interviewing, coding and analyzing data and, at times, writing. Thanks especially to Corrine Bertram, Craig Centrié, Kenny Foster, Julia Marusza, Rukiyaa Morton, Amira Proweller, Rosemarie Roberts, Tracey Shepherd, and Juan Valentin-Juarbe who coauthored some of the original manuscripts from which chapters 3, 4, 5, 7, 8, and 10 have been drawn. Thanks also to Judi Addelston, Richard Barry, Cecilia Castelino, Andy Enriques, Matt Gladden, Sarah Ingersoll, Elise Nawrocki, and Mun Wong. The full manuscript was expertly typed by Barbara Fago, who gave us unbelievably fast turnaround time on chapters and put up with out never-ending changes. Pat Glinski, Carol Norris,

Jenni Hoffman, Eddie Thompson and Linda Pogorzelski deserve our thanks as well for their contributions.

Our final thanks are reserved for those most deeply connected to us and to our work. We cannot begin to express our gratitude to those people who let us into their lives so that we could tell this story of America at the turn of the century. They are living trying lives in trying times. We can only hope that this volume has an impact on those policies and practices which undercut their attempts to live productive lives in peace and justice. To Andrew Hrycyna, our editor at Beacon, we express our profound gratitude. Andy encouraged us to tell a complex story simply, working with us chapter by chapter in order to achieve this end. This manuscript, in its final form, reflects him almost as much as it does us, and we deeply appreciate his insight and ability to ask the questions that force our thinking.

Finally, we would like to thank our families, without whom our lives would be far less rich. Tereffe Asrat and David Surrey offered intellectual and emotional support to Lois and Michelle, respectively, reading drafts of the manuscript and engaging in constant dialogue about America at the turn of the century. We weave their insights throughout the volume and have profited deeply from their contributions. Their love, encouragement, and respect have always been sources for inspiration. Our children, Sara Asrat, Jessica Asrat, Sam Finesurrey, Caleb Finesurrey, and Demetrius Rutling each contributed in their own way to this project. Sara, Jessica, and Sam engaged in discussion about these issues that have consumed their mothers' lives for five years, offering valuable insight along the way. They exhibit the enthusiasm of youth, encouraging us to love, with them, all that the world offers and to challenge that which remains stubbornly unjust. We've been blessed with much; it is with gratitude that we offer *The Unknown City*.

Voices of Hope and Despair
Introduction

IN THIS BOOK CITY DWELLERS OFFER A MONTAGE, A COLLECTIVE BIOGRAPHY
of urban America at the close of the century. Men and women, African
American, white, and Latino/Latina, poor and working class, they ren-
der oral histories of their struggles, victories, and passions, detailing
lives filled with work—and its absence—schooling, family life, spirituality and sexuality, violence on the streets and in their homes, and social
movements that are no longer vibrant.[1] We offer you this biography of
urban America, intending to center the voices, analyses, disappointments, and hopes of the young adult poor and working class. These
young adults, men and women, constitute an unknown city. Unheard
from, they have been the negatively represented constituency of late
twentieth-century America. Sitting at the bottom of "Generation X,"
with neither the resources nor the sense of entitlement typically pos-
sessed by that generation, they are displayed and dissected in the media
as the *cause* of national problems. They are depicted as the *reason* for
the rise in urban crime, as embodying the *necessity* for welfare reform,
and of sitting at the *heart* of moral decay. While much of contemporary
social policy is designed to "fix" these young people, they have much to
say back to policymakers and the rest of America.

The late 1990s has witnessed a flood of books about those whom we
group together as the poor and working class. But this group, particularly the young, remain unknown in many ways to social scientists,
strangers to their middle-class neighbors, and ignored in the general
political consciousness. As our nation retreats from their needs, de-

sires, strengths, and yearnings, we avert our eyes. At the same time, millions of poor and working-class children are growing up amidst the wreckage of global corporate restructuring, in the shadows of empty urban factories, vulnerable to a reinvigorated U.S. nationalism and racism, and witnessing a wholesale depletion of the public safety net while, at the same time, experiencing increasing violence in their communities and often in their homes.

We invite you to meet these men and women, and read them, not as causes of our social problems, but as people whose lives are shaped in many ways by national economic and social policy decisions, and as agents – sometimes hopeful, sometimes exhausted – looking for a life that is, at present, often beyond their reach.

The Unknown City reveals a fractured urban America in the late twentieth century. In spite of legislation and social policies designed in the 1960s to lessen inequality and promote social cohesion, we stand, as a nation in the late 1990s, deeply divided along race, ethnic, social class, and gender lines. As debates about the reversal of these earlier policies swirl around us, the voices of men and women in the poor and working classes are never heard. Our goals in this volume, then, are to examine the deeply fractured nature of American society, focusing on what we call "communities of difference," as low-income people compete for crumbs in one of the richest nations of the world, and to place these voices at the center of national debates about social policy rather than at the margin, where they currently stand. Although excluded from the conversations, poor and working-class people have a great deal to say about their experiences with jobs, job training programs, child rearing practices, early childhood programs, race politics, neighborhoods, domestic violence, street violence, police, welfare, drugs, and schools – all of which are being hotly debated as we write. America of the next fifty years will look very different from that of the 1990s. As we fashion our collective futures, we can learn much from those who are (mis)represented in but excluded from the national conversations.

This book reveals, at once, the common ways in which this generation of poor and working-class men and women – white, African American, and Latino/Latina – have suffered from deindustrialization, federal and state retreat, and the buttressing of police and jails, and, at the same time, the very particular ways in which white men, white women, African American men, African American women, Latinos and Latinas experience, narrate, view, critique, and lived through the 1980s and 1990s in urban northeastern America. We write interweaving stories that credit two forms of knowledge nourished in these "communities of difference," giving equal weight to what Collins (1991) might call "common knowledge" – that which all working-class and poor young adults have access to – and "specialized knowledge" – those fragments of social brilliance, insight, critique, and perspective available particularly within demographic groups.

As we write about the particularities characterizing what might be called generational identity groups, we caution readers about our overstating, or your overreading, generalities. Our interviews with men and women reveal enormous variation within any one group. And yet, we were struck that across Buffalo and Jersey City, each group made sense in a particular dialect, from a grounded angle, with a specific race and gender twist of distinction. As you listen to the words of African American, white, and Latino/Latina women and men, you will hear these "differences" marked boldly. These men and women speak as if they are living in very different cities, even if they share a zip code. In our analysis, we have come to realize we must credit these "differences."

Much as we sought to escape the narrow confines of demographic, essentialist categories, our data tended to bring us back. That is, much as we both know, read, teach, and write about race, class, and gender as social constructions, loaded with power and complexity, we read the stories of African American men living in Jersey City or Buffalo, and they are not the same as those of white men, or Latinas, or African American women living in these same places. Indeed, the very material bases and cumulative historic circumstances of each of these groups, notwithstanding the enormous variety "within" categories, must be respected. For our purposes, we specify the material bases which shape self, Other, and sense of possibility, to include the *economy and economic opportunities*, of course. To the economy, we add a second material base for identity and possibility, the *state and available or with-*

drawn social policies; for example, welfare, quality public schools, student loans for higher education, job training programs, parenting supports, and so forth, which disenable poor and working-class women, men, and children to restabilize themselves and/or reposition themselves and their kin. And to the economy and the state, we offer a third material base for identity and possibility, that is the *body*, as a site for sexuality, performance, surveillance, and violence. Tearing through our interviews are stories of bodies watched, protected, and assaulted – at home, on the streets, by loved ones, strangers, and by the police. Thus, we write with and through post-structural understandings of identity and possibility, ever returning to these three "common" material bases as we move through the nuances of "difference."[2]

While we (try to) resist the tip toward essentialism, that is presuming that *all* white men, African American women, Puerto Ricans, and so forth, are the same and markedly distinct from others, we nevertheless want to credit that distinct circumstances of history, biography, and politics have carved out very distinct forms of consciousness and meaning for young adults. We could present to you life within two urban communities, Jersey City and Buffalo, as though the notion of community were an unproblematic, geographic space of shared experience. Or we could, with equal ease and discomfort, present to you a book about African American men and women, white men and women, Latinos and Latinas, as though each group experienced a social world totally insulated from that of others. Some of our data press toward the latter; our theoretical and political inclinations make us look toward the former, searching for common ground, shared languages, and parallel experiences. Our text tries to speak, at once, in these two dialects, to issues of the common and the specific, without diluting either. So, we offer two chapter forms; one which privileges the unique experiences of groups – for example, African American men – and a second which explores the ways in which poor and working-class people travel over similar terrain in their lives. In the second vein we offer chapters on topics such as schooling, "'You Can Never Get Too Much,'" and "Working Without a Net," on the labors of mothering in poverty.

The Common Story

We have in-depth detailed data from 154 poor and working-class men and women of the generation popularly called "Generation X," aged twenty-three to thirty-five (whom economists would consider "young adults"), all living in Buffalo, New York, and Jersey City, New Jersey.[3] We have selected a group of men and women whom we consider, by virtue of family history, to be members of the poor and working class.

The categories "poor" and "working class" are fluid, with shifting boundaries; they cannot be isolated from each other. Our experience and interviews tell us that individuals travel between these class categories over their lives. Losing a job in the steel industry can make one "poor" within a relatively short period of time. Conversely, landing a job in what Edwards (1979) calls the subordinate primary labor market (unionized labor, garment workers, jobs in auto and steel, assembly-line production work, personal secretary jobs) means that a family can move from poverty to the stable working class. As we will show later, given the decimation of the subordinate primary market, movement from the working class into poverty is all too common today, while the reverse happens far more rarely. While class categories are suspect these days, and for good reason, we feel, nevertheless, that there are important things to learn from the range of people we have selected: women receiving AFDC, people from poor to middle-class homes of origin; men and women working in what is left of factory jobs; young adults in the "new" and low-paying service sectors of both Jersey City and Buffalo; and a few civil servants.

As the recent writings of Oliver and Shapiro (1995) indicate though, even among the poor and working class, comparability of wealth, across race/ethnic groups, is a deception. While there certainly *are* equally poor white, Latino/Latina, and African American people, in urban America poor and working-class whites are, *on average*, living more comfortable lives than poor and working-class African Americans. Well over half of our white respondents in Buffalo, for example, are living in homes/apartments owned or rented with funds from parents or other relatives, who were able to amass a small "nest egg" during the vibrant days of heavy industry. This amassing of a small "nest

TABLE 1.1

PERCENT CHANGE IN REAL HOURLY WAGES BY EDUCATION LEVEL

	High School Drop Outs	High School Graduates	College Graduates	College+
1973–93	−22.5%	−14.7%	−7.5%	−4.7%

Source: U.S. Bureau of the Census, *Current Population Reports*, Series P-60, No. 178, *Workers with Low Earnings: 1964 to 1990*, U.S. Government Printing Office, Washington, D.C., 1992, p. 6.

egg" is much less common for blacks and Latinos, who did not have access to *either* well-paying jobs *or* mortgages in areas which enabled capital gains on property. So, while we recognize the porousness of class categories, we also wish to stress that racial sedimentation in the U.S. class structure cannot be ignored.[4]

Buffalo, with a total population of 328,000 (not including well-populated surrounding suburbs), is a predominately black-white town, with only 4.5 percent of the population foreign born. It sits in the Rust Belt and has experienced deindustrialization since the later 1970s. With the loss of jobs has come a steady decline in population – over 35,000 since 1980. Jersey City, a short bridge walk to Ellis Island, with a population of 228,000, is a port town, diverse in racial and ethnic terms, long burdened by the flight of factories and industry, and long proud of its rich immigrant population which constitutes 24.6 percent of the city. Buffalo, relatively speaking, is a community of home owners. Jersey City is dotted with small houses, apartments, some public housing and, more recently, rapid gentrification. The city has watched an increase in population between 1980 and 1992, netting just over 5000, with the most substantial growth among Latinos. Jersey City experienced its dramatic loss of population around World War II.

Census data allow us to track national and city-specific patterns in employment, education, and income over time, by racial/ethnic group and gender, and place Buffalo and Jersey City in a national context. Evidence suggests that nationally, as in Buffalo and Jersey City, from 1970 through 1990, poor and working-class people sweated through G.E.D. (high school equivalency) programs, enrolled in college and proprietary schools in order to accumulate higher education and in-

TABLE 1.2

NATIONAL MEDIAN FAMILY INCOME

Time Period	National Median Family Income
1979–89	+$1448
1989–92	−$2028
1989–93	−$2737

Source: U.S. Bureau of the Census, *Current Population Reports*, Series P-60, No.
178, *Workers with Low Earnings: 1964 to 1990*, U.S. Government Printing Office,
Washington, D.C., 1992, p. 6.

crease their participation and productivity in the labor force, only to watch their jobs disappear, their unions leave town, their incomes dwindle, and their purchase value shrivel. Tragically, those hit hardest have been those who can least afford it. As table 1.1 demonstrates, relying upon national data, from 1973 through 1993, real hourly wages dropped for all workers, across education levels, but for high school dropouts, the devastation is substantially greater than for those educated beyond college. In parallel fashion, as table 1.2 shows, the national median family income rose from 1979 to 1989 but dropped from 1989 to 1993 (using 1993 dollars).

The most dramatic losses occurred in those families who could least afford to take the hit. Reviewing table 1.3, Real Income Growth by Income Group, in 1993 equivalent dollars, we see that families in the lowest fifth percentile consistently lost buying power from 1979 through 1993, while those in the top 5 percent were most recently bolstered in their purchasing power.

During these years of national crisis, particularly for poor and

TABLE 1.3

REAL INCOME GROWTH BY INCOME GROUP (1993 DOLLARS)

Time Period	Lowest fifth	Second fifth	Top fifth	Top 5%
1979–89	−0.4%	0.1%	1.7%	2.3%
1989–93	−2.9%	−2.2%	−0.1%	0.7%
1992–93	−1.4%	−1.8%	5.5%	10.3%

Source: U.S. Bureau of the Census, *Current Population Reports*, Series P-60, No.
178, *Workers with Low Earnings: 1964 to 1990*, U.S. Government Printing Office,
Washington, D.C., 1992, p. 6.

working-class families, Jersey City and Buffalo have been by no means spared. Men and women in Jersey City, across racial and ethnic groups, from 1980 through 1990, were more likely to complete high school, more likely to attend some college, more likely to graduate from college (from 11.7 percent in 1980 to 21.4 percent in 1990, an increase of 107 percent!), more likely to have been in the labor market and more likely to be unemployed. So, too, in Buffalo. With equally dismal results in monetary terms.

The Buffalo economy, like that of Jersey City, was not able to benefit from the global economy's transformation to post-industrialism (Perry and McLean 1991, 349–50). Many local owners lost businesses to multinational corporations that had no stake in the Buffalo environs per se. Rather than control its own means of production, Buffalo became largely dependent on outside capital and dwindling state resources to maintain its economy in the late twentieth century.

This condition of economic dependence has had profound implications for the working men and women interviewed in this book. Gone is the heyday of heavy industry with its attendant strong working class. Gone are the jobs which pass from father to son, that allow men, particularly white men, to support their families. Now that Buffalo is largely in the hands of external capital, corporate decisions to expand, relocate, or close industries are based on an overall multinational strategy rather than on advantages to the region (Perry 1987, 131).

The loss of heavy industry has meant a rising proportion of people living in poverty and a depressed income generally across demographic groups. Important, though, is the fact that although there is a relatively higher proportion of whites living in poverty in 1990 than in 1980, the mean gap in household income between races has widened within this same time period. White men have suffered relatively more loss in the economy under restructuring, but white families are, overall, still able to piece together income advantages due to a higher proportion of two-earner families than in the Black and Latino communities (see appendix 1).[5]

Jersey City marks a somewhat different history. Sitting just across the river from New York, at the joining of railroads and accessible to ports, Hudson County, and Jersey City in particular, offered rich land

and corporate opportunity at the turn of the century. This community soon became the manufacturing center for Colgate, Maxwell House, American Can, Dixon-Crucible, Westinghouse, and Emerson, among others.

Beginning in the 1920s, however, the economic tides turned. Large employers began to flee. In 1930, Hudson County numbered 90,464 manufacturing jobs. This dropped to 86,131 in 1940. By 1980, the number slipped to 70,023, and by 1990 the county reached an all-time low of 52,029 manufacturing jobs. That is, in the last decade, Hudson County lost over one-third of its manufacturing positions, during a time when the total county population fell by only 3,000.

So unemployment rates began to soar. National unemployment figures are calculated at 6.7 percent for 1990, but are surpassed significantly at 9.8 percent for Hudson County and 11.8 percent for Jersey City, the biggest city in the county, second in the state.

There has been political movement afoot to restore economic viability to Jersey City, with the development of the Gold Coast – a strip along the river long left abandoned by the flight of factories and railroads, now rejuvenated by American Express, Merrill Lynch, Pershing Industries, and the Bank of Tokyo. But, as noted by state assemblyman and majority leader of the assembly Joe Doria, the anticipated "trickle down" of the Gold Coast has been anything but enriching to the residents of Jersey City. "Colgate-Palmolive, Maxwell House . . . all the factories, they're gone. They were on a bonanza and could have moved wherever they wanted. And they did. Then came the Gold Coast, all these financial industries moved into town along the Hudson, great space, tax abatements, beautiful view. They were supposed to hire Jersey City first . . . but for the most part, they brought their employees. People need work and in Jersey City, we just don't have it anymore."

At the same time, Doria supported New Jersey's "welfare reform": "We need welfare that has a requirement for jobs or college, that has Medicaid for health needs, day care for children. . . . We need to see more people getting job training and education replacements. Even if at the lower levels."

When we reminded Doria that he had just noted the severe flight of jobs from Jersey City, he admitted, indeed: "It's a serious *glitch* in the law; the business community made a deal, then didn't come through with the jobs."

This "glitch" – the drop in positions for "laborers and operatives" as well as "craftspeople" – has been devastating in Jersey City (see appendix 1). As the private sector continues to collapse in Jersey City for poor and working-class young adults, the city rises to be both a national and statewide "pilot site" for a number of public sector reforms that have had adverse consequences for the poor and working class, including limits on length of time on welfare, family cap provisions, and reduced support for college-based educational opportunities.

Buffalo and Jersey City have recent histories that lead to important differences. In Buffalo, recent deindustrialization has dramatically shifted and destabilized life on the ground, generating a poverty rate of 25.6 percent. Jersey City, with a poverty rate of 18.9 percent, on the other hand, is a site where deindustrialization began fifty years ago. The recent dramatic exit here has been of the public sector – state and local governments have been depleted as sites of collective trust or engagement over the past decade, whereas Buffalo's public sector remains relatively stronger. A clear example of the public sector contrast can be found in our narratives regarding schools in the two cities: Buffalo's poor and working class are still relatively supportive of schools and other public institutions while Jersey City's poor and working class are decidedly not. They supported the state takeover and might even support a voucher referendum if one were floated.

In other respects, however, the stories from Jersey City and Buffalo, both within and across race, ethnic, and gender groupings, are remarkably similar. Two parallel and interconnected stories emerge – one in which the private sector collapses, undermining the material well-being of the citizenry, and the other in which the public sector abandons, undermining the once loosely knit "safety net" of the working class and poor. If these two cities represent two distinct forms of late twentieth-century urban America, the recently deindustrialized and the long-term deindustrialized, both cities have, nevertheless, endured at one time or another the loss of jobs, unions, and industry, the erosion of a tax base and urban infrastructure, the shattering of the public safety net, and, although more pronounced in Jersey City, the devastating consequences of federal and state retreat from local life (see Katz 1995). Each has seen corresponding/coincident increases in violent crimes, growth of the street-selling drug industry, particularly of crack, the rapid expansion of the prison system, and the intensification of police arrests and reports of police harassment. Both witness the strength and subsequent disappointments of civil rights, feminist, and once hopefully progressive social movements.

In fact we hear quite similar stories of lives gone right and wrong from a generation of men and women in Buffalo and Jersey City. The language of pain and possibility circulates up and down the northeast corridor, in code switching from Latino dialects to black vernacular to white slang. The voices we bring you, from poor and working-class young adults, offer a set of stories not yet told across varying race, ethnic, and gender groups. Our hope is that readers can hear, for themselves, how these young men and women carve out lives in a world seemingly dedicated, at the moment, to the disruption of their communities and their homes.

The Stories of "Differences"

This volume is based upon data gathered in a study generously funded by the Spencer Foundation (1992–95). Our quasi-life-history approach relies on a series of in-depth interviews conducted with young men and women of varying racial/ethnic backgrounds between the ages of twenty-three and thirty-five. Seventy-five to eighty adults were interviewed in each city. Interviews were generally done in two segments, each segment lasting from one to two and one-half hours. Thus, we have between two and five-hour taped interviews with 154 individuals. We conducted many of the interviews ourselves, but were also assisted by talented graduate students, whose first names appear in the interview segments throughout the volume. Interviewees were split more or less evenly among Latino/Latina, African American, and white men and women in each city, and were drawn from meaningful urban communities, to use William Julius Wilson's term, including schools, early childhood programs such as Head Start, literacy centers, churches, workplaces, job training centers, and social agencies such as Hispanics United and the Urban League. We had, in each city, unbelievably helpful advisory groups of activists and community leaders shaping questions, identifying sites for recruitment, reviewing drafts, and inviting our testimony at local public hearings.

Extensive focus group interviews were also held among targeted groups. For example, we held focus groups with African American men who are currently active in their church as a way of expressing social activism and preserving hope for the future, and white working-class women who presently have their children enrolled in a diocesan elementary school. Focus groups ranged from one long meeting, to groups which carried on over two months time, and, in one case, even met again a year later.

We highlight these selection principles to indicate that all of our interviewees are currently connected to meaningful networks and do not represent, in all likelihood, the most alienated individuals within any given community. Many poor and working-class white women, however, were self-described as estranged from kin in so far as they were the ones "left behind" in communities of concentrated poverty, while more fortunate siblings fled "up" and out to the suburbs.

All individuals were asked to respond to exactly the same set of initial probe questions. The open-ended questions (see appendix 3) were used in order to encourage people to talk about their lives – their experiences, hopes, problems, defeats, and dreams. And talk they did. But, by group, they sang different songs, one rooted in their group experiences within the United States. Thus Puerto Rican men and women, white men and women, African American men and women each have their own tale to tell. We heard that, at present, communities of differences are struggling for space, voice, and a better life for their children. The stories groups tell in response to our questions are indeed very different, suggesting that America at the close of the century is an extraordinarily fractured place.

To begin this book, we recognize the race, ethnicity, and gender fractures in urban America and ask questions about these "communities of difference." How is it possible that working-class and poor men and women, whites, African Americans, and Latinos, surviving within the same city, aching in the same economic plight, still manage to see the world through entirely different lenses? How is it that men see so little of gender-based discrimination and domestic violence, while women across racial and ethnic groups document incredibly high rates of abuse? How is it that white men in the working class and among the poor can systematically hold African Americans accountable for their own job loss and downward mobility, when all evidence points to massive deindustrialization and substantial economic shifts, dramatically affecting their economic lives? How is it that Latinas, living amidst economic and domestic terror, can nevertheless imagine rich possibilities for their children, listening closely to the voices of ancestors, surrounded mindfully by incense, candles, and spirits? And how is it possible that African American men, in spite of media and public representations of them, manage to come together through the black church, to worry and work for a better life for the next generation of young men?

We are looking at and with a generation who has been asked to test the limits of human coping. We hear them stretched beyond where anyone should be asked to stretch, and we hear enormous reserves of resilience and creative survival skills. We, and they, speculate on the consequences for their children.

Of course, not all of what we uncover here is located only among the poor and working class. The racism so powerfully narrated by some of these white working-class men, for example, circulates, albeit in different form, throughout the U.S. class structure. So too, domestic violence is not confined to the working class and poor, as physical abuse of women can be found amongst the very rich as well. In addition, it is not only poor and working-class African American men who struggle against the odds as they work to provide a better life for the next generation of African American boys; they share this struggle with their middle-class counterparts. Some of what we find, then, is endemic to American society, rather than being lodged within specific social classes.

Nevertheless, while white racism and male violence against women, to cite two examples, are not confined to the poor and working class, they take *particular* forms within this class, and it is these specifically class-linked configurations that we probe here. So we do not deny the pervasiveness of certain issues across America, but rather, concentrate on the ways in which they manifest themselves among those with whom we spent our time.

We want to make our own authorial voices clear. As women, mothers, professors, grown-up Jewish children, and activists, we know what it means to be outsiders, and have felt the outsidedness of our lives more or less prominently at particular moments. Our empathy with those who are marginalized stems partially from this fact. At the same time, we know that we are, and have been privileged, as academics, and also that we gained privileges reserved for white people in the United States (Sachs 1994). Both of us know first hand what it means to gain privilege and try to pass it on to our children. But our collective memory includes community and politics, and we share a profound sense that we have done nothing alone. Invested with and surrounded by sets of families, friends, and for Lois, spiritual forces, we lean on, and are guided by, people and movements.

Across this text, our authorial voice, then, is both muted and clear. It is muted in that we let the men and women whom we interviewed speak for themselves, and we reproduce large segments of interview text. We do this deliberately because we engaged in this project desiring to have marginalized voices surface in national debate. Thus, African American, Latino/Latina, and white men and women speak quite a bit here, although obviously filtered through our own theoretical lenses. Our authorial voice is clear in that we do not fear expounding our outrage over the practices and policies that systematically discriminate against poor and working-class adults and children in the 1990s. With our outrage also sits our search for space, for peace, for the good, as we work with people who survive the everyday despair of their lives. So if you read our outrage, sadness, and hopes for those with whom we prayed, spoke, and worked, you read collective pain as we weave this text. We hope that you too can empathize with the struggles and strengths of those with whom we spent our time.

As we close the twentieth century, the women and men in this text help us reflect on the past decades. They remember *loss* as the most characteristic feature of their lives. Working-class and poor white men lost what was once assumed theirs and guaranteed, that is, employment and a livable wage. Working-class and poor African American women are losing both jobs (especially in the public sector) and the public assistance that has supported them in times of need. African American men have lost access to public spaces and their meager hopes for the next generation, witnessing and feeling powerless to help. Born only ten years after major civil rights activity, this generation has witnessed the "failure" of civil rights to produce long-term positive change in their lives and communities. Latinas watch "la familia" dis-member, while they desperately avoid its critique and resurrect its fantasy. Latinos watch the economy *and* the family falling apart, expecting little and getting less.

In this book we hear from poor and working-class men and women of the generation just entering adulthood; the men and women of *The Unknown City*. What will *they* say about the society in which we all live? Listen. We do not need to *fix* these young men and women, but the whole of America.

Narrating the 1980s and 1990s
Voices of White and African American Men

TRACEY: *How would you describe your relationships among various racial or ethnic groups in your community?*

VINCE: *At a boiling point, hectic. Ready to explode any time. Between blacks and whites, it's like a hatred thing. No trust. White person can sit up there and say, "Hey, I love you like a brother," and the black person would say, "I love you like a brother too." But when everything is done and said, they don't trust each other. So how could you love somebody you don't trust? And everybody's trying to get over on everybody. The Asians and the blacks, the Asians and the white, the Jew and the Arab, the Arab and the black, the black and the Jew. Everybody's strained. Everybody's watching each other, you know. And at the drop of a dime, you know, if I just drop a dollar on the floor, everybody will fight like cats and dogs to get it. It's at the boiling point right now, and that's the scary thing because what happened last year that we saw in L.A. [Rodney King]. It could happen again, and next time it's going to be organized, and the next time it's going to be bloodier. . . . So it's like ready to explode.*

THE STATE OF WORKING AMERICA (MISHEL AND BERNSTEIN, 1994, 1997), RE-leased by the Economic Policy Institute, confirms what economists like Henry Levin and Russell Rumberger (1987) have been saying for a number of years now. Real wages for the average American worker have declined by almost 10 percent during the 1980s, and, as a result, living standards have worsened for most workers and their families. At the same time, the income gap between the very rich and the average American worker has grown considerably larger. Most American families, if they are fortunate enough to have employment at all, are having to work longer hours, or have more family members contribute to the family wage just to keep family incomes from falling precipitously.

Economists Lawrence Mishel and David Frankel (1990) assert, based on extensive analysis, that the poverty rate, no matter how it is measured, grew substantially in the 1980s. In 1988, an additional 5.8 million people were living in poverty as compared with 1979, and a greater percentage of the poor – 40.1 percent as compared with 32.9 percent – had incomes below half of the poverty threshold. In addition, the real wages of the bottom 80 percent of the workforce have fallen by 1.9 percent over the last ten years. This drop in real wages has not been caused or counterbalanced by a growth in fringe benefits such as pensions and health insurance. Between 1980 and 1989, the real value of hourly fringe benefits fell by 13.8 percent, even faster than the 9.3 percent fall in hourly wages.

These declines have been more devastating to the economic situation of families headed by younger workers, ages twenty-five to thirty-four, and particularly to the three-quarters of the workforce who do not possess college degrees. In 1988, a family headed by a young worker had an income $1,542 less than their counterpart did nine years earlier in 1979 (a drop of 4.8 percent). A young family headed by a high school graduate in 1987 had an income of $2,191 (or 7.3 percent) less than their counterpart in 1979.

Although the economy is expanding in the 1990s, many of the problems evident in the 1980s, according to Mishel, Bernstein, and Schmitt, authors of the –97 *State of Working America,* continue to be felt. "For example, despite growth in both gross domestic product and employment between 1989 and 1994, median family income in 1994 was still $2,168 lower than it was in 1989, suggesting that overall growth does not, under current economic circumstances, lead to improved economic well-being for typical families. The 1980s' trends toward greater income inequality and a tighter squeeze on the middle class show clear signs of continuing in the 1990s" (3).

In fact, declining wages in the 1990s have affected new groups of workers. "After more than a decade of wage growth for most women," Mishel, Bernstein, and Schmitt argue, "the bottom two-thirds of women in the workforce saw their wages decline between 1989 and 1995. In the 1980s, families compensated for stagnant and declining male wages by working longer and sending more family members to work, a trend that appears to have reached its maximum capacity" (3).

The Economic Policy Institute studies are some of the newest in a series of studies offering the observation that the economy has changed in major ways over the past two decades and that a massive restructuring in corporate America and toward a deindustrialized society has taken place (Bluestone and Harrison 1982; Reich 1991).

What is missing from these accounts, however, is the way in which employed workers, unemployed workers, discouraged workers, and nonworkers who are rearing children or other kin are actually constructing their lives and "making sense" of this new economy – an economy that, as William Julius Wilson and others have demonstrated, is even that much harsher on the chronically poor (Wilson 1980, 1996; Jencks and Peterson 1991). What we have are numerical accounts, but to date, we have virtually no data regarding the human condition itself.[1] The question remains, beneath the stark statistical portraits of the economy, how have the real lived experiences of young adults, for example, been affected by these changes? What decisions have they made and are they making in order to live their lives? Are the experiences of people of color different from those of the traditional white working class? What do men and women from a variety of social backgrounds expect for their children's future? How do they interact with public institutions, particularly schools, to encourage their children's success? Or, have they simply given up? To the extent that men and women feel the economic bite as bitterly as statistics would suggest, where do they lay blame, and where do they imagine signs of hope?

In this chapter, we focus on young adult African American men and white men, groups particularly hard hit by the restructured economy. Both groups of men are currently leading lives of pain, frustration, and passion, lives which are directly linked to historically rooted racism, patriarchy, the privileging of white skin, *and* the new economy, as well as the dismantling of the urban public sector. Given their historically distinct racial trajectories, we ask first of all, where do these men lodge social critique? Where do they locate the "cause" of and imagine the remedy for the troubles they endure? Our analysis of "critique" does not stem from data gathered in response to direct questions about critique per se. Rather, it is critique as woven throughout these narrative responses that constitutes the site for our analysis. As we will argue below, across the narratives of African American and white men, it is easy to hear pain, alienation, and blame. While these broad parameters are common cross-race, there are nevertheless clear race-based differences in terms of *blame*. Most of the white men whom we interviewed blame blacks for a failing economy and crumbling urban neighborhoods, and yet remain silent on the role of elites or the economy in their plight. Black men, on the other hand, focus more broadly on a system of economics, racism, police harassment, and disinvestment in urban communities which produces their current situation. As social psychologists and sociologists have long contended, *where* people locate critique, that is, where they place blame and responsibility for tough times bears serious consequence for how they conceptualize remedy, if they can imagine alternative possibilities for themselves and their children, and whether they see themselves as potential activists engaged for social change (Brickman et al. 1982; Crosby 1976; Fine 1991; Janoff-Bulman 1979; Weis 1990).

Throughout this chapter we talk of groups, for example, African American or white males, as if they are monolithic, as if there is no range of opinion within a given group. Clearly this is not the case and we wish to make clear again that we are reporting general trends within groups. Given the evidence we saw from our sample, views expressed here are both typical of the group and often distinct to the group.

So we begin this volume with an emphasis on difference; difference in the ways in which young adult African American and white men, growing up in the same restructured economy, explain their current condition. Given a restructured economy, we ask, how do young adult men, situated at the material bottom of Generation X, make sense of these changes? What political and social argumentation do they muster as they think about the position the new economy has put them in? Given exactly the same set of overall probe questions (see appendix 3), white and African American men offer strikingly different answers to explain their plight. This disagreement as to the cause of their predicament is emblematic of fracture in American society as we close the century, and offers a lens through which we can begin to understand the varied textures and perspectives among young adults in urban America.

White Men

AMIRA: *Are there tensions?*

LARRY: *Probably not so much between them [blacks and Hispanics], but like for us, it gets me angry sometimes. I don't say I'm better than anybody else. But I work for the things that I have, and they [blacks and Hispanics] figure just because you're ahead, or you know more and you do more, [that it's] because you're white. And that's not really it. We're all equal, and I feel that what I've done, I've worked for myself to get to where I'm at. . . . If they would just really try instead of just kind of hanging out on the street corners. That's something that really aggravates me, to see while I'm rushing to get to work, and everybody is just kind of milling around doing nothing.*

AMIRA: *In your neighborhood?*

LARRY: *In the neighborhood. I see that a lot. On the corners. And I say you're just as physically healthy and able to do the work [as I am]. It's kind of a cop-out. Sometimes they say, "Well, you could get a job because you're white." I don't know. I never really had to hire anybody. I've never been in the authority or the position to give someone a job. I just don't see them really getting involved in the field that I'm in. [Larry has a service vehicle and repairs plumbing and air conditioning and heating units; he works for a company.] I never really had to work with any blacks or Hispanics in the mechanical fields.*

The rapid recent deindustrialization in Buffalo has meant a drop of 21 percent in blue-collar jobs from 1960 to 1990. Although this loss of jobs has hit all racial groups, it has had particularly devastating consequences for white men, who were the major beneficiaries of jobs in the industrial labor market. As this market constricts, white men stand to lose the most. This partially explains the sharpest rise in poverty of white males relative to other groups during this time period, although, as noted in chapter 1, women's labor has simultaneously enabled white families to increase the gap in mean family income relative to that of blacks and Latinos. Given industry closings, nevertheless, almost one-quarter of blue-collar jobs have disappeared. While many of these men, over time, have landed employment elsewhere, they have most often taken jobs in the rapidly growing and lower paying service sector, rendering real family income considerably less than before.

In this context, it is noteworthy that the critique of their situation fashioned by many white men is cast largely in terms of marking the boundaries of what constitutes acceptable and unacceptable behavior. Rather than offer a critique of white elites who have directed the restructuring of the American economy, rendering the white working class superfluous, the white male version of social critique is, by and large, a clear, targeted, and critical litany of judgment on the focused actions/behaviors of others, particularly African Americans, and particularly men. This critique circles around three frequently raised and interrelated points: (1) "not working," (2) welfare abuse or "cheats," and (3) affirmative action. Although many, if not most, of the white men interviewed have themselves been out of work and have received government benefits and at times welfare benefits (including food stamps), they see themselves as deserving of such benefits, in contrast to blacks whom they see as freeloaders. Their critique thus serves to draw the boundaries of what constitutes acceptable conditions for "not working," welfare receipt, participation in government-sponsored programs, and so forth, to include only themselves. Having created an "Other" who holds a set of unpleasant personal characteristics, these white men can, at the same time, deny (or legitimate) their own participation in the welfare state, their own experiences with unemployment, their own moments on the dole. Race affords them the opportunity to project and deny, defining themselves as the men who know how to take care of the family and not "live off the government." The new white working-class male can't do what he was supposed to do – support and protect his family (see Roediger 1991; Weis 1990). In engaging in a reconstruction of identity under the new economy, white men again set themselves up as superior to African Americans, a construction which is, of course, dialectically linked to material and discursive constructions in the larger society, to what Smith (1988) calls textually mediated discourses. Their process of identity formation resembles what Weis

(1990) found occurring among working-class high school males, where the work of identity formation was the work of "othering" African Americans. Roediger and others have also suggested that the work of identity formation among white men is tied in large part to the social construction of the black "other" (Roediger 1991; Morrison 1992). As we will see, white working-class men are discursively – but not materially – propped up and remain aligned with white elites who have, indeed, abandoned them. It is important to note that it is white working-class men who themselves do this discursive "work," thus cutting themselves off from a critique of elite abandonment. Their strategy for declaring their own status prevents them from seeing potential allies.

At the heart of the white male critique we heard from our interviewees is an old myth in a new setting – the notion that people of color, blacks, in particular, simply do not wish to work, that they are lazy. Larry, above, takes the evident absence of blacks in his field as indicating a lack of motivation rather than a lack of opportunity. We can hear the victory of psychology over economics in this explanation. Personal, moral attributions of blame thrive despite rampant evidence of private sector and public sector abandonment of the working class. This is juxtaposed to notions of self which assert that although white men may be out of a job, they always *want* to work. From this flows an overt racial critique of affirmative action programs, as well as a somewhat more racially coded critique of welfare abusers and cheats. These points are raised clearly by Pete, John, and Tom below.

CRAIG: *What has the experience been for you as a white male?*
PETE: *For the most part, it hasn't been bad. It's just that right now with these minority quotas, I think more or less, the white male has become the new minority. And that's not to point a finger at the blacks, Hispanics, or the women. It's just that with all these quotas, instead of hiring the best for the job, you have to hire according to your quota system, which is still wrong.*
CRAIG: *Do you have any sense of social movements? Like the Civil Rights Movement?*
PETE: *Civil rights, as far as I'm concerned, is being way out of propor-*

tion. Granted, the Afro-Americans were slaves over two hundred years ago. They were given their freedom. We as a country, I can't say all of us, but most of us, have tried to, like, make things a little more equal. Tried to smooth over some of the rough spots. You have some of these other, you have some of these militants who are now claiming that after all these years, we still owe them. I think the owing time is over for everybody. Because if we go into that, then the Poles are still owed [he is Polish]. The Germans are still owed. Jesus – the Jews are definitely still owed. I think it's time to wipe that slate clean.

CRAIG: Do you think that movement has hurt you as a white male?

PETE: To a small extent.

CRAIG: In what way?

PETE: Because it's, you have to hire a quota of minorities. And they don't take the best qualified, they take the quota number first. So that kind of puts you behind the eight ball before you even start.

———

JOHN: I really, I completely disagree with quotas. I don't feel they're fair. I mean, me as a white male, I'm really being pushed, turned into a minority. We have to have so many blacks working in the police department or in the fire department, or women. And even though, well, I'm not just saying this because I'm a white male, but white males will be pushed, you know, pushed away from the jobs or not given the jobs even though they might qualify more so for them, and have more of the capabilities to do the job. And they just won't get it because they're white males. That's the majority; there's a lot of white males, so we're going to give it to the black males or females.

CRAIG: Do you think these social movements are important or relevant despite what you've said to me?

JOHN: Yes, yes because I feel they have their place. I wouldn't say completely it should be out of the question. They have their place, where I feel that women can speak with women or children a lot better than men can sometimes, and really, with the areas of the crime, you have to have blacks and Hispanics working in community programs, so you have to have certain jobs and responsibilities where they can deal with people of their own race or background. Even myself, I feel like talking *with Italians, just as an example, more so than with someone who is Irish or German or Polish or something else, because you have some of the common background, or maybe, say, the same upbringing or values: traditions, traditions is a big part of it.*

———————

TOM: *There's white trash and there's white, and there's black trash, and there's blacks . . . and you know, there's a lot of educated blacks, and you don't hear them yelling discrimination because they've got good jobs. Because they got the know-how behind them. But the ones that are really lazy, don't want it. They start yelling discrimination so they can just get the job and they're not even qualified for it. And then they might take it away from, you know, a woman or a guy.*

The critique of affirmative action, often referred to as "quotas," is that it is not "fair," that it privileges blacks, Hispanics, and at times white women above the white male, and that this contradicts notions of equal opportunity, and a flat playing field. In fact, the mean black income in Buffalo is just over $19,000 – 71 percent of what whites earn. In a discursively marked reversal, white men portray themselves as the "new minority," the ones who are marginalized by a "quota system." White men's historic access is framed as deserved; men (and women) of color have invaded a once "fair" system – although the economic data do not bear this out. White male critique swirls around a sense of being pushed out of an economic marketplace which they see as formerly functioning fairly. Now, they argue, an unfair privileging is taking place, putting blacks and Hispanics in jobs rightfully thought to be theirs.

Where men give credence to affirmative action, it takes highly specialized forms. John, for example, feels that affirmative action programs "have their place," that they "shouldn't be completely out of the question." For example, he feels that "women can speak with women or children a lot better than men can"; and that, "in the areas of crime, you have to have blacks and Hispanics working in community programs . . . where they can deal with people of their own race or background." In other words, women should be privileged for *certain* jobs dealing with women and children, and blacks and Hispanics should be privileged in jobs dealing with crime and community. That is where, he suggests, affirmative action is useful. In general, though, white men concur with Tom when he states, "They start yelling discrimination so they can just get the job and they're not even qualified for it. And then they might take it away from . . . a woman or a guy [white]." It is important to note that most of these men have little *real* interracial experience. Their coworkers are white, their friends and families are white. Although their children may attend desegregated schools, none are truly integrated. Thus their constructions of blacks are rarely rooted in any real life experiences.

The assertions about affirmative action offer these white working-class men a way of "othering" African Americans, in particular, and resemble assertions made by many of today's academics, Congress-people, and lay persons. We hear a discursive co-construction, almost parasitic, of blacks as lazy, as wanting a handout, unlike hardworking whites. This co-construction serves to elaborate white superiority under a new economy which has hit hard *both* blacks and whites and is further elaborated in discussions of welfare abusers and cheats. In these discussions we hear that these white men have received welfare and critique blacks as "undeserving" of the same benefits.

AMIRA: *Can you tell me what a meeting with the welfare people is like, and why you feel that you're treated like garbage?* [He had earlier stated that he is treated like "garbage" by caseworkers.]
PETE: *Very, very informal. They ask you everything except your sexual preference to be quite honest with you. They ask how many people are in the house. What time do you do this? What time do you do that? Where do you live? Do you pay your gas? Do you pay your electric? How come you couldn't move into a cheaper apartment? Regardless of how much you're paying to begin with. If you ask them for a menial item, I mean. Like your stove and refrigerator. They give me a real hard time.*

————

AMIRA: *Have you ever applied for welfare?*
RON: *No.*
AMIRA: *Or, have you ever had to?*

RON: *Never had to. Probably very early in our marriage, when the first company I worked for closed up, we went through a period where we probably could have. I think we would have been eligible. I mean, our income was really low enough that we probably should have.*

AMIRA: *But you didn't. How come?*

RON: *I guess both of us pretty much feel the same way. You know, we look at welfare as being something less than admirable. I think for the most part, I think most people get out of life what they put into it. You know, because some people have more obstacles than others, there's no doubt about it. But I think a lot of people just expect things to come to them, and when it doesn't, you know, they've got the government to fall back on. . . . You know, I think it [falling back on the government] is more common for black people. . . . I mean social services, in general, I think, is certainly necessary, and Sheila [wife] and I have taken advantage of them. We've got food stamps several times. When I first got into home improvement, before I really developed my skills better and, and the first company, like I said, when they were doing some changeover. And, just before they left Buffalo, we were at a point where business was starting to slack off, especially in the wintertime. I mean, it's tough to try to sell, you know, siding in the wintertime. So, a lot of times in the winter when my income was quite low, we'd go on food stamps, and I think that's the way it should be used. I mean, it's help there for people. But, you know, as soon as I was able to get off it, I did. And not for any noble reasons, but just, you know, I think I'd rather be able to support myself than have things handed to me.*

AMIRA: *Do you have any kind of government assistance in your family right now?*

RON: *No. Like I said, I wouldn't be opposed to going back to it if it were necessary, but I hope that day doesn't happen. I've realized that I'm conservative in a lot of my viewpoints and all, and tend to think that people rely too much on government. And yet, oddly enough, our best chance of getting a house is through the Farmers Home Administration program, which we have been accepted in, but it's just, there's no guarantees that, you know, just to be qualified doesn't mean you're necessarily going to get it. . . . So that, to me, is ironic, that my best chance of getting what I want is, I have to rely on a government program. But I'm not really totally against those types of things. It's just that I think people tend to abuse them.*

Ron goes to great lengths to distinguish himself from a government program abuser, while at the same time, with reference to food stamps and the Farmers Home Administration program, specifies his deserving to participate in such programs and his reliance on them. For Ron, it is blacks who abuse government programs; whites who use them do so only temporarily and really do desire to support their families on their own. As Ron states, "I think it [falling back on the government] is more common for black people." A logical extension here is that "black" programs are abused; "white" programs are deserved.

The primary function of discussions about welfare abusers, by these white men, is to draw the boundaries of acceptable receipt of government services *at themselves* – the hardworking white man who is trying to support his family. Pete, for example, states, "There's definitely some people who abuse the system, I can see that. But then there are people who, when you need it, you know, it's like they have something to fall back on. And they're [the caseworkers] basically shoving everybody into one category. They're [all welfare recipients] all users. But these [the caseworkers] are the same people that if the county closes them off, they won't have a job, and they're going to be there next too." Since most of the caseworkers are white, Pete is discursively aligning himself with the hardworking people who have just fallen on hard times, unlike the abusers, largely black, who exploit the system. His criticism of the caseworkers is that they don't discriminate; they treat all welfare recipients as cheats. Ron also resents this and struggles in his narrative to set himself apart from what he sees as the caseworkers' construction of the welfare recipient.

The discussions of affirmative action and welfare abuse enable many white men to distinguish, in important ways, self and other. This, then *is* social critique to most of the white men we interviewed. None challenged economic restructuring or the historic privileging of white maleness in the economy. Left totally unexamined, and even unrecognized by working-class white men, many of whom are highly marginal in this economy, is the role of white elites who self-consciously closed industries and/or enabled legislation which moved capital across state and international borders, thus interrupting far more white male jobs than affirmative action ever was intended to or ever could (Perry 1987; Bluestone and Harrison 1982). Oddly enough, of course, white working-class men, through their unions, fought elite whites for years, in the struggle for higher wages and better working conditions. In the current economy, they have traded in this class perspective for the politics of race privilege.

African American Men

Unlike the white men examined above, African American men, as a group, offer a broad-based social critique. Rather than locate blame in an individual or group, their critique is of racism and society, powerfully woven around notions of job availability. Astonishingly consistent in their narrations, the critique tends to swirl around three interrelated points: (1) availability of jobs; (2) the existence of the crack economy, and (3) police harassment. These three are, as we shall see below, seen as inextricably linked in the world these men inhabit, although the lack of jobs provides the centerpiece of their analysis. George, Lee, and James below offer compelling insights in this regard.

> GEORGE: *Buffalo's fucked. Buffalo is real fucked up. The public school system is fucked. The judicial system is fucked. Oh boy, is it fucked. Everything here, basically in Buffalo, is fucked. And if you ain't already got it [money, jobs, resources], you ain't going to get it.*
> TRACEY: *Do you think about moving? Do you think it's like that in a lot of cities?*
> GEORGE: *It's not like that in a lot of cities, because like I said, I had my chance to travel and meet different cities, and go to different places. It's just Buffalo has always been fucked up. And like I said, the only way a person here can make it, if you ain't into nursing, if you ain't into computers, if you don't own your own business, you know, if you ain't already working for a big corporation, big companies, or stuff like*

that, you ain't got a chance. When you walk through that door crawl-
ing, you be busting your ass for that first couple of years. You got to
bust it real hard, you know, and back in the old school, you had to bust
your ass to keep a job, but now it's even harder for a young man to
keep a job. You know, a woman's got a better chance of keeping her job
than a man do. And that's kind of messed up. The women [have] taken
over.

Later, George expands upon this discussion in his response to the question, "If President Clinton were to come to Buffalo, what kinds of
things should be dealt with here, and what specifically would you like
him to do about it?"[2]

GEORGE: Strictly the first thing — jobs. . . . and it's hard to get a job that
do got medical coverage because you've got to work in an office where
you're messing around with computers. So you've got to be working
with some type of high tech job or something to get them different
types of benefits. So that's one thing. And [here] they're just shutting
down the plants. You know, taking Ford away from here, taking Chevy
away from here, Bethlehem Steel, you know. Different jobs like that,
they're just taking it away. And then, like I say, a young man like me, I
ain't really got a chance unless I open my own business, and it's not
going to be easy to open up your own business. Because who wants to
do carpentry all their life, and they ain't got no benefits behind it, you
know. I want something that's going to give me benefits. I want some-
thing that's going to give me, if I hurt myself on my job, I can still know
I could sit back and receive social security, all my pension and stuff
like, and my kids still got a chance to go to college and be something
five times better than me . . .
TRACEY: What do you think about why there are so many men in jail
these days?
GEORGE: No jobs, point blank. There ain't no jobs. There ain't nobody
who's telling them how good their potential [is]. "Okay, you've got
potential!" You know, they ain't got nothing like that. You've got some-
body who would rather sit down and say, "Here, sell this." "Do this,

Do that." You know, "Shoot this gun." You know, that's all they're hearing all day of their life, you know. And at the same time when they're here in the daily life, they still got to face the outside world, or going out there and trying to find them a job. They can't find a good job nowhere. You know, nobody wants to work, a single man, a teenager, here. He can work for $4.25 an hour, but a single man, a single man with children, or a single man over the age of twenty-six or twenty-seven years old, nah. He can't live off nothing like that. I can't.

TRACEY: Okay. What social or political problems are you most concerned with today?
LEE: Jobs. Ain't no good jobs for us.
TRACEY: Well, if it were up to you, how could there be more jobs? How could you solve that?
LEE: Start opening more buildings. I don't know. Yes, I'll start opening up much more businesses, where everybody can get a job. I'd cut back on trying to build all these missiles, and start opening me up franchise of businesses. Just something small, so the youth, the young youth, could work. Keep them off the streets.
TRACEY: Do you think that people have given up in our generation? It seems like you're focusing a lot on the youth.
LEE: No, you know what it is? It's just too many of them now. People having babies at twelve. You know, so that's just making everything worse. But I know here, there's no jobs here but McDonald's and Burger King, fast food. Italians and Arabians own everything here. It's like, well, about five or six plants in Buffalo, not even that much. Then that brings us to drugs and guns involved. Because you've got to get money. And when you get some money, you've got to stand up for your money. So that just about covers the jobs, and the drugs, and the guns. [In other words, that explains all these problems.]

TRACEY: What social or political problems are you most concerned with today?
JAMES: Social problems, I have to take a look at the drugs, the killings.
TRACEY: How do you think these problems can be solved?
JAMES: Education. Jobs, we got to give out the jobs. Like I say, you

know, of course you ain't going to get no job where you can make $400 a day. But, you know, get the motivation to get a chance to get like some programs and train them for these jobs where they can make good money. Instead of just keeping the jobs out there in the suburbs and, you know, because like I say, it's hard for a black person to come into the field and move up the ladder, where they're blocking, you know. So I feel if you can give them training and programs and all that, I think it would help a lot.

In addition to the economy and lack of jobs, as noted by George, James, and Lee, much of the direct assessment of racism hinges on the treatment by police, and what is at times called police brutality. It must be pointed out here, that while some individuals state that it is white cops who harass blacks, others take pains to point out that both black and white police harass them—the young African American men in the poor community. Police harassment is, in these narratives, tied also to the drug economy, and the cultivated stereotype/image of the African American male as drug dealer and thief. These points blend powerfully in William's analysis:

TRACEY: *Do you experience any particular daily hassles?*
WILLIAM: *Daily? Nowadays the daily hassle depends on whether I'm wearing a tie or a baseball hat. With the police . . . I'm telling you the truth, I put on a tie, they will call me "sir"; with a baseball hat, you don't hear "sir." [They assume] everybody's a criminal. Like, you know, I wear a beeper, my beeper's important to me because of my business [he helps promote music in the city]. I have to be in contact with my partners at all times, so therefore if I'm wearing a beeper and a baseball hat, you know, got some jeans and some sneakers on, you know, I'm looking like a typical drug dealer on the east side. And that bothers the hell out of me, because the fact of it is, I can be, I've been pulled over and harassed, but I'm telling you the truth, I have never got harassed wearing a tie.*
TRACEY: *I guess clothes make the man.*
WILLIAM: *I mean, you don't want to think that way, but I'm talking from a personal experience.*

Later, in discussing the neighborhood, William expands as follows:

You got a lot of people in my neighborhood that's dealing in drugs and they're making money and they're comfortable, so it's hard to say what could change them. But, the people that's having the problems, and just having hard times, can't find jobs. Some working, making regular income, begin to be able to do a few of the things that they want to do. You have households that the female's not working, the man's not working, and she's gettin' a check from downtown [receiving welfare], and that's what they're living on, and it's rough. Jobs. Some kind a, you know, you ask people what they want to do, they want to work. There's a lot of people in my neighborhood that has skills to do a lot of stuff. I mean, anything you need done, you can just walk into the neighborhood and somebody in the hood can fix it. But, these people don't have jobs. They've got these skills and they's just sittin' around with it. So they end up sittin' around drinking all day long.

William argues that people in the community *want* jobs – that jobs would eliminate a lot of problems. Additionally though, William centers forcefully on the social construction of the black male – on the ways in which young black men are *constructed* as being the root cause of America's problems.

I'm concerned about the view that a lot of people have against young black males, as far as drugs. Because every time I hear these views, a lot of times I wish I could just jump into the TV set and make my comments, because I think that the young black male is getting a bad rap on a lot of the stuff that's going on in this country, basically because when he do his thing, everybody see it. But, he's only a small portion of the big problem. It's just that the people that's doing the big stuff, the people that's making the hundreds of millions of dollars a day, are not being seen. So the young black male, or the poor Puerto Ricans, are being seen. But when I hear this is the problem of our country, the young black male, that just flips me upside down, because how can the young black male, the young drug dealer, be the sole problem of the whole country which we can't even control? And, where's he getting his drugs from? Who's supplying him? And these questions are being left out. I mean, when you, when the government spends millions of dollars to investigate the war on drugs, I feel they're going in the wrong places. I mean, why would they even want to come down to the street level?

Personally, I mean if you've got a tie on and suit, you know, and what really pisses me off is because guys wearing ties and a suit are the real drug dealers. They the big man. The big men are not on the corners. They're in the office buildings, getting more money than these young boys are, you know; and I hates that, you know, 'cause I gets caught up in that 'cause I'm always out here [on the street].

William searches broadly for the "cause" of contemporary problems. Jobs, media representation of the "black male as problem," police harassment, and the local breakdown of "morality" all sit at the heart of his criticism. Sounding a bit like the white males in his critique of "sitting around and drinking," William ties this condition to the absence of jobs.

The construction of the black male as drug dealer and responsible for all social problems leads, inevitably, to police harassment. Since black males are set up as entirely problematic, this offers a clear field for police to enter as they cruise the neighborhood. With the "all black males are criminals" image firmly etched in their minds, police, both black and white, viciously sweep through poor black neighborhoods, as Richard and Vince suggest below:

RICHARD: *Well, I've seen a lot [of harassment] with the police. I've seen harassment with them, a lot, you know, coming up. You asked me before about violence. Not violence [there wasn't much violence in his life], but harassment. You be walking down the street, maybe two or three [of you], and they [the police] stop [you] and nobody's really done anything, but there can be two or three of them, you know. They just stop them and harass them, you know, just no particular reason but, you know, I've dealt a lot with the cops because of my brother. I've seen like cops over, come to the house, arrest him and, you know, stuff* like that [*his brother was in and out of jail until he died in his early twenties*].

LOIS: *White cops, black cops, both?*

RICHARD: *White, yep, both black and white cops, both. I've seen a lot of it, and in prisons and, you know, because of my brother. I mean, I'm scared like, people are scared if a cop is behind you.*

VINCE: *I say now comparing the neighborhood [with the one he grew up in], it's a constant war. It's like a war zone. Hear shots ring out in the middle of the night. You're always protective of what's going on around you all of the time. You're all the time aware. My neighborhood now, something is always going on. It's never quiet. You might hear some gun shots twice in one night. Arguing, little kids using profanity, drug dealers going out in the open, police harassing people. You don't view the police as protecting you, but as your enemy. And you watch them because it's almost like they're legalized gangs.*

TRACEY: *Would you call the police if a situation were to happen, or some emergency?*

VINCE: *If it was a life-threatening situation, I probably would, but if it was something minor, I would take care of it myself. I know how to communicate with people and talk to them. Get people to calm down, get them to see the rational side of it.*

TRACEY: *Because it wouldn't be worth it to call the police?*

VINCE: *Yeah, it wouldn't. It wouldn't be worth it. They don't understand. Usually when you have a white cop who comes in your neighborhood, they don't understand what's going on there. They view us against them. And I try to talk to some police where I know that they shouldn't have that type of attitude, but they don't care. I think it's the pressures from the job. They view every black male as a drug dealer, or a thief, or you know, harassing them. Pull up on the corner, "Alright, everybody pull out your I.D.," you know, and I know for a fact they don't do this in a white neighborhood. Because when our neighborhood was white, they didn't do that. As soon as it turned mostly black, everything changed. [Vince's neighborhood was predominantly white when he was a child; as he grew older, the neighborhood became composed almost totally of African American families.] The police system*

here in the Buffalo area is a joke. The community doesn't view the
police as trying to protect them. My son is six years old. He doesn't
view the police as trying to help him; he views the police as his enemy,
and he has a good reason to feel that way because the police are con-
stantly harassing black males or anybody in a poor area. They stereo-
type; they have the attitude where it's us against them. And I have
friends that are police officers and I watched them change. You know,
it was like they were cool coming up and they were cool in high school
and college, and as soon as they got this badge and this gun, it seemed
like they just changed. With responsibilities the changes do come, but
they make the changes for all of the wrong reasons. Our police force is
very corrupt. I could never become a cop. . . . I don't trust them. If
they pulled up to a group of guys, I can understand why a group of
guys would run. The police have this thing, you know, grabbing guys,
handcuffing them, taking them somewhere, beating them up, and then
letting them go. Or ask them, "Have you ever been in jail," and young
guys would say, "No." "Well, you're going to jail today." I believe the
police have been given too much power in our community and become
a legalized gang. And I'm willing to stand in front of the head police
commissioner himself [and say it]. He's corrupt, he knows it, I know
it, the community knows it, but still nobody is able to do anything. I
think we need a police to police the police. Somebody who's not with
them and watching, and then has the power to do something. They
talk to you any kind of way, treat you like you're an animal, and you're
supposed to respect them? I don't see it.

At root, community problems, according to the men interviewed here, derive from the lack of jobs for men. Due to the lack of good jobs, many men turn to trafficking in drugs, basically selling at the street level. These men are often critical of this "turn," even as they might understand it. It is here where the analysis of racism and the racial order begins to weave through the narrative. The police harass residents, particularly men, who live in poor central city areas, and they do so armed in part with the discursive construction of the black male as criminal, thief, and drug dealer.

Several interviewees point to Rodney King as the logical outcome of this link between the discursive construction of the black man and subsequent police behavior. While many note that the drug economy does not originate at the street level, but rather involves people much higher up, including the police, businessmen, and the government, the poor are targeted in the "war on drugs." "Street sweeps" land African American men and youth in jail. Their expendability is obvious: "There will always be more such people."[3]

What about the others, ask young black men like William – those who bring the drugs into the country? Those who enable the drugs to be brought into the United States? Though here, too, as Taylor (1992) argues, often lies the social construction of the "foreign other." What about those business people who launder money, thus allowing the drug economy to thrive? These young, black men point out that we have spent so much time constructing and punishing the poor that we do not seriously consider the fact that the drug economy, like any economy, can hardly survive on the poor alone.[4] A structural analysis, while certainly not full-blown, is embedded within African American male critique, a critique that is shot through with understandings about racism. Tragically enough, of course, it is these same African American men who are represented as the viral "other," the discursive dumping ground, so to speak, for all that is bad in American society. Their expansive critique, given their own position, is wholly undermined, a point we pursue further in chapter 4.

African American men consistently raise the degree to which they are tired of being America's scapegoat. The political and "daily" construction of the black male as useless, dangerous, and lazy injects paralysis into the black community (see chap. 4), at the same time as it encourages whites who wish to imagine their salvation in their whiteness, not in their class position, to imagine all that is wrong with American society to be linked with the African American male. Elite whites absolutely collude in these constructions and need to be held squarely responsible for them. The language spewed in Congress, from state legislators, and the parade of black criminal bodies which daily floats across our TV screens during the news, encourages whites to center "pathology" on blacks rather than look carefully at decisions made in the economic and political realm which directly affect the type of access blacks have to the labor market. Fundamentally accomplished is that attention is deflected from structural sources of "personal problems" (see McCarthy et al. 1997). It can be argued, in fact, that it is in the best interest of elites that working-class whites hold African Americans responsible for their plight – it interrupts cross-class and cross-race political organization. Although African American males offer a set of critiques regarding the economy, racism, and the construction of the black self, their critiques can be easily excised, ignored in a sense, since they emerge from the group which is most demonized and feared.

The ways in which social critique is currently playing out in these two communities is extremely dangerous, and, perhaps even more to the point, discourages alliances across racial groups wherein social and economic decisions can be challenged. White men have pinpointed black men as the cause of much of their trouble, and black men, while having a broader critique, appear to have nowhere to go with it, no broader struggle with which to ally themselves. Given also that this deep critique is lodged within that group which is most demonized, most ready to be seen as "wanting something for nothing," the chance of this critique being taken seriously in the broader political and social realm is slim. Pushed into a corner of having critique which garners no attention, back males are increasingly likely to lash out at the system which has denied them their due. Having no allies and no organized struggle around race with which to connect at the moment, this lashing out may become increasingly destructive.

The question arises, why do African American and white men lodge critique so differently? All, in fact, have been substantially hurt by an economy that has changed rapidly since the 1970s. Buffalo, in particular, is a city hard hit by the policies and practices of deindustrialization which caused many thousands of jobs to be eliminated. Manufacturing jobs have been hardest hit, and these are the very jobs which were most often filled by the poor and working class. In fact, companies made very specific decisions to relocate, leaving in their wake a high state of joblessness and, later, relatively poorly paid jobs in an expanding service economy (Perry 1987). Why don't many white males, the hardest hit group according to Lester Thorow (1995) and others, pinpoint the economy and the specific decisions made by companies as they weave social critique and explain their own located position? What are the component parts of this "white male discourse of loss," and how does this discourse link to the continued scapegoating of blacks, men in particular, which is the very group offering the most compelling analysis of the white male position? How is it that the broad-based systemic critique in evidence among African American men loses strength? In the next two chapters we explore more fully the groups under consideration, probing the narrated biographies of race as they ultimately serve to splinter poor and working-class males; probing how the "differences" produced by race and racism can keep men and women of the poor and working class at each other's throats and out of each other's social movements.

Loss of Privilege Inside White, Working-Class Masculinity

IN THIS CHAPTER, WE TAKE UP THE CHALLENGE OF FURTHER UNRAVELING
white male identities inside working-class culture in the 1990s, a time
of economic restructuring and deindustrialization. Gone are the jobs in
heavy industry that sustained white men's fathers and grandfathers,
that allowed men to earn the "family wage" which bought them the
privilege of dominating their wives and children in the home. Most of
the truly "masculine jobs" that demand hard physical labor and provide reasonable wages are gone and have been replaced by jobs in the
service sector. These jobs not only pay less but do not offer the "hard"
real confrontation with physicality that was embedded in jobs of former years and which encouraged the production of a certain type of
masculinity (Connell 1995). We wonder, then, not only how these men
in the 1980s and 1990s, in the midst of feminism, affirmative action, and
gay/lesbian rights, manage to sustain a sense of self, individually and
collectively. We wonder further how they sustain their relentless belief
in a system that has, at least for their cohort, begun to crumble, eroding
their once certain advantage over white women and women and men
of color (Newman 1993).[1] As scholars begin to recognize that "white
is a color" (Roman 1993; Wong 1994), that whites are worthy of study
as whites, this book attempts to make visible the borders, strategies,
and fragilities of white working-class males who are struggling to survive in very insecure times, at, in Smith's (1988) words, "a moment in
history."[2]

While white working-class men may be considered privileged via their color, and work to affirm their whiteness, they are fundamentally, materially less privileged than their economically advantaged middle- and upper-middle-class white male counterparts, a point which they are doggedly *not* focused upon. Further, they are losing the edge they once had in the economy over men of color, in the sense that there are fewer working-class jobs to be had. Thus white working-class men represent a position of emptying privilege, indeed the loss of the little privilege they once held. It is this loss that we excavate as we turn our attention more carefully to the white men with whom we worked.

As we argued in chapter 2, white working-class men, for good reason, feel themselves to be under siege in the economy. They feel themselves to be de-centered, to no longer hold the jobs, and job security, that they sense is rightfully theirs. This discourse of loss, however, stretches widely over a variety of life spaces. These men are not just responding to perceived loss in the economic realm, even though their first instinct is to express loss this way.

Actual loss in the economic realm is, in itself, quite complicated. White men *have* lost ground in the economy in two senses: (1) many of the jobs working-class white men held in an industrial economy are gone and have been replaced by a far lower paying set of service sector jobs; and (2) real income has declined for all Americans since the 1970s. Thus the economic loss felt by these men is real; they have indeed lost ground, experiencing more loss than other poor and working-class groups given that they had an edge to begin with. We witness, then, growth in the poverty rate of whites, at least in Buffalo, relative to other racial groups during the 1980s and 1990s. At the same time, though, as described in chapter 1, the gap in mean family income of whites relative to blacks and Latinos in Buffalo has widened from 1980 to 1990, suggesting that although things are bad for whites, they have worsened in many respects for other groups. This does not contradict, merely contextualize, the relatively greater loss experienced by working-class white males. Mean family income is up for whites relative to other groups partially because more white women are in the paid labor force than ever before, and more whites than blacks or Latinos live in two-earner families. So, while the loss is real for white men, this loss does not translate materially into a benefit for blacks or Latinos. Although it is perceived that way by many of the white men whom we interviewed.

Given this, the fact that white working-class men blame African American men for their condition is striking. How does this happen? How does this "discourse of loss" target African American men as responsible for white men's current situation?

Under Siege in the Neighborhood

Many of the white working-class males whom we interviewed, spoke through a discourse on work in which they drew bright-line distinctions between themselves and a largely black "other," constructed as lazy, unwilling to do what is necessary to get and keep a job, and content to live off government entitlement programs. In so constructing the black "other" with varied unpleasantries, they simultaneously author the white male self as authentically earnest – wanting to work, to support a family, as taking government benefits only when absolutely necessary and, therefore, as deserving them when they do. Their authorization of self as deserving economic privilege in the face of a population decidedly "less worthy" than they renders the felt assault that much more stinging.

This sense of assault, however, runs far deeper than in the economic realm alone. It invades the perceptions of many white men in their talk about neighborhoods, of physical living spaces. They express a sense of no longer belonging, or that their neighborhood is "deteriorating," further evidence that it is no longer a space that belongs to them in either physical or psychological terms. Most often encroaching instability is attributed to an influx of blacks or Hispanics who they clearly, again, position as "other." As Larry says, "I really feel – I'm not going to say out of place. I do. I've grown up in the neighborhood [the Italian west side], but I don't really feel as though I belong here anymore. I don't know, not strictly because I'm a white male, and there's not many of us. I mean, there's not really that many in my neighborhood that I can say, 'Well, I have a neighbor, the guy who lives next door to me or the somebody across the street.' There is, I'm kind of like the minority. I'm – I don't really – there's not a lot of people I associate with."

A focus group discussion with three white men in a west side church in Buffalo uncovers similar sentiments:

CRAIG: *What was it like when you guys were little?*

MIKE: *I think it was different – ten times different.*

LARRY: *I loved growing up on the west side. It's still the case now – everybody knew each other. On the block there was always tons of kids. That's what I remember growing up on the west side – kids, all over the place, and everyone had somebody to play with, and everybody knew each other, and everybody's parents looked out for the other parent's kids. You could leave your doors open. There were people out on their porches and all that.*

MIKE: *It wasn't like – it's more like, I don't know if you know the area [talking to Craig], but it's more like the way North Buffalo is now, in a way, when we were growing up.*

LARRY: *There were a lot more Italians when we were growing up. We're both from Italian backgrounds, but I think there's more differences now.*

MIKE: *It's not just because of that, it's more because of their poverty, you know. There's a lot more different people nowadays. You've got poor people living in the area, they're always going to try to make money somehow.*

LARRY: *I still like this neighborhood. I discussed this before with you [in an individual interview]. I wouldn't leave the neighborhood, but the neighborhood is going bad. It's gone bad. It's been in the process of going bad for about five or six years now. If you live here, it's OK. If you lived here all your life, it's normal. But, if you get somebody that comes in from Tonawanda [suburb], a friend of yours, they see it, and they say, "Wow, how do you live in this?" It has progressively gotten worse.*

MIKE: *When I went into the Air Force in '89, it was at a certain point, but when I got back in '92, it was like, wow, what happened? It was a big difference.*

CRAIG: *What did happen? What did you see happen?*

MIKE: *I just seen more kids on the streets, more of them starting to dress up like the rappers on TV, white kids, black kids, Hispanic, it didn't matter. I just seen, you know, more hanging out.*

LARRY: *The west side has always been like a low-income type of area, and it's always been a tough neighborhood. But what I think is, more or less, it's getting more violent. We both went to Grover [High School], so we know what it's like to grow up in kind of like a tough atmosphere, but nothing like it is now. There's a lot of drug dealing, a lot of guns.*

MIKE: *The thing is, they're getting younger.*

LARRY: *Thirteen – fourteen-year-old kids are carrying guns. It's really not that out in the open, but you hear about it. You hear about the shootings. . . . There was a rape at School 18 [elementary school], maybe about a month ago. I heard it on the news.*

MIKE: *I did see a drug bust. As a matter of fact, right on my street. The cops more or less blocked me in my driveway, because they just pull up, and they park unmarked cars, and they just rushed into a couple of houses down.*

Mike, in an individual interview, elaborates as follows:

MIKE: *School 18 . . . when I went there, it was a very clean, you know, very big building. Now . . . now I see it, I drive by there, and there's graffiti all over the walls and the parking lots written on the ground. So that's pretty much a good way to explain it from the way it changed from when I was little until now. Just look at the school. . . . And you hear the loud music all over the place now. I mean, it's not as bad as I might be making it sound . . . but . . . my car got broken into, stuff like that . . . that never happened back then.*

LOIS: *It didn't?*

MIKE: *I'd say up to four or five years ago, it didn't happen.*

LOIS: *Interesting. What proportion of the people are still Italian?*

MIKE: *There's a lot of older ones still there. . . . I'd say 30 to 40 percent.*

LOIS: *Still? Well, that's quite high then.*

MIKE: *See, you have the lower west side and the upper west side, . . . you*

know what I'm talking about . . . that's predominantly Puerto Rican.
The upper west side still has got a lot of Italians, though, there.
LOIS: *But you said a lot of the Puerto Ricans and blacks are moving into*
the upper west side?
MIKE: *Oh yeah, they're coming. I mean, which is . . . which is fine. I*
have no problem with that. A lot of Italians are moving to the north
side, so that's starting to be Italian Heaven over there. But there's been
a definite change, no doubt about it.
LOIS: *Do people talk about that?*
MIKE: *Oh yeah. . . . I hear my aunt downstairs, when I first got back*
from the . . . I was in the air force . . . when I first got back, I remember
her describing the neighborhood – "Oh God, Mike, it's so terrible
here." She sort of exaggerated, "It's so terrible here . . . they got the
music going, and you can't even walk outside, you're afraid to get
mugged." I mean there's been people who got mugged in the parking
lot of the church – ladies.
LOIS: *Really?*
MIKE: *Not during regular church hours or anything, but just . . . like*
night, like maybe making their errands or something . . . but, I've
heard other people make comments, you know, "It's just not the
same" type of comments or . . . "You've got to be more careful now."
It's definitely not the serene place that I perceived it as when I was
younger, that's for sure. I mean, it's sort of back to when I was talking
about my friends. It's really bad when you're afraid to walk through
your old neighborhood where you grew up, even down the street. . . . I
mean my girlfriend lives right down the street from me, and I was com-
ing from her house one night and . . . I needed to cross another street
to get to my block, and there was a group of kids fighting there so I'm
going to go around. You know, I was thinking that, I can't even walk.

Mike is interesting since he, himself, is a border crosser in the sense
that his girlfriend (to whom he later became engaged) is Puerto Rican.
However this presents no conceptual difficulty for him since she comes
from a Puerto Rican family who has lived on the lower west side for a
while and who also objects to the new Puerto Ricans and blacks moving
in. As he notes, "Yeah, she'll talk to me. Coming from her mouth her-

self, she would say the same thing I did. It's really sad, I can't walk through my old neighborhood, you know, it's really sick. It's ignorant, you know. They, her family, feels the same way. Her mother, because her mother doesn't have a car, so she has to walk a lot of places, and she knows what's going on."

Many of the white men interviewed hope to exit the areas they define as "under siege" as soon as they can. Larry, for example, has bought some land in a suburb where his two brothers live because he can't imagine raising children where he currently resides. Several others plan to move to the suburbs, or to North Buffalo, which represents a more upscale set of city neighborhoods, when they are married, and especially, when they have children. This will not be easy to accomplish, however, since many are living in properties owned by their parents, properties bought with monies that white privilege was able to amass in the parental generation, when white men could secure full-time work in industry. Their current wages, if they are working, are not necessarily enough to support the kind of geographic move they desire. Those who foresee staying in the city are working to establish block clubs, neighborhood watches, and small-scale organizations designed to patrol the borders of their communities, to keep their communities safe from "outsiders." Tom, for example, is very active in the block club in his community. He explains how he got involved:

TOM: *I kept reading in the paper about crime. And I kept reading about what different block clubs are doing different things. And we talked with some of the neighbors to get together to form a block club. So we started, I think, a year ago, I think in June, and we started last year to meet. And then we went through all the routine to become an official block club. And then we just grew from there.*
LOIS: *What is the purpose of the block club?*
TOM: *To watch the neighborhood. You know, if you see trouble happening, to call 911. Or if one of the neighbors is having a problem, you know, it's better to come out in groups, you know, don't cause any violence. But if two kids are there against, say, one of the neighbors, and maybe five neighbors [come], the kids aren't going to be that stupid to do anything. [The block club allows people] to just continue on. To*

watch each other; we watch each other's house. And, you know, if we see somebody else, like the lady across the street is an older elderly lady. And we watch for her. You know, we see somebody strange up that driveway or at her house, you know, we'll confront them. We'll ask them [who they are]. And I think that shows too. I think people see that.

While he narrates this as very supportive, and indeed it is in many ways, the borders they are patrolling are those basically encasing the white community against encroaching "others." It is whiteness that people are attempting to protect in these neighborhoods, just as it is whiteness that enables discursive alignment with elites, as shown in chapter two, even though elites hardly work for their benefit in the economic arena. This does not deny the fact that some blacks live in white neighborhoods as well, but rather points out that in these white neighborhoods bordered by the "other," it is the "other" against whom white communities are attempting to protect themselves (Fine et al. 1997). This is also not to ignore the fact that several families of color have lived for years in these white neighborhoods, but rather to note that these families are considered settled—as "just like us" in the case of the "Spanish" family who lived in the Italian neighborhood. It is the racial "other"—the "other" constructed as lazy, violent, dangerous, as not working, as hanging around—that is at issue here. And it is this group around whom block clubs are formed. White working-class men feel that their neighborhoods are under siege—they will either leave, or organize to protect themselves against the bordering/encroaching other. As Tom says, "If I move, it's going to be because I want to move, not because the kids are going to force me out. You know, I'm not afraid of the kids. I'm not afraid of, you know, people moving in. You know, I'm not afraid of the colored coming in. They don't bother me. If I'm going to move, it will be because [I want to]." In the meantime, he is organizing with other white men and, to a lesser extent, white women, to patrol the borders of his neighborhood, a relatively "safe space," from the onslaught of the "other."

Some, like Bill below, recognize that the block clubs can engage in seemingly racist practices:

CRAIG: *Do you belong to any groups of any kind?*

BILL: *No, none.*

CRAIG: *Do you belong to a block club?*

BILL: *The block club I won't join. I totally hate their views. I mean, they're like, "Get them out, kick their ass," just —*

CRAIG: *Who is saying "Get them out, kick their ass"?*

BILL: *Oh, people who live a few doors from me. And they're very prejudiced.*

CRAIG: *So, they're whites?*

BILL: *Yeah.*

CRAIG: *Whites want to kick out the blacks?*

BILL: *Exactly. It doesn't matter to them if they're good or bad. You know if they're renters or owners. They just want them out.*

As Bill notes with distaste, many white men take up a protectionist stance in an effort to secure their "turf" from assault in a time of increasing racial diversification in the city and, with that, the fracturing of white working-class neighborhoods. Block clubs emerge as freely organized and co-opted spaces for group meetings and group exchanges designed to bolster the community, but they also exist as a site for the deployment of tactical strategies meant to arm the neighborhood against the "other" (Marusza 1997). A "good" community initiative in the interests of engagement across difference thus doubles as a legitimate form of border patrolling. Initiatives on the part of white, working-class men need, then, to be seen as counter-strategies for reclaiming lost power and privilege in their communities, which they perceive as being under immediate threat of dislocation.

Under Siege in the Home: Contesting Gender Roles

White working-class men express strong sentiment about the family and, specifically, about male roles and responsibilities within the family. The discourse of loss, in fact, surfaces very strongly in the domestic realm, where men feel that women no longer "know their place," that their own male (read dominant) position is being eroded. As part of narrating loss, they idealize and even valorize the family, at least in theory, if not altogether in practice. These men, who have lost real material space inside shop-floor culture, and the economic arena generally, turn to the family to assert or reassert dominance in that realm. While this may have always been the case, as Lillian Rubin (1976) and others have argued about the working-class family, the move to sustain dominance in the white working-class home is particularly key at this moment in time when there are genuine material losses in other spheres of working-class life. Men no longer have a clear-cut material sphere in which they can assert lived power. Working-class men are forced, in a sense, into the realm of family, in order to assert a form of symbolic dominance. Turning to the family as the emergent domain of male power, they insist or reinsist on reclaiming gender privilege. Much of the patrolling of the borders of community must be seen in these terms as well. The borders of community as patrolled by white men are drawn in the name of the family – men are protecting their wives and children (all of whom are constructed as absolutely less than men) from what they see as encroaching assault. Thus they envelop the family sphere within their own symbolic dominance, a dominance which they substitute, although not wholly consciously or completely, for their former authority in the material realm.

Recall that white working-class families are able to sustain an economic edge in terms of mean family income relative to blacks and Latinos in part because more white families rely on two incomes. The movement of women into the labor force, however, is not necessarily seen as positive by white working-class men, at least insofar as it challenges traditional gender roles and expectations at work and at home. Thus loss is expressed in terms of status in the family, as well as being linked to the economy and the neighborhood. These men feel that they are getting it from all sides – and perhaps they are.

We conducted a set of conversations in a focus group in an Italian church located in one of the borderlands of Buffalo. You can hear that the family sits centrally within the construction of manhood in these narratives, propping up the discourse of masculinity inside working-class culture:

CRAIG: *What do you think the role of the family is right now?*
LARRY: *I think there is definitely a fall in the American family right now.*

MIKE: *That's the major contributor to any of the problems, I think.*

LARRY: *Like I said, I think the family in America is at a total . . . what I see is, is it used to be a man could work, make a paycheck, and the woman could stay home and be a housewife, but now you need either two incomes or a man cannot support the family, he cannot get a job to support the family, so he bolts, he leaves, and goes on his own, and that's what I see. Unless there is a thing where there is better jobs and better opportunities for people, then maybe the family can build up again where you could have a family that stays together. But I think that's what it is. I think that the family is falling apart because a man just cannot support his family anymore, and he bolts. He takes the easy way out. All the other pressures of the world.*

CRAIG: *What other pressures?*

LARRY: *The age itself. Men are tempted away from their wives; wives are tempted away from their husbands because of sex.*

CRAIG: *Is that new, though?*

MIKE: *No. It's not new, but it's more frequent now because of every-thing—it's just thrown at you no matter what. You could watch TV and you could just turn it—I mean even regular cable—and you could see some gross stuff, even for kids, you know. It's the temptation of bad. It's the temptation of money and it's just, you know, it's the temp-tation of well, I've got to please myself first.*

CRAIG: *What do you think is going to happen to the family in the future? Is it going to get better or worse?*

LARRY: *I hate to say it; I don't think it's going to get better.*

Larry and Mike attribute what they see as the fall in the American family to a variety of factors. In fact, we hear them searching for expla-nations as they scan Reaganomics, popular culture (cable TV), com-modified sex, and the lack of jobs. However, it is clear in these narra-tives that the linchpin of the family is the man as breadwinner and protector of wife and children. The economy and popular culture have made it difficult for men to occupy this position since two people now need to work, and sex tempts both men and women away from family commitments. Thus there is a moral component to the breakdown of the American family as well. But the male as provider must, they argue, be restored, if the family is to regain its strength. There is a clear valorization of traditional gender-based roles, as Latinos and African American men in chapters 4 and 5 also articulate, without which the family is undermined. It is these traditional gender roles that are at stake.

CRAIG: *Do you think that the roles of men and women are now changing to some extent because of the changes in the family and the changes in society?*

LARRY: *Definitely. There is more of a leadership role for women.*

MIKE: *There is nothing wrong—I mean, I agree with women being able to be independent and stuff like that, but the women's lib, when that started, it really threw things into a little bit of chaos too because, like you said, the family. For one thing, it took the mother out of the family.*

LARRY: *Right. The role of the woman has definitely changed because the woman has to work now.*

MIKE: *Now there are babysitters or the baby is at day care all day long. I don't know what kind of person I would have been if I didn't have my mother there everyday, you know, knowing that she'd be there, and, I don't know. I don't disagree totally with it because, you know, if my wife wants to work, that's great. Nowadays she has to. Nowadays, and like you say, society is made to where she almost has to work, but the roles are just . . . I think deep down the roles are still the same.*

LARRY: *I think for one thing, the roles have changed because again, of the single-parent households. There is a lot of that, and the mother has to be the father and the mother at the same time.*

MIKE: *Yeah, that's true.*

LARRY: *And it's very hard for a mother to discipline a teenage boy.*

MIKE: *You need two parents.*

LARRY: *I was never disciplined by my father, but I really never needed to [be], but if there is a father around, there is no bullshit going on.*

MIKE: *Yeah, you're right. If I was disciplined, it was mostly by my mother. My dad yelled a lot.*

LARRY: *Yeah, exactly.*

MIKE: *I got spanked by my mother, but that was the role. And I had the traditional family. I don't know if you did, but my mom was home tak-*

ing care of me. And it's not like she didn't do anything, she did a lot of work.

LARRY: Cooked and cleaned.

MIKE: My dad went to work and came home at 5:00, we had dinner. That's exactly how I grew up. They made sure, no matter what, we always had dinner together, but I don't know, I guess it is a – starting to become a role reversal. The women want their equality, but sometimes they just want what they shouldn't have, I guess. God didn't intend them to have some other kind of role.

LARRY: Mike, that's too much, man!

CRAIG: If women were busy cooking and cleaning and spanking the kids, what did the men do?

LARRY: The men were working from 9:00 to 5:00, like he said. They would come home, and they didn't want to hear nothing – eat, watch TV, go to sleep. Well, they disciplined their kids, but, like I said, basically, in Italian families, like we were, I think it was more centered around the mother. She cooked, she cleaned, we went to her for everything.

MIKE: It's not that my father said you have to do it, it's just that she wanted to do it, and he appreciated it.

LARRY: Like he said, the values that were instilled in you when you were a kid.

MIKE: Yeah, right.

CRAIG: Given everything that you just said right now, what is the meaning of maleness?

LARRY: First of all, I think the meaning of maleness is more than, you know, helping to produce a child. I still think that the meaning of maleness is to go out, earn a living, support a family, I still feel that should be the meaning of maleness. I don't know if it is, I really don't think it is.

MIKE: You stand up for what you believe in.

LARRY: Like he said, a lot of selfishness. A lot of men want to go out there and just make a living for themselves. But I still think the meaning of maleness should be for the man to go out, find himself a wife, get married, raise a family and support that family.

MIKE: *Just like pretty much what he said. Just to keep – a real man will keep what he believes in and not stray from it to please everybody. He'll get a wife. He'll love her unconditionally and she, in return, will respect him and want to do things for him, and vice versa, and just to follow the example of maybe the church or of Christ. That's pretty much it. Just an unselfish provider willing to sacrifice for his family, or sacrifice for whoever, and not take everyone else's values, to please the other person.*

LARRY: *I think they should be responsible. The male should be more responsible for the family.*

MIKE: *Right, exactly. That's what he is in society. Like it was back in the days – like the* Leave It to Beaver *times, when the man went out, and the woman stayed home.*

LARRY: *I think that's when there were really no problems in America. I don't know, I wasn't there, but from what I see, it seemed like everything was better.*

These men reclaim their waning dominance in the material sector by centering the family in their collective memory of the past, as youth coming of age, from which point they move toward its valorization as the main resource for financial, but, even more to the point, emotional support. This reclaiming of dominance, however, does not emerge, as we have shown, only in relation to the economic realm. There is felt loss within neighborhood as well as within the family. It is the *package of loss* within which white working-class men are centering critique and claiming privilege.

Conversation that captures the importance of the intact heterosexual family sets the stage for discussion of the central role played by men in the household as they argue their significance to the home space despite the fact that they understand themselves as only symbolically dominant therein. In other words, these men reclaim the waning privileges of white male dominance in all experienced sectors through a traditional vocabulary of gender roles and relationships.

AMIRA: *What's the most important thing in terms of life?*

LARRY: *Family. Because that's your flesh and blood. That's who you grew up with. That's who loves you the most. That's your most trusted, prize possession, your family. That is the most important thing in my life.*

AMIRA: *Anything else?*

LARRY: *Belief in God and sticking together as a family, and that's basically it.*

The centrality of family to the provision of emotional support inside working-class culture is best captured in Larry's admission of family as "your most trusted, prize possession." Attaching material value to the family unit allows white, working-class men to position the family as the fulcrum point on which masculine domination hinges. This line of argument is sustained inside Tom's attention to the family as the provider of emotional support, whose example makes the future possible.

LOIS: *Could you have predicted that your family would have been so important to you?*

TOM: *Yes, yes. I mean, if [his sister] calls me to do something, I'll still do it for her. My parents were close . . .*

LOIS: *So you're not surprised to see this in yourself?*

TOM: *No. My father's brothers and sisters, my mother, on her side, the cousins and that, we're just close . . . I mean, it just goes from brother and sister, from wife and kids to brother and the whole family. I mean, when her [his wife's] parents are up, my uncles and aunts will invite them to parties, and they'll make 'em feel at home. And we just, you know, we just don't feel . . . we don't let anybody out in the cold, you know, . . . we get along. If you don't get along with somebody, usually somebody says something to you, and it's out in the open and, you know, we're not behind your back stabbing you in the back.*

Establishing the foundational aspects of the family unit, these white, working-class men are able to build an argument that validates male authority inside the home. Although home space materially belongs, in large measure, to women, and the men wish it to stay that way, they want to make it absolutely clear that they are seen as dominant. They are the head of the household even though they do not materially inhabit and/or take care of this household in ways they expect of their women. While white men have always asserted dominance in the home, the depth to which this is being asserted, we would argue, is due in part to the erosion of dominance in what they see as their rightful material space in the wage labor sector, as well as in the neighborhoods in which they live.

CRAIG: *What kind of image do men have?*
DAVE: *Well, like I said. It's kind of the normal thing. They're expected to, at least, try to provide, and if they don't, they should try to find a way around it, whether it's taking downtown [welfare], and getting public assistance, or whatsoever. They are expected to provide in some manner.*

TOM: *Well, I think I kind of summed it all up. I'm definitely a family man. Love my kids, love my wife. I'm simple. A man should work. You know, women should, you know, raise the family. Men shouldn't wear earrings. I hate that.*

As we will see below, central to Tom's private understanding of what constitutes appropriate manhood and womanhood is a very real sense that men cannot be trusted, that inborn male instincts need to be tamed (by women). The only way these instincts are controlled is through the establishment of a family, in which the man is held responsible for the protection of his wife and children. Otherwise inborn male instincts will rise to the surface.

LOIS: *I know they're young [Tom's children], but Susie [she is in the fifth grade] especially, is there anything in particular you're starting to tell her about men?*
TOM: *Yeah, I mean, we've had that talk. I've had that talk with all three, not just Susie.*
LOIS: *OK. What have you said. What do you tell her?*
TOM: *Well, it was hard. Susie, this year, saw the movie, you know, they call it "THE" movie. The other two, I explained something about men.*
LOIS: *About reproduction and menstruation?*

TOM: *Yeah. And Susie, we try to tell her what men really look for.*
LOIS: *What do you think that is?*
TOM: *Men are pigs. [laugh]. Famous quote. They are, I mean, not all of them. The abuse, you know, sexual abuse. You know, I can, I mean, I include myself on that subject. You know, it could be me. You know, if you feel something that I'm doing that's uncomfortable, tell some-body. Don't hide it. It could be your grandfather. It could be your uncle. It could be a friend. It could be a priest. It could be one of your teachers.*
LOIS: *And you talk to them about that?*
TOM: *Yeah, I talked to all of them.*
LOIS: *Even Jenny? [She is six.]*
TOM: *Even Jenny. They didn't understand. I pulled out the health book. And I was showing them pictures about this and that. And they, at first, they were laughing, and it was hard to talk about that. They were too young, but you have to, I think. And I don't know how to go about it. So basically I really explained it to them. A lot of people told me I was nuts. But if only one of them got the message, it's going to work. You know, [I told them] men will try this and try that. And they're all sitting there — "Well, I don't understand." That men try to do it this, and try to put it over her and all that. So what I did is I took out some-thing. What the hell did I take? Um, a small opening, I took. And I took this big vase. And I said, "Do you think I can put it in this hole over here?" They were like, no way. I said, "Well a man will be able to." That was graphic. It was. But they just sat there, and it was like, I think they got my message, so I think that's it. They just sat there. And Julie [my wife] goes, "That will help." I'm like, "They got the message."*

Tom's role as a father doubles as male protector whose responsibility is to provide his daughters, in particular, with the foreknowledge that men are biologically outfitted to exercise sexual abuse. As Whatley (1985, 1987) points out in her study of discourses of male sexuality in sexuality curricula in schools, women shoulder the responsibility for controlling male sexuality. Fault for their becoming victims of sexual advantage lies in their failure to tame male sexuality. Tom assumes the underlying premise of much of the sex education literature circulating in schools that the inability among men to control themselves is natural to them (Fine 1994; Whatley 1985, 1987). The discourse on female sexuality, in turn, advocates that girls arm themselves against the unleashed sexual energies of men. The theme of the challenge of the white, working-class male to control himself is captured in conversation with Bill:

CRAIG: *Do you even talk to him [his son] about what it means to be a man? Or what it will mean to be a man [when he grows up]?*
BILL: *Yeah, I probably [will] instill in him the idea of his word, when he says something that he's gonna do it, and stick it to and, you know, . . . not lie, and be true to your word. 'Cause to me, that's basically one of the most important things you can be. I mean, a real man in my opinion is someone who is good to their word, who is strong but yet in control of their strength. There's people who like lift weights and stuff, and they lose their temper and like kung fu somebody, kick him in the jaw and shit. Whereas a man is somebody who would have the strength to do this destruction, but would have the control of knowing when to use it properly, if there was a terrible situation where you would have to pull it [strength] out. Like say you were being mugged or something . . . having strength, but having the brains to control the strength. To me, that's what man is.*

Bill attributes to the "real" man not only "strength" but, most importantly, the ability to exercise restraint over his own innate power. These "natural" properties position the man as protector and defender of his family, according to the men whom we talked with, providing ample argument for reclaiming his lost privilege in the home space. The point is that male power is claimed as "natural" to men, thus justifying their symbolic dominance even in the face of waning economic privilege.

While it is indeed the case that men in general, middle-, upper-middle-, and upper-class white men included, may express similar sentiments regarding male and female roles in the family and the underlying biological imperatives of such roles, those men not under siege in other areas need not specifically claim dominance in the family realm as compensation for loss. For those men earning a great deal of money, symbolic dominance in the home/family sphere can, to some extent, be assumed, and explicit statements to this effect need not be made. Earning money also buys uncontested neighborhood space. What poor and working-class white men are fighting for is what higher-class men can, to some extent, take for granted, although the feminist movement means that male dominance is never totally uncontested. Nonetheless, the assertion or reassertion of dominance in the home/family sphere among poor and working-class men is, we would argue, a *compensatory* assertion, wherein these men have lost status in other realms. Thus the staking out of symbolic dominance in the family is a way of reclaiming waning dominance in the material sphere, something that higher status men need not do.

Many of the white working-class men whom we interviewed are enveloped by and producing a discourse of loss – loss of jobs, neighborhood, and their felt rightful position in the family. While a few resist this line of argument and welcome shifts in race and gender positions, most did not. Most striking, however, this narration of loss does not translate into any broader analysis of their own position in the current economy or into coalition building with other groups which have been equally affected by restructuring. In fact, rather than form coalitions, as we saw in chapter 2, white men set up African American men as the "cause" of their problem in the job market, which then reverberates into the home, where white women challenge their dominance. Their "struggle," whether consciously or not, becomes that of fortifying *white* and *masculine privilege,* actually *preventing* coalition building with other groups equally affected by economic restructuring, such as white women, and African American men and women. In so doing, they leave intact a set of social and economic policies which keep them chronically unemployed or underemployed. How is it that this occurs?

Partly, as we saw, their position in the economy is complicated, as they have experienced loss at one and the same time as they are still relatively privileged. Additionally, what they see in the newspapers are accounts of industry closings and job loss, but not accounts that explain carefully how and why it is that industries have vacated the urban northeast. There is, then, no broader discourse available offering the white men examined here *economically* based reasons for their lived experience of loss. In fact, since the media packages blacks (and feminism secondarily) as the root cause of problems in contemporary American society (McCarthy et al. 1996), those who experience loss are actually *encouraged* to center all that is wrong with society on African Americans, particularly men.

Although white women are not without blame in these narratives (indeed they are blamed for not being in their "place"), it is easier to express *generalized* anger toward African American males than toward their own white females, since it is arguably the case that white men are still linked fundamentally to white women, and even dependent on them. This is not the case for African American men, from whom white men can emotionally and spatially distance themselves with few felt consequences. This does not mean that white women are left totally off the hook, however. As we will see in chapter 7, white men target white women in other ways, and the level of domestic violence in white working-class homes remains a little talked about secret.

Prying open these men's lives reveals a discourse of loss which stretches over several areas. In the search for a fall guy, they target African American men, in particular, as the reason for their waning dominance in all spheres. What, then, is the response of African American men? What do these men's lives look like, the men who are set up as the "cause" of so many of society's problems? To what extent do they fight back? We take up this set of questions in chapter 4.

4

"To Stand Up and Be Men"
Black Males Rewriting Social Representations

We have traversed the soil of North America, bringing advantage to it as farmer, mule trainer, singer, shaper of wood and iron. We have picked cotton and shined shoes, we have bludgeoned the malleable parts of ourselves into new and brash identities that are shattered and bruised by the gun and the bullet. And now the only duty our young men seem ready to imagine is to their maleness with its reckless display of braggadocio, its bright intelligence, its bold and foolish embrace of hate and happenstance. If we are not our brother's keeper, then we are still our brother's witness. We are co-conspirators in his story and in his future.

— AUGUST WILSON, Introduction to *Speak My Name* by Don Belton

There are only two kinds of black men—the broken who fail and the true black men who have stumbled in the past but will rise again.
Will the real black man please stand up?

—NATHAN HARE, "Will the Real Black Man Please Stand Up?"

BLACK INTELLECTUALS SPEND MUCH TIME DISCUSSING THE REPRESENTATIONS of black males. Striving for fullness, writing against stereotypes, exploring black masculinity, recent work pries open discussions which swirl around the black male as discursive subject or object. Stretching across the borders of media studies, literary theory, cultural studies, gender studies, and queer theory, this new work intentionally displaces static representations of the black man and struggles to topple hegemonic and unilinear cultural representations of black masculinity (Blount and Cunningham 1996; Belton 1996).

The working-class and poor African American men we interviewed are not engaged in writing books about black masculinity. However their daily labor also involves opposing representations of black men in the broader society; they work with and against such constructions, carving out ways of being men, husbands, lovers, and fathers that are in opposition to media representations. The work of carving counter-representations is constant, for dominant ideology and culture are powerful (Ginsburg 1989). As McCarthy et al. (1997) have so eloquently pointed out, inner-city black and brown youth are surrounded by an engulfing discourse of crime and violence, through the media, which constructs them as "other." Situating media technologies within "the turmoil of social life as cultivators and provokers of racial meanings and common sense," McCarthy sees "television and film as fulfilling a certain bardic function, singing back to society lullabies about what a large hegemonic part of it 'already knows' " (i). The representation of the black male is key here, as much of what is distributed about the "dangerous" inner city casts the image as dangerous black males – about men who live through crime, who live the fast life, who father children but do not care for them. Media representations, from film to TV sound bites, sizzle with these images. And it is these images – these staccato statements that buzz through our minds – which inner-city black men have to negotiate as they walk out their doors each morning. It is the carving out, or more accurately, the rewriting of black masculinities that is the work of our interviewees. It is the walking through and against media representations, lack of jobs, as the result of a restructured economy and of a decidedly racist society, that constitutes the work of establishing subjectivities.

The men whom we interviewed are also working against stereotype. Dodging bullets and dodging stereotypes. This is a group that is not much heard from, as Don Belton (1996) notes, except insofar as they are authorized by unsympathetic others; the media, the police, the courts, the welfare system.

The men in Buffalo and Jersey City whom we interviewed are poor and working class, but not disaffected from work, community, or family. Some are married; most have long-term partners, with whom they may or may not live. Half of the eighteen men interviewed in Buffalo do not have a high school diploma. This contrasts sharply with the situation for African American women where nearly all of the women with whom we worked have a high school diploma. Over 38 percent of the men are active in the church, and virtually all grew up in the church. All the men have at least one child, but only a handful live with their children currently. The vast majority have wage earning jobs, but have bounced in and out of the low-paying workforce for many years. Most are totally expendable in the economy, and suffer the ravages of postindustrial society. Many have received welfare at one time, but few receive it now. They work when they can, at low-paying jobs in the service economy which renders them chronically poor. Many are deeply committed to church life. We contacted these men through cultural organizations, literacy centers, job training programs, churches, and schools.

Black, white, and Latino working-class and poor men, in sharp contrast to women (see, for example, chap. 8), are concerned with policing community borders. Recall that the white men presented in the preceding chapter constantly negotiate their own positionality vis-à-vis the "other" in their neighborhood and schools, and their own masculinity vis-à-vis their women. While "victory" in this regard is hardly assured for poor and working-class white men in the late twentieth century, their agency is wrapped around a struggle to assert identity as white and male, and to police the borders of spaces which encourage this identity to flourish. While African American men would like to do exactly the same, we will see clearly in their words below that this ambition is expressed as collective desire – as "the community needs to come together," or, more specifically, as "black men need to come together," rather than as something that is already accomplished. Omi and Winant (1986) describe a war of position as they suggest that prior to the Civil Rights Movement in the 1950s, black communities attempted to strengthen their own living spaces, thus consolidating themselves and readying their communities for what Omi and Winant describe as a war of maneuver, a direct attack on the structures of racist America. What black men in the 1990s are describing is the need again for a war of position, only this time one under the control of the men.

In the Midst of Drugs and Violence

Like African American women with whom many of these men share physical space, African American men describe neighborhoods filled with violence. Unlike the women, however, these men focus on state-sponsored and street-spawned violence and rarely touch upon the terror in the home described by black, white, and Latina females. For black men, violence is about streets and cops, and both the "good guys" (read police) and the "bad guys" (read criminals) are seen as bad for inner-city residents. (We explore this point extensively in chap. 6.) Here let us listen to black men's voices as they detail the streets, drugs, and crime that shape their lives.

LOIS: *Has the east side changed [since he was a child], or have you changed, or both?*
RICHARD: *Both, yeah both. The east side has changed. I didn't used to worry about walking down the street. Now I walk down the street, and I think about drive-by shootings. I think about situations on the east side I seen a while back, where a gang of boys would be walking down the street and they'll snatch somebody for no reason. And they call it, like, wilding, you know, I never worried about that before. I, we, never worried about walking down the street like that. And now I worry about standing on the corner and a car coming by, and just spraying bullets. . . . You know, there's a nearby street, Box Street. It's in the newspapers now. That's like right next to the projects. Now growing up, that street wasn't like that. It wasn't nowhere near like that . . . you know, it was like, drugs. It wasn't like that. That's what I mean. I could walk down Box Street.*

————

GEORGE: *I've been involved in violence. I've been involved as far as witnessing my friends, and growing up with guns and stuff like that — shooting at people. A couple of times I caught myself calming down, you know, trying to go a straight path. I found what happens, what goes around comes around. And I've had the experience of somebody shooting me. And then I had the experience of somebody jumping me, and it turned me right back around to go back to my violence friends,*

*because I know they, they'll support. I have them helping me if some-
body messing with me.*

TRACEY: *And so you were actually shot, or you just shot at?*

GEORGE: *Yeah. I was shot. I was shot one time in the chest. I've been
stabbed before. I've been stabbed several times. I've been hit by an ax,
you know, so I've had a violent life, you know, growing up as a
teenager.*

———

TRACEY: *You told me about the violence that you experienced when you
were a child with your stepfather and your mother. Is there any other
violence that you ever experienced personally?*

WILLIAM: *Oh yeah, on the streets. Yeah, I've seen people get shot. I've
seen people pull the trigger. I mean that's as violent as you can get.*

TRACEY: *What are your reactions to these things?*

WILLIAM: *It's hard to say. I don't really have any reaction. Anytime I see
any type of violence towards somebody, whether we know them or
not, you know, feeling, like man, it's sad, you know. I mean, just picture you talking to a guy, you know, and a minute later you trying to
hold him in your arms cause he done got shot, his blood is on you, you
holding him, and there's no ambulance at this point, and he's saying
stuff like, "I don't want to die now. I don't want to die now." I mean
that stuff will never go away in my mind. I been with people who did
the violence on themselves. The lady I was just talking about, about
my daughter, she tried to kill herself in front of me, and I'm not talking
about no pills. She slit both her wrists, and I never forget it. She walked
into the bathroom, closed the door, slit both her wrists. I thought I
heard water running, then I heard bump. I goes in the bathroom and
blood is coming out of both wrists. I'm trying to tie her up, I'm trying
to tie both wrists, and when the ambulance got there they definitely
said I saved her life, and I know I did, but I thought she had died right
there, because she just bent over, and I'm like, oh, but I remember not
panicking, mainly because I had seen so much violence up to that
point in my life. And that was two years ago.*

———

RICHARD: *I guess it's [violence is] not as bad with the women as it is with
the men, you know, well, black men. Because I hate to see it the way it*

is today. I hate to see it. You know, we're killing each other off. You know, and it happens every day, we'll kill each other in a second, in a heartbeat. And they don't see that. They don't see that they're selling drugs in a neighborhood, and they're destroying the neighborhood. And turning everybody into crack addicts. And, I don't know. It's just frustrating. I mean, I don't know if it's gonna always, you know, it was like that back then [in the past], but it was different. I mean crack wasn't, it didn't exist back then. Cocaine was there, but crack wasn't there. You know. It's different.

Our interviews with African American males are saturated with references to violence on the streets. In contrast to those with black women, however, the descriptions generally involve self – the narrator is detailing *his* violent encounters while in the community. Women also describe violent encounters, but women position themselves as witnesses, looking through windows while attempting to protect their children. Women detail being locked in the house, trying to nurture children as street violence swirls about them. Physical violence involving women tends to be located in domestic scenes; physical violence involving men directly is located on the street and may be perpetrated by the police.

Men also spice their descriptions of street violence with strong references to what has happened to friends. Street violence is not, therefore, *only* about self, but is also about others who are walking the streets. Many bemoan the fact that friends have been lost to violence, either killed, or living in such a way as to heighten the possibility of being killed. Significantly, violence is not narrated, for the most part, as being a problem principally affecting children. For women, the opposite is true – street violence is *always* about children and how they have to raise their children in the midst of it. (We will address this point fully in chaps. 8 and 9.)

On the American Dream
As we have pointed out, black men exhibit an expansive critique of racism and society, powerfully woven around notions of job availability. This well-established critique wraps itself around the interrelated is-

sues of lack of jobs (which assumes primary importance), police harassment, the social scripting of the black man by the media, the social production of the drug economy, and the local breakdown of "morals." Black American men understand the factors that produce the inner cities in which they live, including those of specific policies that have been embraced in order to contain and punish the black poor. No other group, as Hochschild (1995) also notes, evidences this set of insights.

At the same time, however, their critique is blunted by a strongly held notion that if you (I) fail, it is your (my) fault; that it is only hard work that keeps one from accomplishing what one wants. While at first blush this appears contradictory, and indeed it is in a certain sense, *both* understandings, the broad critique as well as the notion that you can make it if you really want to, are rooted in the African American community's historically based experience in the racist United States. Further, it is important to remember that this stark critique is being voiced by the social group most disparaged in American society. The representation of black men is such that it is difficult for a critique arising from within this group to carry weight in the larger society. Not only is it easier for those outside the group to dismiss the critique, but it is harder for those inside the group to have confidence in their judgements over time, to have these judgements be anything more than angry stabs at American society. This is even more the case given a powerfully packaged dominant ideology which suggests that anyone can make it if only they try hard enough. Embracing the notion that anyone can make it must also be understood, though, as a move from within the black American community to counter white racist notions that although America is the land of opportunity, it is not so for blacks. Thus the ideology was handed *down* to the community, but it was also homegrown *within* the community as a way of insisting on racial equality.[1]

The idea that you can make it if you try hard enough is encoded within both hope for the future and understandings of the role of schooling. When we asked men what they hoped to be doing five years from now, the following emerged:

VINCE: *In five years, I hope to be in law school. Working towards passing that bar.*

TRACEY: What could get in the way of that?

VINCE: Me and myself. I can be my worst enemy.

TRACEY: What could make it happen?

VINCE: Becoming unfocused. Letting pride get in the way. So I have to stay focused.

———

CRAIG: Do you think it's [the future he has described] going to be this way?

DONALD: Yeah, if you put your mind to it, you can do anything.

CRAIG: What would make you very happy?

DONALD: Lots of money. A decent lady I could be with. Own my own home. And that's it. Travel, get up and go when I get ready to go.

———

TRACEY: In five years what do you hope to be doing?

JULIUS: Retire from the Board of Ed [he is a teacher's aide]. Teaching kids the good things about life and the up and down road I came through. Reach out and touch your kids. You can't save them all, but I try to touch one or two, or what I can do, a day. And just design T-shirts and be traveling and having fun. Take me a group of kids on the road and teach them how to sell T-shirts and be promoters in their own eyes.

LOIS: What do you see as getting in the way of doing that?

JULIUS: Me. I'm my own worse enemy. If I don't want to do it, it can't be done. So I'm my own worse enemy. That's the only way I see myself stopping.

Each of these men envisions the future as being largely in his own hands, and this is very common among the men we interviewed. The ideology that you can make it if you really want to is well worked through in American culture and provides a ready discourse when individuals are trying to make sense of their own experiences, whether individually or collectively. Jennifer Hochschild (1995) argues this point forcefully, calling the American Dream a "control ideology of Americans" (p. xi). She states that the American Dream does not refer to the right to get rich, "but rather the promise that all Americans have a reasonable chance to achieve success as they define it—material or otherwise—through their own efforts, and to gain virtue and fulfillment through success" (p. xi). In fact, the African American community, in opposition to racist America, historically adopted this ideology within itself as well. In the face of American society telling African Americans that they could *not* do certain things, *not* actualize the American Dream, an oppositional culture developed wherein blacks were told within the community that they *could* do a great many things, irrespective of dominant ideology about blacks. This braiding of understandings of oppression with a sense that the individual must keep trying to overcome obstacles is reflected in black male discourse today. Unfortunately, however, in the current time, the broader economic realities as well as those associated specifically with central cities effectively blocks individual mobility in the vast majority of cases.

The notion that the individual is responsible ultimately for his personal outcomes is nowhere more clear than in narrations about schooling, both past and present.

TRACEY: *Did you finish high school?*
RASHON: *No. I left in the twelfth grade.*
TRACEY: *You left?*
RASHON: *I left Alabama in the twelfth grade.*
TRACEY: *And you didn't come back and finish here [Buffalo]? Were you kicked out, or were you just—*
RASHON: *I just left. They [my grades] kept going back and forth.*
TRACEY: *What kind of student were you in high school?*
RASHON: *About a C. I could have been an A if I had put in the effort. I feel I didn't even put any effort for certain classes. Like science, I mean. Social studies and math, I liked. English was alright. But I liked literature better. And if I didn't study, I could go in and make an 80 or a 70. I figured—why study? But science I didn't like, because the teacher didn't like me, and that made it even worse. We kept bumping heads. And I wouldn't put no effort in the class. But the rest of the classes I would. I could pass it. But like my grandmother said, by the skin of my teeth. But I wouldn't put no real effort into it until like, maybe, finals*

*time. I would study to make, to pass a test. But I didn't put in no effort.
I could have been an honor student. But I didn't put any effort. And
that was my fault, now.*

TRACEY: *It was your fault? Do you think the school's at fault for any
of it?*

RASHON: *A little, but . . .*

Rashon holds himself responsible for not doing well in school. While
this may be partially true, and one might consider him "mature" for
understanding the part he played in constructing his current condition,
this notion of self-blame runs through many of the narratives and
matches the assumption that the individual is ultimately responsible
for his own position. Consider Richard, an artist, and a home-care
worker earning minimum wage with no benefits:

LOIS: *Can you tell me a story about your education? Something that
stands out as being a turning point for the way you looked at the
school, or the way you looked at yourself?*

RICHARD: *I'll say art. Art was the one thing, out of everything in school,
that I could do well. I was really good at it. I mean, I got like 90s, you
know, in art class. Even though, I guess, you're talking about specific,
like history or English . . . like I say, I love to read. You know, I could
sit back and read all day. I could go through novels. I love to read. I
love history. I was good at history, you know, because I love to read.*

LOIS: *But you mean, there's no reason why you shouldn't have done
well in high school. You're very smart, very well spoken, you love to
read. What happened? Do you know?*

RICHARD: *I don't know. Guess it's hard to say. I guess I got tired of
school, I got tired of going. And I just didn't want to do it anymore,
which was stupid. It was very stupid, you know, when I think about it
now. Because a couple friends around me, they done the same thing;
they dropped out, and none of them today, they don't have a high
school diploma [neither does he]. And they're like, you know, "I really
wish I would have, you know, at the time. I really wish I would have
stayed at it." But I got tired of it. I didn't want to go anymore. I didn't
want to get up in the morning. I didn't want to deal with it. I didn't*

think it helped me. You know, I didn't think, you know, the English and the math and the science, you know, I told myself, what use is all this to me? How is this gonna benefit me once I get out? You know, I really didn't see how it would help. Well, I knew why I needed the math, I guess, in a sense, and the reading. But I guess the whole basic set up of it is like, how is this gonna help me once I get out? Because a lot, you know, I got a lot of kids ask that today. It's like, how does this affect my life, you know, today, you know, once I get out? You'll find out later, you know, it's funny.

Richard dropped out of high school in the tenth grade and never went back, not even to complete a G.E.D. When he talks about schooling, he centers the critique wholly on himself — he was stupid; he should have known better; he didn't understand the importance of English, science, and so forth. Many students, of course, could make the same statements about schooling, but most do not drop out. The schools and parents hold middle-class students in, and often expel the poor, particularly black males (Fine 1992). With the systemic critique floating among black men, it is absolutely striking that not one man holds the school accountable for his (failed) interaction with it. It is always, in the final analysis, the fault of the individual man if he went astray of the school system (which the majority of the men interviewed did).

As these very same men narrate their desires for their children, it is always in terms of school — they should pay attention in school; they should go to college; they should do their homework. While this is arguably good advice, of course, the point is that the individualistic ideology is barely punctured by the sweeping systemic critique in evidence among this same group. It is, in fact, difficult to sustain these two sets of discourses simultaneously. Action is either provoked under one or the other, and each is inevitably blocked by the competing discourse. In other words, on the one hand, a man will desperately desire to make it in the future. He goes back to school. His experience in school is negative and he reverts to the systemic critique, thus prompting dropping out. Once he drops out, however, unless some broader movement is there to propel action under the critique, he is subject, once again, to the individualistic ideology and blames himself for failure. This dual discursive frame leads to a great deal of paralysis in the actual lives of poor black men (Weis 1985).

This discursive duality is particularly prominent in narrations about why it is that so many black men are in prison. Highlighting the two men below serves to point out the ways in which these two competing discourses can be at warring odds even within the same individual, emerging at different points in time with respect to different issues:

CRAIG: *Why do you think there are a lot of men in jail these days?*
BUTCH: *Because a lot of people, a lot of men were deprived of the family unit, that type of thing. There are certain people that are in prison that have a strong family foundation, and still that [crime] was something that they wanted to do, you know, but the majority is, you know, problems at home. It starts out at home. Some people just, I don't know, like I said, some people just wanted to* choose *[our emphasis] that type of lifestyle and, you know, they wanted to follow in somebody else's footsteps. They didn't want to be known as a punk or . . .*

———

RICHARD: *I guess some of them just want what they want, and they want it now, and they don't really care about having a job. I mean, there are some out there that just, they love being criminals, you know, that's the kind of life that they want to lead. I don't care if they were in a job, you know, if everybody had a job, there are just certain people that just love to take [steal] than work for a living. Then I guess that there are some that, just because of the job situation, they are kind of forced into it, or they are led into it. You know, 'cause after a period of time it's like, they don't want to work at McDonald's and make, I don't know, three something an hour. They look at the drug situation and they see, like, fourteen- and fifteen-year-olds making like $5000 to $6000 a week, or something like that. You look at that, versus making $100 or something.*
LOIS: *Is that an accurate estimate, you think? I mean, can a fifteen-year-old kid make $5000 or $6000 a week?*
RICHARD: *Yeah, they can make a couple thousand a week, you know, fourteen or fifteen years old. Walking around with big diamond all*

over, gold, cars, everything. I mean, versus working, like I said, McDon-
ald's job or some fast food place or, you know, you weigh that, and
they'll go for the other. It's like, why not?

Richard, in particular, exemplifies the dual discursive frame alluded
to above. He suggests that there is some measure of "choice" as to serving time in jail, but at the same time, such "choice" is rooted in real experiences within central cities, and specifically the fact that the drug
economy offers money and opportunities that the legitimate economy
of the city does not.

We have suggested in this section that a dual discourse floats
through black males in a way that it does not float through other
groups. Those who are not immobilized by this dual discourse do indeed land in some very important spaces, where they are attempting to
carve out what it means to be black men and raise the next generation
of youth. One such space is the black church, where men's groups are
flourishing as men take stock in their position in the community.

Men and the Church

In the black community, we hear a striking commitment to, engagement with, and embodiment of religion and spirituality by both men
and women. From men we can hear a strong, if ambivalent, relation to
church, commitment, and belief in God. A full two-thirds of our informants grew up in homes in which religion was woven into domestic
practice. Arnold, a reverend in Jersey City, sees the church as his salvation. There he saw women as role models. He worries, today, about the
diminished importance of religion to impoverished black communities.
Indeed, he worries that the church has not worked effectively within
poor black neighborhoods.

I worry about religion and how much impact or how much worth you
can place on religion, how much it will, and how much it does influ-
ence people's lives. Because if it doesn't, then all the work that I do, all
the sermons I preach, all the weddings I perform in the name of God,
the funerals I preach, the counseling I did, it's all for naught. But I

*know the stuff is real and I know it makes a difference, but you know,
in the back of my mind there is always this worry, you know, that one
day, nobody's even going to come to church, people are not even going
to care, they're going to wonder who is God and who says you are
working for Him? Do you know what I mean? All those kinds of
things I worry about because I am very young at this. I have only been
serving in the ministry for about five years. And I know people who
have been at it for sixty years. I know people who have been in it for
ten or fifteen years and are tired of it. They are aggravated, they're at
the point where they see that their work may be in vain, that they don't
need to continue, that they need to do something else. And that's not a
good sign. They are not encouraging me. They are not saying, "You've
got the rest of your life ahead of you. It's going to be a wonderful
thing." They're saying to me, "Get the hell out and do something else."
It's going to be a problem; it's an uphill struggle. It gets worse, when
does it ever get better?*

Sam, too, grew up in a family of prayer:

*And at one point I was, I was really very sick. And it was the week; I
was sick on the weekend and then I went on my second mass retreat.
And I went anyway, you know. And I didn't tell anyone I was sick and
I didn't tell my mother, you know, my parents or any of my friends that
I was sick because it was an illness where, that I had when I was
younger. And I said, oh Lord, I have to have an operation. And I didn't
want that to happen, you know. That'll take a few months, you know,
away from [laughs], what it was, but what happened was, I went to the
retreat and I just let everything go, you know, and I didn't think about
being sick. I tried to put my whole mind and body and soul into the
retreat itself. And spirit, you know, in the retreat. And I came home
and I finally told my mother that I was sick and I was going through
the problems. And that was the first time me and my mother sincerely
talked to each other, you know. And my father was in the hospital
because he was in and out of the hospital throughout my life. And that
was the first time we really sat down and talked and prayed, you
know. And I don't remember anytime that we prayed together, you*

know, even when I was younger she'd say, now go say your prayers. But no time we seriously prayed together. And then I called my pastor and she [my mother], you know, asked him to pray for me.

These young men, many of whom testify that they have been saved by the church, as peers have succumbed to streets, drugs, and violence, worry that the black church as an institution has outlived its utility for the black community. From Alex, we hear both the critique and the hope:

Growing up I had a great sense of community. I think I've lost that sense, which is why it was very easy for me to move out of the community and move into another area. I guess the only segment of the community I feel comfortable with is the, or are the church folks. The people at my home church where I grew up. And those people, I am very familiar with them; I know them. And it is interesting because the church is located two blocks from the house that my parents live in and that I grew up in. Even though the people that go to the church don't necessarily live in the immediate area, I don't think, most of them don't live as close as I live. I'm one of the people who live closest to the church. It's actually two separate communities because the people who live closest to the church don't attend church. So it's the people who live closest to the church that I don't feel a sense of community with. I feel more of a sense of community with the people in the building, rather than the people who live around the building. Interestingly enough, I'm one of the people who live around the building. And I don't have sense of community with my neighbors. I can't explain, I guess, why I don't. I guess we just don't have the same interests. Some of my neighbors don't attend church. Religion is not really a part of their life. They have different ideals as it relates to raising children.

Alex and Obe worry that spirituality has moved out of the church, that the church has moved out of the neighborhood, and that the next generation of black boys has consequently been abandoned.

MICHELLE: *You say the church has abused you?*
OBE: *Yes, teaching all that foolishness and having me give donations*

and stuff and wasting all my beautiful Sundays when I could have
been out. It sucked
MICHELLE: *Did you used to go to church on Sundays?*
OBE: *Yeah, I went for the wrong reasons and everything, but I ain't got*
nothing against the real church, because I know the church is in my
heart and that this is just a bunch of shit; they can open it up and have
dances and feed the homeless for real and have them sleeping on them
benches, you know. That kind of thing, shelters. So I felt abused by it
and abused by the sequestering and segregation of people.

One young black male community activist, recently deceased, authored a poem in 1995 which reflects a broad-based disgust at institutions throughout his city "designed to keep you deaf, dumb, and blind." In that poem, Che Lumumba wrote:

Asphalt jungle, knee deep cracking sidewalks
　　unseen but real dividers
to keep us on the reservation
　　in Jerkey City, New Jerkey . . .

He continues:

Churches and Bars on every block
competing for lost souls
One with the word the other the bird
Both designed to keep you deaf, dumb and blind . . .

While Che Lumumba despaired about what he saw in the church, he had no doubt of its standing in Jersey City. For many other African American men, however, the church offers a site in which they can renegotiate what it means to be a man and reassume control of their communities. The men in our focus group acknowledge the contradictions and disappointments:

ODYSSEUS: *I was raised in the church. It consumed my life. I had no*
choice but what you might consider "early spirituality."

ARNOLD: *Really, I was dragged by a little old lady, Mrs. Watson. She took ten of us, dragged us to church, to Sunday school. . . . We met friends and made friendships that lasted a lifetime. That was a key element that saved us from the streets. We all knew that all the mothers, and all the fathers, were watching us. Mrs. Watson brought each of us, and taught us to bear witness; she taught us something about character, believing and God. That God could change the lives of people. We were making, we were creating people by going to the church. Church was like a factory to make good, principled people. To create leaders. Trouble is, Mrs. Watson doesn't believe in the institution anymore.*

Odysseus, Arnold, Alex, Obe, Sam, and others, young black men raised with deep and impermeable beliefs in the church, now worry about its value to the community. They worry that the black church has allowed spirituality to slip from social activism and thus abandoned the community. Odysseus poses the dilemma most profoundly when he allows us to listen in on his internal struggle:

I keep faith, but at times, I do have questions, especially around social issues. I cherish faith, trust hope, despite the despair, and the church taught me this. Taught me to be community minded and help others; to pass beggars and give, and hope that God will bless you. Keep me out of trouble . . . I can only thank God, I wouldn't have the strength to do all this on my own. But when it comes to social issues, we don't deal. We used to work for affordable housing, then the church got into the business of housing for profit, corruptions, greed, and hypocrisy. I don't know when I'll open "Star" magazine and read an exposé. No one will talk about AIDS. We have people dropping dead while playing the piano on Sundays, and we don't mention it. One week you're playing at your friend's funeral, next week it's yours. And we don't mention it . . .

These young men explain that as the black church gained a meager slice of social power within the Jersey City political machine, smuggled out of a white bureaucratic elite, some of the elders, the church leaders, grew to be seen as hypocrites, less willing to struggle hard for the community, to share the resources, to make room for the next generation.

ODYSSEUS: *We are stuck, then, with the question, for whom is the church a community of worship and commitment? We want it to be a utopia, but it's not. Aren't we responsible to help find solutions? . . . At some point, we lost faith in children as the critical element in our community. We used to march against homelessness, now we have a soup kitchen, every 4th Sunday of the month. The church tried to put a band aid on its own guilt. We can say we tried.*

ARNOLD: *Church is like an old shirt, with lots of buttons. It doesn't fit as comfortably as before. We may need to put another panel in the waist, or go on a spiritual diet. But we do need to take back the church for ourselves and the community. . . . There has to be hope. As we look back . . . My soul looks back and wonders how I got over . . . If we could only make it over.*

These young men represent the generation of black men born in the midst of or just after the intense civil rights struggle. Knowing their elders gained much, but left much undone, they dream of a church *for* community. Ever mindful of *their* accountability to the community, and their not-yet-fulfilled-obligation to the next generation of African American youth coming up, these young men struggle to imagine a program, a project, an institution, that could make a difference in these very hard times.

Church and the Reworking of Social Representations
The church is still a site of hope for many, despite growing reservations. In Buffalo, we met with a black men's group in the Still Waters Tabernacle Church where we conducted several focus group discussion sessions. This group is self-consciously carving out and affirming a counter-hegemonic black masculinity, a black masculinity rooted in the black man as father, as leader of young men, and as patroller of the borders of community. Where they critique black women, it is only insofar as they do not believe that black women are supportive of this endeavor. As we sit with them in these focus group discussions, the role of father surfaces quickly, and much of the discussion revolves around raising the next generation of boys:

JAMES: *You know, as Julius was saying, basketball is not the answer to the problem for the youth per se [referring to midnight basketball programs intended to keep boys off the streets]. Every time, you know, [there is] some problem . . . they [city officials] get midnight basketball to get the youth out of trouble. But you can't play basketball all day, you know what I'm saying. They need . . . actually need a father in the home, and* be *a father, what have you. The mother is a mother.*

TRACEY: *When you say, "Father be a father and mother be a mother," what specifically do you mean by that?*

JAMES: OK. *You need your father. If they make a kid, they need to be there still, you know. You have ladies being the mother, the mothers being the fathers too. They need their father, they need the man in that picture too. But, you know, like I say, it starts at home, and then the mothers need to teach. I put it like this, I feel like the parents need to teach their kids, respect is the bottom line, you know.*

JULIUS: *Like James is saying, a mother can't teach her son how to play basketball, when her son wants to go to the court and play, you know. His father needs to be at the court where he can go to play basketball, and teach him just the way to shoot and just the way you dribble to the bucket. The mother cannot do that. The mother can raise her son to a point, and discipline, and then the father has to step in too, and put some discipline. I think, I'm from the old school where, you know, I still give my father much respect, and he asks me to do something, tells me to do something, there's no problem. There ain't no talk-back. Might be a question every now and then, but it's well, okay, you're still my father, I don't care about how old I am. You're still my father and I still have respect for you. This is your house. And I have, you know, to abide by that, and my son . . . I have a sixteen-year-old son, and my son have to do the same thing. And, you know, your kids only do what they see you do. You know, if you sit and smoke a cigarette or a joint on the porch, then that's what they're going to do, where . . . they'll think it's alright to do it because their daddy, you know, did it. You know, just like, you feel it's alright to bring women in and out of your house, and you've got a son or daughter there, well . . . you know, they think that's going to be alright when they . . . you know, well, you did it. So why can't I do it?*

This group of men are terribly concerned about the future of youth – there is no respect for authority, no respect for parents, the lure of the streets is great. But they are not only concerned about youth – they are also concerned about this generation of men and women, arguing that the men, in particular, need to "come together" and take hold of their own communities.

TRACEY: *Do you all think that men need to change? And, if so, what would make them better?*
JULIUS: *I think we need to change; we need to come together as a community. That's where unity is. A lot more men to seek God and to have an understanding what God is all about. They don't know the unity. They need to find out. You need to have classes on that where they need to, you know, we need to get 'em off the street, and have them in here [the church], so they can become better fathers and role models. Because I look at it that football players and the basketball players are not role models. We are role models, where they can see, touch, and feel everyday. And be able to come up and ask and question. And say whatever they'd like to say. We are role models. You know, their mothers and fathers are role models. They spend most of their time with them and see them everyday. So, you know, that's what I look at it. That, as far as men need to do, we need to come together and raise our kids, and our boys and girls, and our communities right. We need to take it back. Because if the community is strong, there's nothing that can get by us. Because if we're so strong the politicians will come to us. "What do you think we need to do to make this city or community better?" They're going to be coming to you all the time, asking you for your backup, your leadership, asking you, can you put a program over here. Would you help us fund another program? That's what we need. And that's what we don't have. We have a few good black men, but not a lot of good black men that we need.*
DWAYNE: *As black men, there definitely needs to be a change. The bottom line is we just, it's time we just need to stand up and be men. One thing I learned is that authority respects authority. And we have to take authority in our own communities, and our families. And like he*

said about the politicians, when they do come into our neighborhood to look for things, there is no authority. There is no authority figure. So there is no respect. So, therefore, they can do whatever they want to do and basically get away with it. And like he said, it's time to come together and be men, and stand up and come together, and, you know, stop sugar-coating that there's not a problem in our neighborhoods. Because there is. And, we have to realize it and deal with it, and not look to anyone else to solve our problems. We have to. And it's time we stand up and be men and do that.

JULIUS: *And we don't bring the guns in here; we don't bring the drugs in here. We have no planes [to bring the drugs from overseas]. We have no busses, and all, that we own and can drive right into the neighborhood and drop it [drugs] off on the corner. That's our problem. We don't have none of that, you know.*

James, Julius, and Dwayne are engaged in long-term discussions about community, masculinity, and themselves. For them, the church offers a powerful site within which notions of manhood are reconstructed and affirmed, and it is a space about which they care deeply. They voice over and over the notion of "coming together" as a community, "coming together" as men. By this they mean that black men need to stand up collectively and take responsibility for their communities and families, thus enabling them to patrol the borders of community in a way that other groups of men do. Drawing upon essentialist notions of manhood (men can teach boys basketball; women can't) and working with border-patrolling strategies typical of white working-class male communities, as we suggest in chapters 2 and 3, these men are not so far apart from their white male counterparts.

In their desire to affirm position in the community, they ask women's support, which is not, in their experience, always forthcoming.

DWAYNE: *I don't know, somewhat I see more and more black women realizing it, but just, just to realize that they [women] have to get behind their men and support them in what they're doing, and that there is a struggle out here and, and a lot of us are trying as hard as we can. And so I would basically say, just to realize that they need to get behind their men and support them.*

JULIUS: Yeah, because behind every strong man is always a strong woman.

TRACEY: What do you guys mean, "get behind their man?"

DWAYNE: Support, I mean.

TRACEY: Is that in a traditional sense? Like staying at home, or . . .

DWAYNE: No, no, not —

JULIUS: Just help him out. You know, "Honey, it's going to be alright." "Today . . . you had a bad day." "Can I help you with something?" "What are you doing today?" You know.

DWAYNE: Support.

JULIUS: Like if you got a wife that, you go to church, and she don't get up and go. Now, how's everything, how's anything going to be right when you come home because you're leaving home, you're leaving Satan at home, and you ain't taking Satan with you, so when you come back home, you're going to hear Satan coming in that door, because it ain't right. You know, you're [in] balance, but she ain't [in] balance. So that's where we have to learn to get behind each other [men and women]. And just like, you know, if you're running an office or you've got a business, your wife should be in that business. Or just like you're a politician, your wife should be behind you in what you're doing, you know. Be able to know, well, he's sick today, so I'm going to pick up the load today and do what I've got to do, because I know what he's supposed to do.

DWAYNE: But even in the sense about how, if I'm doing something, then, you know, just let me know that you're with me. And you [a man] might fail once or twice, but I'm still with you. I remember one time I went to the movies [on a date]. She looking at the movies, and there was a white man in the movies, and she was like, you know, that's the way I would like you to dress. Well, he got on a two-thousand-dollar suit, you know, and, which he didn't pay for! They're like just props, you know. Excuse me, but sorry, I'm not there yet, you know. So, you know, just unrealistic things like that. We look at what someone else is doing, well, in the white community, and we want to say, well, that's what we want you to do. Okay, fine, but it takes time, it takes effort. A lot of women don't realize that. It's about "When are you going to give me mine?"

Many men with whom we talked complained – that women do not stand by them; they do not silence themselves with respect to public complaints about men in the community (see chaps. 7 and 8 for differences between black and white women regarding the issue of domestic violence, for example); they are too materialistic; and they leave men if they don't get what they want. But these men do not wholly blame women for all that is wrong in their lives. Again, the expansive systemic critique that black men weave enables them to place more of its blame *outside* of the black community rather than within it. This is not to suggest that rage and frustration are not expressed both within the family and community as black males attempt to carve social and economic space. The point is simply that when articulated, a critique of why black men are in the position they are in does not, generally speaking, place blame primarily on the shoulders of women.

We have suggested here that these men are working both within and against dominant ideology, culture, and the representation of black males – as Du Bois said they would – with double consciousness. They are trying to return the spears of blame back to the economy, the politicians, the media, the police, and corporate America to get the load of blame off of their backs. Jon is smart, African American, gay, and angry:

You have to understand, yeah, we're getting all that, but it's not a movement, it just tied up in technical bullshit . . . joining black associations to change stuff, I got to tell you . . . that people need houses? . . . tell that these cops killin' people? . . . that you're responsible for the drugs? I got to tell you that AIDS is your problem? I got to tell you that the children are murdering and raping because you are giving subsidies to these big companies? . . . I got to tell you the pharmaceuticals are dumping their waste, biomedical and nonbiodegradable substances and all that stuff? . . . I got to tell you that you are all crazy? Why don't

you just look at your televisions and see that you are mad. Look up at
the sky and you can't see the stars in New Jersey. I got to tell you that
you are just out of control, that you're an idiot monster, I got to tell you
that you're dying . . . do I really have to do that? . . . and then I have to
sit down and analyze it, and then have to let you sit there and use your
technology to transcribe and come up with some bullshit about it and
you ain't gonna do nothing to save nobody. It makes me tired.

In the absence of stable jobs and a listening government and in the
presence of raw racism throughout the class structure, the task of au-
thoring a counterhegemonic race/gender script is immensely difficult.
These men are, however, doing the "lived" equivalent of writing
against the grain that black writers expound. "Writing back" in 1990s
racist America without a social movement of meaning constitutes
much of the work of today's working-class and poor black male, just as
is true of the black intellectual.

Issues of empowerment signify the lives of these and other African
American men. For many, the response to racism propels a sense of
powerlessness and despair, an opting out (Pastor 1994; Fine 1991;
Hochschild 1995). For others, the response has been heightened participation in social groups, neighborhood- or church-related organizations, or in fledgling social movements to foster a sense of personal and/
or collective empowerment. Most African American men, we have
found, live in both worlds. Contradictory beliefs and projects collide in
the very same minds and communities (Hochschild 1995).

Today young African American men are, again, as the Black Panthers were in a different way, trying to regain control of their communities. The men we introduce in this chapter are using the church, men's
groups, and community-based organizations to restore community
life to neighborhoods long abandoned by the private and now public
sector. Frighteningly, however, in haunting but depoliticized memory
of activities thirty years now gone, substantial numbers of younger African American youth are also patrolling and armed. But not for collective or communal self-defense. The movement seems far away, visions
of possibility appear long evaporated, communities have been for-
saken, borders go unchecked. For African American men who have, to

date, neither engaged in nor developed a counterpart to the black femi-nist/womanist movement, the process of becoming psychologically in-formed – as many of our informants have done in the church, in school, and in community groups – does not alter the imbalance of material resources and social power. It certainly does not eradicate the racism they endure regularly. While church, school, community programs, and other "free spaces" enable a sense of control over one's circum-stances, as we elaborate in chapter 12, the larger picture is well known, by these men in particular. Their social critique, their insights, run fun-damentally counter to the sense of perceived progress in which they so desperately want to believe. James Baldwin knew this well when he wrote, "To be Black and conscious in America is to be in a constant state of rage."

5

"It's a Small Frog That Will Never Leave Puerto Rico"
Puerto Rican Men and the Struggle for Place in the United States

NUYORICAN

I fight for you, Puerto Rico, You know?
I defend myself, for your name, You know?
When I enter your island, I feel like a stranger, You know?
I enter to encounter more and more, You know?
But you with you false hood (disillusion),
You denied me your smile,
I feel angry, bitter
I am your son
from the migration
of forced sin.
You send me off to be born in foreign lands,
Why, why, because we are poor, right?
Why, did you want to rid yourself of your poor,
Now I return, with a boricua* heart, and you,
You despised me, you look at me with contempt,
You attack how I speak,
while I eat McDonald's in American discotheques
I couldn't dance the salsa in San Juan.
I danced the one that I danced en El Barrio.**
Filled up with all of your ways,
Well, if you don't want me, well
I have a Puerto Rico delicious and tasty where I can find refuge
In New York, and in many other streets
that honor your present, preserve all of
your values, by the way, oh please, don't make me suffer,
You know?

—TATO LAVIERA

CRAIG: *How did you feel when you moved into your own apartment and began taking small jobs?*

RICARDO: *I felt a sense of responsibility, a sense of destiny. I felt that if I could make that work at that age, then actually nothing could really stand in my way. In fact, it was the first test of becoming a man. My father once told me that just being a man is not of age. It's a matter of mental state. You are a man when you're ready to be a man. You could be forty-five and still act like a teenager. You live with your parents and expect your parents to pay for your meals and board you. You can be twelve and you can bring home the money to take care of the family. That's the difference between a man [and a boy].*

[Now] it's the same attitude [for me]. There's nothing I think I'll ever do that'll compare to what my father was able to do. To be able to not only father fourteen children, not only just to stay there, you know, some men would have ran away. And then do it today, costly, he stayed there and reared fourteen of us. He wasn't satisfied with the public school system, even though as an option, he wouldn't have to pay tuition. He wouldn't have to buy meals. He wouldn't have to buy uniforms. He wouldn't have to buy books. He could just send us to the public school system. He chose not to and put all fourteen of us through a Catholic school. That's quite an accomplishment.

PUERTO RICANS WITHIN THE AMERICAN MOSAIC CONSTITUTE A SUBSTANTIAL proportion of the population of northeastern cities, particularly New York City, where a million Puerto Ricans lived as early as 1960. While other minorities experienced a period of socioeconomic advancement during the 1960s – which was followed by a phase of limited gains during the 1970s – the Puerto Rican experience is one of continually growing disadvantage since 1960 (Sandefur and Tienda 1988; Torres and Rodriguez 1991; Bean and Tienda 1988; Moore and Pinderhughes 1993; Melendez, Rodriguez, and Figueroa 1991).[1]

No matter how it is measured, the disadvantaged and deteriorating relative position of Puerto Ricans is clear. Their median family income was lower than that of blacks, other Latinos, and Native Americans in 1960, and, most importantly, these differences widened by 1980. By 1987, the Puerto Rican median family income was half that of whites. Puerto Ricans, among Latinos, constitute the only group for whom the family income gap did not narrow relative to whites during the 1970s

(Bean and Tienda 1988). Poverty is higher among this group than any other, and Puerto Ricans consistently report lower labor force participation rates than any other group. Labor force participation declined for males from 1960 to 1980, while that of females has grown. Marta Tienda has speculated that Puerto Ricans are becoming an "underclass" within the Latino population in the United States, a situation about which many are justifiably concerned (Tienda 1989).

Nicholas Lemann (1991) has pointed out that, for a period in the 1980s, half the Puerto Rican population on the mainland was living in poverty. Lemann's agenda was to front and center Puerto Ricans as being what he calls "the other underclass" in the United States. Poverty is not the only issue here. Charging that there is no institutional network that could challenge the position of Puerto Ricans on the mainland, he explosively states:

> Practically everybody in America feels some kind of emotion about blacks, but Puerto Rican leaders are the only people I've ever run across for whom the emotion is pure envy. In New York City, black median family income is substantially higher than Puerto Rican. . . . Puerto Rican families are more than twice as likely as black families to be on welfare, and are about 50 percent more likely to be poor. In the mainland United States, Puerto Ricans have nothing like the black institutional network of colleges, churches, and civil rights organizations; there isn't a large cadre of visible Puerto Rican successes in nearly every field; black politicians are more powerful than Puerto Rican politicians in all the big cities with big Puerto Rican populations; and there is a feeling that blacks have America's attention, whereas Puerto Ricans, after a brief flurry of publicity back in *West Side Story* days, have become invisible. (97)

Lemann pits Puerto Ricans against African Americans, thus letting elite whites totally off the hook. His basic point about the relative invisibility of groups, however, holds.

Although in 1992 *Euromoney* reported that Puerto Rico had registered the highest per capita income in 1991 in the Caribbean, $6,000, there remains widespread poverty on the island. Nevertheless, all the technological comforts of today are available for those who can afford to purchase them. Urban Puerto Rico looks eerily like Anywhere, U.S.A., with its American stores in American-style malls and ubiquitous fast-food chains. In the countryside, "mini-mansions" have spread in recent years to the most recondite corners of the small island. However weak, there is a striving insular economy. But the economy does not thrive for those whose voices you will hear here. These are the peasants and workers with literally nowhere to go given that land has been appropriated by large American-owned agribusiness ventures and that Operation Bootstrap (a plan presumably intended to industrialize the island) has failed to provide enough work for islanders. The poor of Puerto Rico were catapulted, by virtue of their poverty, from their island to the mainland shores where they live in barrios in U.S. cities. They attend the poorest of urban schools, are relatively uneducated, have little money, and are cut off from their mothers and fathers, brothers and sisters who remain on the island. As Tato Laviera says, only the poor "eat McDonald's in American discotheques" and dance the salsa "en El Barrio." Filled with the ways of Puerto Rico only to be looked at with contempt by those who dance the salsa in San Juan, those living on the mainland, nevertheless, make their way between worlds (Lorenzo 1995).

Perched marginally in the shrinking U.S. economy and affected by large-scale cuts in public funds for housing, training, and education, Puerto Rican men sing a different song than that sung by either white men or African American men. They affirm their Puerto Ricanness, staking claim to what Benmayor, Torruellas, and Juarbe (1992) call "cultural citizenship." Puerto Rican men want to preserve and protect with pride a form of *being* Puerto Rican in the United States, a form that includes the patriarchal authority with which they grew up. (As we will see in chap. 10, Puerto Rican women also have a stake in reclaiming cultural citizenship, yet they are staking out identities carved in quiet resistance to traditional notions of patriarchy.)

We have seen this dance choreographed through all the communities with which we worked, and yet, it is particularly striking in the Puerto Rican community, where "hombres" are attempting to hold onto a form of being Puerto Rican rooted in patriarchal authority in their everyday actions. While the white, African American, and Latina women whose interviews are presented in chapters 7 through 10 tell horrific stories of patriarchal abuse in the kitchen and the bedroom, white men and African American men remain silent on these issues. But Latinos speak. In this text, unfortunately, Latinos carry the burden of male violence we *know* to to exist across ethnic lines because, among the men whom we interviewed, only Latinos "fessed up."

African American women have never been wholly snared by this form of patriarchy in the United States primarily as a result of the historical denial of well paying jobs to African American men. White women are not, at the moment, wholly rejecting of it (see chaps. 7 and 8, respectively). In the Puerto Rican community, the song of patriarchy is both sung and defeated at one and the same time, loudly and with great passion, sung in actions as well as words on a day-to-day basis and sung to affirm cultural citizenship. Puerto Rican men in the United States are demanding with this song to be heard as "men" in a country where they are stripped of all the costumes and accoutrements that enable men to be "men."

The men whom we interviewed are predominantly island born and are members of the working poor. Most work doing odd jobs or picking fruit at orchards just south of Buffalo. Many hold service positions or work part-time as mechanics or in security in what remains of industrial positions in Jersey City. Several either volunteer or work at low-paying jobs at a social service agency designed to help people of Latino/Latina background. In Buffalo and Jersey City, this population is overwhelmingly Puerto Rican. Almost all have moved from New York City or, in sometimes the case of Buffalo, from New Jersey, where their parents moved in the 1950s. Some were born in the United States; most moved to the mainland when they were young. Moving to the United States does not mean never returning to Puerto Rico, however, as crowded red-eye flights from New York testify. Many of the men interviewed have at least one child in Puerto Rico, the result of an earlier relationship. While some of these mothers lived on the mainland and then moved back to Puerto Rico, most of the men, in fact, lived in Puerto Rico for at least a brief period of their lives, where they had children. They express strong emotional attachment for their children in the

United States, although half of the men do not live with their children and do not necessarily provide support for them, or even see them. We have here a group of men strongly connected emotionally to notions of family and kin, but many of the men have no relational connection with the children they father. They hang on tightly, though, to the ideology of family. Family *should* be certain things, even though, given economic realities, life may not allow it to be.

Demand to Be Recognized

In poor northeastern communities like those in Buffalo and Jersey City, Puerto Rican men, in spite of great poverty, affirm a form of what Benmayor, Torreulos, and Juarbe (1992) call "cultural citzenship":

> Cultural citizenship expresses a process through which a subordinated group of people arrives at a common identity, establishes solidarity, and defines a common set of interests that binds the group together into action. Critical to this process is the affirmation and assertion of perceived collective rights which have been ignored or denied by the dominant society and its legal canon. Defined in this way, cultural citizenship is clearly oppositional, articulating the needs of people who do not hold state power. (72)

Cultural citizenship, then, refers to attitudes and practices that affirm the right to equal treatment and participation in the society through the right to cultural difference and dual allegiances.

Our interviews with Puerto Rican men alert us to the fact that these men affirm, on a day-to-day basis, their "cultural citizenship." Far more aggressively than the Puerto Rican women whom we interviewed, Puerto Rican men put themselves forward as being Puerto Rican, as deserving of respect on the mainland *for* preserving their heritage. The affirmation of cultural citizenship, for men is, however, threaded with inherited and constructed notions of masculinity, and it is these very notions that Puerto Rican women are unravelling in the fabric of their day to day lives. (Interviews with Puerto Rican women are examined in chap. 10.) For while women elaborate, in many ways, traditional ways of being "mujeres," they also re-script being "mujeres" and "mamis" at one and the same time. There is no comparable rescripting along gender lines for men. An "hombre" is an "hombre," much as he was in a Puerto Rican man's grandfather's generation, but with neither the material resources nor the social respect or domestic absolution of grandpa.

A key to understanding the Puerto Rican struggle in the United States lies in hearing the demand to be recognized as Puerto Ricans. Puerto Rican culture is embattled, but continues to insist on being acknowledged, as Phillipe Bourgois (1995) states. Yet some Puerto Rican men on the mainland are anything but nostalgic about the island itself. Emilio, in Buffalo, explains his relationship to Puerto Rico this way:

> *When I went to Puerto Rico, I went not long ago, I was there, about five years ago. . . . I took about $1,300, and I was going just for fifteen days. I gave it away, because people there . . . they expect that you have lots of money because you come from the United States. So I bought food where I stayed, and I gave money away, and when I found myself broke, I had only $150, I bought a ticket and I came right back. I only stayed ten days, and things didn't go that well because people expected something very different from me, actually.*

For some, though, Puerto Rico occupies a nostalgic space, a space of incomparable beauty. Sabastino, in Buffalo, articulates nostalgia:

> *I had to go back to Puerto Rico to find out what Hispanic or Puerto Rican meant. And when I went back to Puerto Rico and saw the way people live over there, I loved it. Because you have a lot of nice plants, a lot of nice trees, a lot of nice culture in Puerto Rico, that here in the United States, you'll never find. They have a lot of that. You'll never find nice animals there, here, or any place else in the world. It's a small Puerto Rican frog [coqui] that will never leave Puerto Rico. Scientists have tried to take it out of Puerto Rico, but they never succeeded. So I think the main thing, Puerto Rico signifies that frog, or better yet, that frog signifies Puerto Rico. Plus the tradition of Puerto Rico, nice people, country. You go to a person's house and without you even ask-*

*ing, they bring a cup of coffee. They bring you food, you know. So I
had to go back to Puerto Rico to see what really being Puerto Rican
is like. I wouldn't give up Puerto Rico for nothing.*

The island occupies a somewhat contradictory space for Puerto Ricans living on the mainland. Some experience extreme distance as they
attempt to reenter the island of their nostalgic dreams. For others,
Puerto Rico is all that it should be – magical, beautiful, and a source of
inspiration and strength, like the *coqui* that Sabastino describes.

Whatever the place of the island, though, Puerto Ricans are proud to
assert their identity as Puerto Ricans on the mainland. Indeed, these
men demand recognition outside the bounds of U.S. racial dichoto-
mies, and are angry at the slightest hint of discrimination based on their
cultural identity.

Roberto, Conception, Juan, Sabastino, and Manuel, below, indicate
how angrily Puerto Rican men reject being treated as inferior. They refuse to accept second-class status and assert their right to live as cultural equals to whites, while at the same moment asserting their right
to be culturally and linguistically different.

LOURDES: *Tell me, was there something negative that you didn't like
while you were studying for your G.E.D.?*
ROBERTO: *Yes, there was something. In the manner, in the way that one
comes to this country, and so one learns first to speak the language,
and there are many people, white people, that make fun of you. They
teach you that only they can do things, that only they are people, and
that you can't do it [do well in school]. And so I shout that "Yes, I can,
and that if you try to do anything, you can do it and get ahead."*
LOURDES: *Did you get to be in touch with these type of people who
really didn't have confidence in you, that didn't think that you could
learn the language?*
ROBERTO: *Yes. The majority were white.*
LOURDES: *Were they teachers?*
ROBERTO: *Yes. One, one female teacher, and some classmates.*

LOURDES: And what type of things did they say to you to make you feel these things?

ROBERTO: They used to laugh about the way I spoke English. But I was sure that they could always understand what I was saying, what I was saying to them. But they used to do it just to make fun of me, to tease me, and to belittle me, to put me under, always. That's what I figured they were doing.[2]

LOURDES: Do you see a lot of racism?

CONCEPTION: Yes.

LOURDES: Where?

CONCEPTION: Everywhere.

LOURDES: For instance?

CONCEPTION: Well, for instance, in the county and the farms where I work [picking fruit], you know, if there are white people and there are Latinos that can do probably the job better than the white people; you know, the white person will always get that job without knowing, but only because they are white. Maybe just to watch over us, even when there were Latinos who could do the job better. Sometimes when you arrive someplace, you know [by] the way people look at you, the way that they talk to you [that they are racist].

JUAN: I experienced a lot of verbal abuse. Basically whenever we went into white neighborhoods we were told by elderly people, they used to send their kids out after us with bats and sticks. . . . I remember one time we were thirteen years old, not even, about eleven years old, and three of us, we were trying to walk to the nearest public swimming pool, [the closer pool] wasn't built in Cazenovia, we were trying to walk there from Lackawanna and we got jumped by a bunch of grown men on motorcycles. They broke my friend's collarbone, and shoulder, arm . . . and even when the cops came, they didn't give us a ride. They [the cops] told us, you know, you better start walking pretty fast. And them guys chased us, they caught us like four or five times. And police would keep coming. I think we held out now, all in all, three young kids against seven or eight adults. But yeah, I've had some very negative experiences with racism.

Later, when Juan was asked to recount his school experiences he stated:

JUAN: *Straight out prejudice. A lot of racial incidences. There was a group of about sixteen or seventeen white males that would try to take advantage of opportunity. I remember guys getting jumped in gym classes and so on and so forth. Getting beat up in the shower in the locker room.*

CRAIG: *And there's no explanation why they did that?*

JUAN: *To me, there's an explanation. It's a tough [macho] behavior. Even then I kind of knew it. They were acting out as something they were taught by someone. Retaliating from fear. I used to tell my Hispanic friends that if an incident ever arose, I said no one likes getting hit. In a win or lose battle, pain is pain. And I said as long as you can give out a little and take a little, I said then they'll never come back. So we had one incident where I stayed after school for a wrestling team, and a friend of mine, we were going to a late bus and we were crossed by a couple of them [the white boys], and then a couple more, and then a couple more. Before I knew it we were surrounded by eight or nine guys. I grabbed something and just started swinging. And after that the guys weren't prejudice. I don't like people who hide behind it. I learned that there are some people who'll say, "Listen, I don't like you, nothing personal, I just don't like your kind." And I was able to deal with that a lot better. And it kind of helped me when I went into the military. It was very helpful.*

––––––––––

EMILIO: *I had come here in 1977 as a kid, and I used to see that this [west side] was filled with Italians, and then Puerto Ricans started to come, many Puerto Ricans, and they [the Italians] started to leave. They started to sell their houses. They started to get away from us. They even had their festival [the well-attended Italian Festival] around here in Connecticut [street], but since then it [neighborhood] began to fill up with Puerto Ricans, you know, and they don't get along with Puerto Ricans. I don't know if it's that they think that we are pigs, or we don't want to get ahead in these States, and so they have left. [They moved the Italian Festival to North Buffalo.] They've even left trying to get away from the Puerto Ricans because, you know, they have their positions since they were raised here and everything; they think that we're going to ruin their things. They don't give us a chance for us to get ahead, 'cause you know something – I tell myself that if I were given a chance that I could take something – a profession, something, something that I could do, like in the farms, I know how to deal with the farms, with the land. If I were given a chance to be in charge or to maintain a group, I would get ahead, but there is not opportunity. I would need my house because I don't have my own house, and just with working alone, I wouldn't be able to pay the rent, so we're kept beneath always . . . they don't want to give us a chance. And if you have a couple of dollars, they want to take them away too.*

––––––––

MANUEL: *I used to work at River Restaurant, right. Well, there was two owners, Eddie and Lou, but Eddie was there every day, and Lou was taking care of the other one in Williamsville [a suburb]. And Eddie used to just turn around mostly and say, "Well, let the Spic do it." "Let the Spic do it." All the sloppy jobs – "Let the Spic do it." And then he'll start laughing and say "Come on baby, go do it." I'm thinking in my head, you know, like "Damn, you're an asshole."*
CRAIG: *How did you feel when he talked about you that way?*
MANUEL: *Well, at first I used to get pissed off. And then, after, I just said, ah, let it go, you know. You know what I mean. Words are cheap.*
CRAIG: *So you didn't do anything about it?*
MANUEL: *No . . . I just turned around and I told him. I said, "Listen, you know, you can call me, you know, whatever you want, because you know, I don't care. I'm what I am and that's it." You know what I mean? And that's all [there is] to it. You know, Spic is just a slang for a Hispanic. You know what I mean, you know. Words doesn't hurt, you know.*

Puerto Rican men critique racism and the ways in which opportunities are denied Puerto Rican males. With a clear sense of whites as the dominant other, several men talk about being beaten up by whites; others point to denial of opportunities in the job market, watching less qualified whites climb the ranks. As Conception states, "If there are white people there and there are Latinos that probably could do the job better, you know, the white person will always get that job."

While Puerto Rican men assert their right to have opportunities on the mainland and to experience their lives free from discrimination, they do not exhibit the searing broad-based institutional critique characteristic of African American men (see chaps. 2 and 4), of the ways in which American society denies opportunities to people of color while simultaneously constructing these people as "less than" whites. Not one Puerto Rican man in Buffalo, for example, commented on police brutality in the neighborhood in which they live (even though it exists), nor did they discuss the social construction of the Latino as "other" in U.S. society. Rather, critical comments addressed transgressions by individual whites against individual Puerto Ricans. While this is certainly shared in the sense that individual transgressions add up to something larger, and Puerto Rican men are well aware of this, this set of shared understandings has not produced the fevered pitch anger so characteristic among poor African American men. Anger in the Puerto Rican community is, instead, channeled into demands for cultural citizenship, demands to be Puerto Rican and at the same time partake of the opportunities of mainland America. Insisting on both equality and difference has oddly contradictory effects. On the one hand, it enables hope to survive within the culture. On the other, on the mainland, far from home-based networks that could challenge the status quo, these men are de-moored from bases of identity and place (Deaux and Ethier 1992). Removed from the material, social, linguistic, and other forms of capital that buffer self, poor and working-class Latinos on the mainland are free-floating, dislodged from cultural anchors in the economy and, as we see in chapter 10, at home. In response, they insist on reinscribing a traditional form of Puerto Rican citizenship.

This cry for recognition as Puerto Ricans must be understood historically. As Benmayor et al. (1987) explain,

In Puerto Rican communities throughout the United States oral histories tell the story of a working-class people who have been migrating in significant numbers since the turn of the century, ever since the United

States took possession of the Island in 1898. In 1917, the U.S. unilaterally decreed citizenship for Puerto Ricans, giving impetus to an economic migration that stretches out to the present. Emigration was a means of survival for peasants, displaced from their land and relegated to season employment, at best, by the expansion of the U.S. sugar monopolies around the turn of the century. Colonial economic disruption also affected urban workers, bringing cigar makers, tailors, carpenters and other skilled artisans to the incipient Puerto Rican communities of New York City. . . .

It was not until the later 1940s and early 50s that hundreds of thousands of men and women flocked to New York, economic causalities of Operation Bootstrap, the post WWII plan to industrialize and modernize Puerto Rico. Out-migration and population control through female sterilization was part and parcel of this plan, for Bootstrap was unable to provide sufficient jobs and economic growth for the Island's unskilled and semi-skilled work force. By 1960, close to one million Puerto Ricans had relocated in New York and it was in this period that Puerto Ricans began to be seen as a growing "minority" and "social problem in this country." (1)

The coercive history of the "relationship" between Puerto Rico and the United States is essential to our understanding of the relentless commitments made by Puerto Ricans to retain their cultural identity and assert their resistance to colonization. It explains why they have only lukewarm energy for the collective fight for improved social position on the mainland and persist in their claim that Puerto Rico is their nation of origin.

On this point we take exception to the otherwise compelling writings of John Ogbu (1984, 1988), and follow instead the lead from our informants, that they have been historically coerced *and* they have elected to migrate to the United States, *as Puerto Ricans*. Further, it is important to note that given the economic, and as we will see, the gendered relations at "home," many Puerto Ricans in the United States – economically subordinate to all other demographic groups – still feel relatively advantaged vis-à-vis their kin back home. These men are not alienated; they are, however, as Ethier and Deaux (1994) would argue, fundamentally de-moored. They may compare themselves in disgust to the economic and social status of U.S. whites, but they simultaneously compare their station to their "less fortunate" friends and relatives back on the island. This double consciousness, to borrow from Du Bois's insight, serves to blunt what might otherwise contribute to the development of an incisive critique of U.S. race relations.

There is a further issue embedded within the struggle for cultural citizenship – the negotiation over assumed racial definitions and categories existing on the mainland. The very contestation of these definitions encourages Puerto Ricans to carve out a specific Puerto Rican racial/cultural space and to refuse the bifurcated racial tapestry woven on the mainland. It is to this issue that we now turn.

Contesting Racial Dichotomies

Clara Rodriguez (1989, 1992, 1994) argues that as Latin Americans, Puerto Ricans come to the United States mainland with a critique of colonialism *and* notions of race that differ from racial understandings in the United States: "They entered a U.S. society that had a biologically based biracial structure that assumed a white – non-white division of the world. Euro-American whites were at one pole and African American blacks were at the other." In fact, as Sachs (1994) and Ignatiev (1995) show, Jews and Irish became "white" in the United States by distancing themselves from those considered "black," strategizing within racial polarities. This binary persists, in particular, in the urban northeast.

Padilla (1958) argues that in Puerto Rico there is a biracial continuum, with the two poles black and white, but that the categories in the middle of the continuum are not castelike social groups. In fact one can experience mobility within one's own lifetime from one racial designation to the other, and racial categorization is tied to social class and education as well as skin color per se. Also, members of the same family groups are often identified with varying racial terms, and an individual might change their racial status dependent upon their education. This contrasts sharply with categorization in the United States where one cannot be black at one moment and white the next.[3] In this sense it is helpful to note that the Puerto Rican sense of race is one which is similar to that which exists in much of Latin America, where the large mestizo and mulatto populations constitute a a sizable majority that is capable of articulating social norms and values. Mediated by money and education or fine distinctions in appearance, race in Latin America can be viewed as fluid rather than rigid, and not bipolar and castelike as it is in North America. It should also be noted that mestizo or mulatto is a European construct which stems from the concept of miscegenation, or racial mixing and polluting. Populations of Latin America and the Caribbean inverted this notion, viewing themselves as a *new* race or people, rather than as a polluted one. As Rodriguez (1990) posits, it is somewhat ironic that Puerto Ricans epitomized the concept of the melting pot. "Puerto Ricans were an ethnic group compromising more than one racial group. From such a perspective, Puerto Ricans were racially both blacks and whites; ethnically they were neither."[4]

When Puerto Ricans come to the United States, they meet a racial order which forces them to be either black or white, thus denying their own Puerto Rican culture. The struggle of mainland Puerto Ricans is a struggle to be seen *as* Puerto Ricans and to distance themselves from the black-white dichotomy. As Rodriguez (1990) states:

> Being classified according to U.S. racial standards meant being identified racially instead of culturally. For many Puerto Ricans this means being reclassified into a different culture. This reclassification and its consequences have affected Puerto Ricans of all colors and have been persistent themes in the autobiographical literature found in the *Memorias de Bernardo Vegas* (Iglesias 1977), Jesus Colon's *Puerto Rican in New York* (1961), Piri Thomas' *Down These Mean Streets* (1967), and Edward Rivera's *Family Installments* (1983). The most cited experience was that of the darker Puerto Rican who is taken to be "Negro," "colored," or "black." (135–36)

This struggle on the part of Puerto Ricans to name themselves, to claim their own voice and culture, thus resisting U.S. racial bifurcation, is most obvious in the census data. Although it was assumed that Puerto Ricans would be assimilated over time, that is, become either black or white according to U.S. standards, Puerto Ricans have resisted this pressure and put forth their own culture in response, identifying themselves as "Puerto Rican" or "other" in 1980 and 1990 censuses (Rodriguez 1992).

The mainland Puerto Ricans we spoke with proudly assert their own Puerto Rican roots and reject the strict black-white bifurcation characteristic of the United States.

JUAN: *I circle Hispanic [on application forms] and write Puerto Rican.*
CRAIG: *Tell me why you do that.*
JUAN: *Because I think my culture, my race, the Puerto Rican race is misconceived and then stereotyped by a lot of other people. We have a very strong and proud culture. We come from an island a hundred miles long, fifty miles wide. We've been conquered over and over again by not just the Spaniards. We are a melting pot. Puerto Ricans are mixed with Indian, Hispanic, black, white, Spaniard. And, and through all of that, we kept our culture strong. . . . For instance, there's very little Puerto Rican on Puerto Rican crime, as compared to other cultures. For us, as a rule of thumb, it isn't right. To us, once you express violence towards another Hispanic, you express violence to his whole family. So, therefore, we're more prone to talk it out. You know, where, if your brother stole something from me, I would go to your family and explain to your family, "Listen, your brother broke in my car, stole my stereo. He's gotta pay for it or else I'm going to have to take care of it." Usually the family will make amends and they'll discipline.*

———

LOURDES: *What will you tell your daughter about your culture and race?*
CONCEPTION: *That one must always remain united with the race [Puerto Ricans] because one is never going to forget where one comes from, one's roots. That one comes from another culture, another country that has its own culture. That even though we live here, we can never forget our culture. That is very important.*

———

MANUEL: *Just tell [my daughter] where her family comes from, and this and that, and just not to, you know, be embarrassed about how you are. You know, just stay for your race, you know.*

Preserving Gender Regimes

The Puerto Rican family is the primary cultural unit; for men, it is simultaneously a site for pride and for remembered violence, as Puerto Rican men are the only group of men we spoke with who consistently talk about the violence they witnessed and were subject to as children. As they report it, their fathers hit them often, and this was mirrored in violence between husband and wife, both in the United States and in Puerto Rico. While men are critical of violence, they patrol the borders of gender and sexuality rather vigorously. For Puerto Rican males, the struggle over what Trinh Minh-ha (1989) calls "boundedness" is simultaneously a claim for cultural identity and the scratching out of gendered imperatives.

For Puerto Rican men, as for whites and African Americans, work constitutes a gender role that they see themselves having to fulfill, a gender role prescription which links them with past and future. In her study of youth in Puerto Rico, Muñoz (1995) finds that "work as a tradition where young men can fulfill their social obligation to support a family was expressed by youths of all ages and across all sites. In this way work was seen very much as a male bastion, a place where males needed to develop their identities, to fulfill what they see as manhood, ser hombre. As a tradition, work was understood to mean an important avenue to enter into society and participate in it by being able to produce a family and that this was a pattern that would continue on with their own children whether they were boys or girls." (130) As Muñoz points out, this set of gender expectations has been exceedingly slow to change, and persists in Puerto Rico and on the mainland, in spite of economic realities which have forced many Puertoriqueñas who are poor or working class to leave home and work in factories.

While Puerto Rican women challenge these strict definitions of gender in that many have to be provider as well as mother, Puerto Rican men do not appear to be regrounding these symbiotic gendered definitions. On the contrary, they are reaffirming themselves as "hombres" and continuing to weave fantasies of male-run households in which women stay home to do household-related chores and raise children.

As noted above, Puerto Rican men are the only group of men whom we interviewed who acknowledge the violence in the homes in which they grew up. It is indeed noteworthy that a group which struggles hard to maintain patriarchal structures is so critical of the ways in which these structures played out in the homes in which they were raised. Their job, as men, is to blunt the edges of male brutality with which they are all too familiar.

SABASTINO: *It [the violence] would be like if she [his mother] was in church, and he [father] was home drinking, and the rest of the family was in church with her, if anybody left a dish in the sink, I would be paying for it.*
LOURDES: *How old were you at the time?*
SABASTINO: *Nine years old. Yeah, I suffered a lot of physical abuse and verbal abuse.*
LOURDES: *How does that affect you now as a person, as an adult?*
SEBASTINO: *I'm twenty-five now. As an adult, it has affected me to the sense that I don't want to be like him, in that way, where I did see a lot of violence between my mother and father, growing up. Right now they're divorced because of that, and I wouldn't want my spouse to go through the same thing I went through . . . that my mother went through . . . on my behalf, that I would abuse her physically, verbally, mentally. I guess that taught me a lesson.*

_____

CECILIO: *Childhood, yes. My uncle's wife. I told her I didn't want to eat the eggs. She catched me. She squashed the eggs in my face . . . [he begins to cry].*

_____

RICARDO: *Like I used to come home . . . she [his mother] would tell me to come home at a certain time and I used to get home later, and then she would tell me, go take a bath or a shower, and I used to go take a shower, and like two or three minutes later, she would walk in and she [would say] "Out of the way," and she used to hit me with the cord — with the extension cord or a belt. Because she used to make sure I was wet so it could burn more.*

_____

DOMINGO: My father abused me.

LOURDES: Did he ever hit you?

DOMINGO: Yeah, a lot in the face. And he beat me, pull my hair, all over my body, and everything.

―――――――

EMILIO: Oh yes, she [his mother] used to beat us up, and how.

LOURDES: Can you explain to me a little bit more about that? Did she used to beat you with her hands, or how?

EMILIO: Oh, with whatever she would find, she would hit us. She once hit my brother with a hot iron. She was ironing early in the morning before we went to school. She was ironing our clothes and she got very upset at something, and she burned him with it. She burned him with an iron all over his body. And she used to beat me up, and she used to beat us up like crazy. It was terrible. . . . I didn't get hit that much [compared to his brother and sister] because I was the one who lived the least with her, just about a couple of years. Otherwise, you know, my head would have been messed up too, because with the walls, with the windows, she used to hit them with whatever she found in front of her. She forgave a lot of things. She forgave me a lot of things, but I saw a lot of things which affected me. Yeah, because I have the most mind of all of them and, you know, it was messed up as a result of that, I tell you. And that's why it's hard for me to express myself. You know, like there are many things that I know about, but I don't say my ideas, or I don't explain them, because I'm afraid. I'm afraid of expressing myself.

There is no other group examined here which evidences this degree of openness about violence in the family. Puerto Rican men, additionally, are strong defenders of the patriarchal family and do not support breaking up families, even when violence is present. It is expected, in fact, that "mujeres" will stay with the family, no matter what the cost. This expectation is clear in the following interview with Sabastino. Lourdes, the interviewer, speaks from within the Puerto Rican culture. She offers Sabastino a possible explanation for why his mother, after twenty-five years of marriage, divorced his father—an explanation Sabastino does not seem to fully accept.

SABASTINO: *The divorce was about four years ago. But it's something that still hasn't been erased from my mind, or any of my family members.*

LOURDES: *Why?*

SABASTINO: *Because after twenty-five years of my parents being married, I really didn't think [they should split]. Even though my mother did give my father a lot of chances, he had his drinking problem, and he was abusive with her and the family . . . but it was like a sudden decision. From her part. All of a sudden she just put a restrictive [restraining] order on him and put the divorce and everything. It was just like a sudden move. It was a sudden jolt for the family. That's why we all scattered and everybody took their own way. Like my brother stayed in Buffalo, and the rest of my family is in Puerto Rico.*

LOURDES: *Do you hold a grudge, or do you resent the fact that your mother made that decision?*

SABASTINO: *In a way she did the right decision for her well-being. And in a way she did not, maybe, did not think about us. She was more thinking about her in that moment, about her future she has left than about our future, how it was gonna affect us. Even though she did it at the right time because almost all of us were already adults, or almost becoming adults, and if she would have done it earlier, there would have been a bigger pain for all of us.*

LOURDES: *You know, I have to commend your mother to hold off twenty-five years with the same abusive pattern. It does sound like there was a pattern there, and now that you're adults, I mean, I don't know, I would, you know, sympathize with her. Maybe because I'm a woman, you know, and I can relate to a certain extent to what she has gone through. Because you get so tired of the mental abuse, and you say to yourself, I'm going to wait until my kids get bigger. My kids need a father, they need a role model, you know, but you try to hold on and you try to hold on, and it's like you're holding on to a rope, and at any minute it's gonna snap and you're gonna fall, you know, and one day comes, and you just can't take it anymore, and you say, "No! Kids or no kids, I have to get out of this situation."*

SABASTINO: *She's forty-five . . . He's [his father] ten years older than her. And she remarried. He still hasn't remarried. It's been a while since I last heard from her, but it really doesn't . . . the example she set right*

there is not a good model for us, because it just teaches us to get mar-
ried, divorced, and remarried to somebody else . . . just keep jumping.
LOURDES: *Well . . . you know, I think that in our culture it's taboo, you*
know, [for women] to bring it out in terms of domestic violence, you
know, to bring it out into public and to inform a friend, to inform
people that I'm being abused. Okay, it is the role of a Latina woman to
stay with the abuse, to continue to hang on until death do us part, and
literally, death do us part! It does happen [Latina women do get killed
by their husbands].

Sabastino sees his mother as having transgressed the bounds of what it
means to be a wife and mother, and, in the process, hurt the entire family. Although Sabastino recognizes full well the abuse in the family, he
is unwilling to say that the family should be dissolved. The role of a wife
and mother demands that she be there always.

In her study of Puerto Rican youth, Muñoz (1995) finds that Puerto
Ricans are extremely clear regarding appropriate roles for men and
women.

> The monumental effort involved in taking steps outside the home to
> work is pushed back by an adherence to traditional gender roles which
> keep these women constantly checking their movements against a
> mythic norm of gender, of being a "mujer," an internalized form of fem-
> ininity, of caring for others selflessly, willingly. The message that comes
> at them from within and without is that to be a "mujer" means to care
> for children, to be a mother, to be a caretaker, an "ama de casa"—a
> housewife. The image of mother described by youths in the interviews
> is traditional and based on ideals of self-sacrifice and selfless giving:
> mother love is glorified. (146)

Our interviews with young Puerto Rican males on the mainland indicate that they have the same expectations of women.

LOURDES: *What is expected of the women in your community?*
DOMINGO: *Well, they are, if they've got children, they have to take care of*
the children, clean the house, make dinner. Things like that.

LOURDES: What do you expect of your wife?

DOMINGO: Well, I expect from my wife to listen to me when I speak to her. Sometimes she don't listen that good. She [should] listen if I tell her to do something. She don't want to do it right away. She will start to make complaint. She tells me, "I don't have to do it. You don't tell me what to do." She tell me that.

LOURDES: What, for example, might you tell her to do?

DOMINGO: Well, if I need something like, we do laundry, every weekend on every Sunday. So if I need, like T-shirt for today, if dirty, so I'll say, you pick out the dirty laundry and take out the T-shirt that I like, to wear tomorrow. And she say, "No, I'm not going to do it. If you want it, you do it yourself." So, she's like that.

Both Domingo and his wife work outside the home, he, as a clerk in a grocery store. He has commented that his wife will not go back to Puerto Rico because she has a good job here, one that would not be available in Puerto Rico. He, though, is asserting traditional hombre rights over women in demanding that she provide the clean T-shirt he wants. She, on the other hand, is negotiating these expectations. Sabastino and Ricardo articulate similar gendered expectations below.

SABASTINO: [talking about his ex-wife] Well, during the time I was with her, I was working for a security guard company and made a household in Puerto Rico, bought land, made a house, took out a loan. I had everything for her; so, that was not enough for her. The more I gave her, the more she wanted. It was like I couldn't give more than what I tried to give. Plus, there was always constant arguing, fighting, she's very aggressive – she was like a man, like she would argue with me like a man to the point where it almost got to fist fighting, and I'm sure she probably would have [hit me].

———————

RICARDO: My father once told me that just being a man is not of age. It's a matter of mental state. You are a man when you're ready to be a man. You could be forty-five and still act like a teenager. You live with your parents and expect your parents to pay for your meals and board you. You can be twelve and you can bring home the money to take care of the family. That's the difference between [a boy and] a man.

We have argued here that Puerto Rican men are elaborating traditional conceptions of gender, while at the same time demanding the right to participate in the United States *as* Puerto Ricans – to maintain their own culture, their own identity, and their own racial designations. Thus the affirmation of a particular form of cultural citizenship is twinned with affirmations of a gender regime, one which is often stabilized through violence. Only Juan below, of all the Puerto Rican men interviewed, acknowledges that men no longer have the economic power to demand obedience from women, that the old days are gone. This is not to say that he likes this fact, but rather that he recognizes that the bargain will no longer work:

> *Hispanics, this is where machismo comes into effect. Where the man feels that a woman doesn't have a right to question him, that he should be able to do whatever it is he wants. Which is fine and dandy because in the old times, the men earned that right, to head the household. He worked, supported the family, was there all the time; he was the pillar of strength. And now they [men] want the same respect, without having to work for it. And it just cannot happen.*[5]

Juan reflects upon the gender regime in a way that the others do not. Most elaborate gendered norms akin to those of their grandfathers in Puerto Rico. Thus, the male struggle for cultural citizenship is also a struggle for gendered positionality. The passion with which Puerto Rican men resolve to maintain cultural difference in the face of U.S. society is the same passion with which they resolve to be men. However, as Juan points out, because Puerto Rican men cannot provide for their families, they cannot keep their part of the "gender bargain." And, as we will explore in chapter 10, Puerto Rican women are refusing the failed bargain, refusing to do the work of both hombre and mujer as they feed, clothe, and raise the young.

The men in this chapter are sculpting lives amidst the decoupling in their neighborhoods of capitalism and patriarchy. Trying to recoup a life once lived, with tradition and culture but without the material conditions that allowed "men to be men," these men, on the mainland, are stripped of language, access to material goods, jobs, a place in the economy, and increasingly, a place as head of the household. Eager to defend who they are, they are at the same time robbed of the means to do so by economic and political forces outside of their control. Virulent strains of anti-immigration fever twisted with anti-Affirmative Action sentiment increase their sense of economic vulnerability and assault them with linguistic and cultural shame. In contemporary politics, these men are cornered, with little to inherit and less to hold on to.

The material and cultural conditions for Latinos among the poor and working class are in crisis. A desperate search backward produces little more than public acknowledgment of that which is *no* longer. In some spaces, in some communities, Latinos are carving new sites for a mooring of identities, for instance, in the public political scene. In Jersey City, Latinos are emerging as major players in the mayoral race and City Council elections. Actively involved in block associations and ward level politics, these men (and women) are demanding a place and a voice in municipal politics, working to create new arenas in which to produce Latino citizenship. With the economy and domestic life (as once known) effacing, with those bases for Latino identity eroding, politics may be the new frontier for identity work, for "re-mooring."

Cops, Crime, and Violence

MICHELLE: *If the president were to come to Jersey City to hold a town meeting, what problems would you want him to pay attention to?*
FRANK: *Crime and drugs, violence in the streets. The drug problem is out of hand.*

ALL THE YOUNG MEN AND WOMEN WE INTERVIEWED WERE ASKED THE QUESTION posed above. Almost all offered a response similar to Frank's, their common fear forming an urban mantra. In this chapter we try to understand not only the common experience of fear associated with crime, but also the particularities, that is, how distinct subcommunities of women and men explain the prevalence of crime, where they locate the source of the problem, and how they articulate its effects on their children's lives.

Crime and Poverty
Scholarly work on crime and poverty has spawned a number of important policy and theoretical conversations about causes and also consequences, particularly in communities of highly concentrated poverty. But this literature, however brilliant, has often ignored critical facts that our interviews reveal: that even experiences as seemingly clear-cut as *crime* and *fear* are deeply marbled by class, race, and gender.
    Several main themes emerge from recent work on crime and poverty (Fagan et al. 1993, Currie 1993). In a rigorous review of available literature and a deep ethnographic look at eight urban communities across

the United States, Fagan et al. conclude that communities of concentrated poverty are today marked by a breaking apart of links between generations which formerly bonded new generations to stable jobs and life roles. To paraphrase Anderson (1990), the "old heads" are gone or no longer respected. When jobs and factories vacated urban America, unions disappeared in the urban northeast, and the tradition which had worked best for white men, of passing jobs and connections from generation to generation was threatened. The consequences of this economic community-based bankruptcy are multiple (Currie 1993), among them the well-established institutionalization of drug markets (Bourgois 1995) which follows on the coattails of unemployment. As Bourgois notes, when public space is abandoned by legitimate businesses, drug dealers soon are able to exert control over life in that space far in excess of what their numbers would predict.

Scholars also document increasing rates of violence provoked, received, and/or witnessed in communities of poverty (Hsieh and Pugh 1993, MacLeod 1995, Sullivan 1989), and there is a parallel scholarship on the alarming consequences of urban violence on children and youth. A recent study documents that 40 percent of inner-city youngsters from the sixth to tenth grades have witnessed a shooting or stabbing within the past year, with 74 percent reporting feeling "unsafe" (Schwab-Stone et al. 1995). It has also been shown that those children exposed to high levels of "stressful life events," including violence, are more likely to display high levels of aggression themselves (Attar, Guerra, and Tolan 1994).

Despite its usefulness, the literature on violence does not reveal the ways in which even such supposedly clear-cut experiences as *crime* and *fear* vary dramatically by class, race, and gender. Rarely are these issues examined in terms of demographic groups. It is assumed that we all know what crime and fear are, and that all urban Americans experience them in the same way. In this chapter we look at crime through the eyes of white, African American, and Latino/Latina men and women with whom we worked in the Buffalo and Jersey City poor and working-class communities. We worry that research on crime and violence in poor urban America and the policies stemming from even the best of this research have been written through a narrow, even singular, lens and therefore speak only from the perspective of *some* living within these communities. Our goal here is to decenter and complicate what we take to be a unitary representation of crime and violence, a representation which quickly crumbles when we speak across ethnic/racial and gender groups.

In this chapter, we analyze the narrative responses to three questions:

1. Think about Jersey City/Buffalo as it has changed over the past twelve years, particularly around crime. Do you see Jersey City/Buffalo as more violent today than it was in the 1980s? Do you see more, less, or the same amount of what could be called police brutality?
2. There are a lot of institutions in Jersey City/Buffalo that shape our lives – police, welfare, courts, schools, hospitals. Can you tell me about a time you had to struggle with one of these institutions for yourself or a relative? What happened?
3. There are a lot of young men in jails. How do you explain this? Why do you think this is the case?

Our data sweep us toward two conclusions. First, the experience of urban terror associated with crime, violence, and drugs is articulated passionately and profoundly by poor and working-class men and women, across racial and ethnic groups. Urban fears are democratically distributed among the poor. Second, while the terror may be universal, the *articulated site of violence* varies dramatically by demographic group. While all informants were similar in age (between twenty-three and thirty-five years old) and class (poor to working class), they varied by race, ethnicity, and gender. When asked about violence in their communities, African American men and Latinos (to a far lesser extent) focused their comments on *state-initiated* violence, detailing incidents of police harassment, the systemic flight of jobs and capital from poor communities of color, the over-arrest of men of color, and the revived construction of prisons. In response to the very same questions, however, white men in our sample report incidents of *street violence*, attributing these incidents almost universally to men of color. In sharp contrast to all three groups of men, white women, when asked about crime and violence, offer scenes of *domestic violence* among their parents, themselves and husbands/boyfriends, or sisters and husbands/boyfriends. African American and Latina women likewise detail scenes of *home-based violence*, although African American women, like men from the same community, as often describe incidents of state-initiated violence, typically in the welfare office. And African American women, like white men, passionately narrate incidents of street violence.

We hear, then, that depending on where you sit in the social hierarchy, the experience of urban fear of violence will be traced to different sources. And yet the particular standpoint that has influenced social policy and scholarship most directly, that is the standpoint that is best reflected in prevailing laws and academic writing, is the standpoint spoken in our data almost entirely by poor and working-class white men – those who discuss neither state-initiated violence, nor domestic violence; those who focus exclusively, almost fetishistically, on street violence initiated by men of color.

We introduce our data to demonstrate that the full trilogy of violence and crime – state, community, and domestic – must be taken seriously in order to be responsive to the range of needs embedded within poor and working-class communities. If national policy and social science refuse to recognize and address state-initiated violence, community violence, *and* domestic violence – all three – then we must cynically conclude that federal, state, and local legislation is being written in ways that reflect prevalently the terrors, needs, and projections of white males while silencing the voices of men and women of color as well as white women in their cries for violence-free homes and communities.

As you will hear, living in communities of concentrated poverty, now exacerbated by a drug economy in which individuals are armed with easy access to guns, has many consequences: it has diminished the material well-being of community members; created neighborhoods in which little to no trust exists between adults – reducing a person's ability to rely upon a neighbor for support, help, assistance, and information; has produced neighborhoods in which children are often locked in their homes and unable to play outside, limiting them physically, so-

TABLE 6.1

VIEWS OF VIOLENCE AND THE POLICE ACROSS DEMOGRAPHIC GROUPS

	White Men	White Women	African American Men	African American Women	Latínos	Latinas
Focus of Violence	*Community*, focus on street violence perpetrated by "other"	*Domestic*, focus on gender	*State*, focus on racist policies	*State, Community, and Domestic*, focus on race and gender	*State*, focus on race	*Domestic*, focus on gender
Views of Police	Friends/Family, High trust	Moderate Trust	High Mistrust/ Corruption	Mistrust	Mistrust	High Mistrust/ Corruption

cially, and psychologically – gluing them and their mothers to television as a dominant transmitter of social beliefs and worldviews; and has resulted in communities in which women and children are unable to take advantage of the few educational/social/recreational programs that may still exist because they fear for their lives.

Reviewing responses to the *three questions* listed above and using grounded theory, we have targeted various themes: (1) *focus* of the violence – that is, state, community, domestic; (2) *trust* in the police; (3) whether or not the respondent speaks in a *racialized discourse*; (4) whether or not the respondent indicated that the *police advised* him/her about how to "take justice into my own hands"; (5) whether the respondent sees *police brutality* as being on the rise, declining, or stabilizing over the past decade. Using these themes as our lens, we hear quite distinct stories pouring out of each demographic category: white men, white women, black men, black women, Latino, and Latina. Torn by the desire not to essentialize, we are nevertheless forced by our data to recognize the ways in which violence operates through race, class, and gender. For a cursory look, see table 6.1. We review the data by demographic groups and then we speak across groups.[1]

White Men

Of the six groups, white men emerged as the most distinct, that is, atypical narrators. A full half of these men spontaneously volunteered that they had a friend or relative who is a "cop." Quite distinct from the rest of the sample, 75 percent indicated high levels of trust in the police, and only 25 percent alluded to police corruption in Buffalo and Jersey City in which 75 percent of Latinos and African American men reported instances of corruption and police brutality. Alan says,

> *Oh, the police. Last week when we had the break-in, the police came down. I thought it was kind of strange, you know, that the one cop said to me that it was too bad that you didn't catch him inside the house because then you could have killed him and we wouldn't have said anything. He said it was too bad I didn't catch him, I could have beat the crap out of him. But I don't really think I've had a run-in, so to speak.*

As you can hear, Alan feels protected by police. Like Alan, three other white men independently volunteered that the police, following their reporting of a crime, instructed them in how to "get the guy" next time. Twinned with their trust in the police, these men consistently identified the race of perpetrators. It is noteworthy that the white men were the *only* group who insisted on naming the race/ethnicity of their perpetrators – or at least naming those who were black or Hispanic.

When discussing fears, many of these men consistently projected fear onto others – parents, children, sisters – while denying their personal fears. In other words, in the aggregate, white men would narrate a racialized discourse of crime and punishment, attributing virtue and responsibility to the police who represent "us," criminality and degradation to men of color, all the while discussing this in terms of protecting elders, women, and children. In this triangle, these men do not see police brutality. Or they do not, in the words of one, "see enough." A full 75 percent indicated that police brutality was on the wane – or that allegations of police brutality were nothing more than fabrications, again unusual in a city in which most of our respondents recited incidents of personal and/or witnessed acts of brutality. Sixty percent of white men considered charges of police harassment to be "racially trumped up." These men, more than any other group, narrated an empathy with police officers that was sometimes combined with a dismissal of harassment charges, and at other times was honestly conflicted. Bob, for example, offers the following analysis of police brutality:

> I don't know. I mean police brutality is such a crock sometimes. Most of the time people that are getting brutalized have done something one way or another to intimidate the police officer. He doesn't have the easiest job in the world, so it's tough to say what's brutality and what's not. I mean there's instances when innocent people do get roughed up, too, but unfortunately that's because of the violence that's out there. Police are no longer reacting with any courtesy. They're just grabbing people, and that's because of what they have to face. Anybody could potentially be a killer in a policeman's eyes. It don't matter if you're ten or a hundred. So that's what they have to live with. Forty hours a week they have to worry about that. From the second they start to the second they finish, there's not really a time when they can't worry about it, so that's a big problem. You say, "Are police too rough?" What about the people, are the people too rough? Is there, like, civilian brutality towards the police? Are they allowed to do whatever they want? I don't think so. I think there's some type of law you have to uphold.

White Women

Unlike white men, fewer than half of the white women interviewed "trust" the police; 60 percent narrate stories of police and courts in terms of violence in their homes, or in the homes of their mothers and their sisters. They, too, see little in the way of brutality, but 48 percent of those interviewed recognize corruption in the ranks. Many express the kind of frustration with police evident in this account by Caroline:

> Well, like with my sister, my middle sister. She lived with a boyfriend who was a drug addict. Well, he was reformed, and then he moved in with her and he became a problem. My parents were away and he was, you know, threatening my sister and stuff. And he locked us in the house and he was threatening to kill us, and all this sick stuff. So anyway, we had to call the police about eight times that day. And they had to arrest him. But it was, I mean, as far as the police go, it was a very

. . . it was frustrating at first, and then it was a good experience because they helped us. You know, they protected us. At one point I didn't think they were going to, and I really was going a little bit crazy, you know. They kept sending him on his way and he kept coming back, you know. . . . And I started screaming, you know. I'm like, "You're giving him change [money] and sending him on his way? He'll be back in an hour. Where is this guy going with a crack problem and a dollar?" You know, so I'm, like, screaming at this cop and everything. And then the other two came and, you know, I was pleading with this, the one who came back. I was like, "You swore you were going to put him in jail. My sister and me are scared to death. My father isn't here." We have nobody, you know.

Because the police potentially protect women from violent men, these white women, unlike the women of color, see the police as "responsive." Indeed one woman whom we interviewed had pressed charges against her husband for domestic violence and had brought him to court on charges of nonpayment of child support. She described working with neighbors on a petition to get more police protection. But this woman was an exception. More common among the white women we interviewed was to only whisper about the incidents of domestic violence which pervade their lives. They tend not to call the cops, not take out restraining orders, and not to bring their husbands or boyfriends to court (see chap. 7). Most of the white women, in fact, have had few dealings with the police. They are more likely than the white men to note police imperfections, but still more likely than women of color to trust the police.

CECILIA: *We had a situation where these people were coming from Duncan Projects, harassing the neighborhood kids. And what we did was we called up the North District Police Department and we asked to have them drive through occasionally because the kids were being harassed. They were being robbed and everything else. At first it was, like, a problem, but then we got like this big list. I think it was like 4,000 people.*
SARAH: *Oh, a petition?*

CECILIA: *Yeah, and we brought it up to them and we got it [protection].*

SARAH: *Four thousand people. Wow. Who did that?*

CECILIA: *Well, me, this girl Brenda, we went through the buildings.*

SARAH: *Do you think it is important to do this kind of work?*

CECILIA: *Yeah, because you see, if you don't protect what you have, nobody is going to protect it for you. If you show, if you just move in and you see that other parents are interested in everybody else's kids as well as our own, you feel more comfortable knowing that someone is looking for your kids, too. So then you say, I'm going to look for their kids.*

SARAH: *The police are responsive to your needs?*

CECILIA: *Oh yeah, they are, yeah, they are. At first it was a little bit of a problem because they said they don't have enough cars. So we just blew it off and they thought it was over with, but then we went and had the petition made and brought it to the commissioner and it was over with. We got it taken care of.*

African American Men

In our interviews with African American men, we heard two powerful discourses of violence. One was what we might call the everyday work of counter-hegemony *for* and *by* black men – working against the violence of racist representations, as displayed in chapter 4. In the constant confrontation with harsh and humiliating public representations of their race, ethnicity, class, gender, and sexuality, understanding full well the images of black men constructed and distributed by the media and popular culture, these black men battle their image as criminal, as super athlete, and/or super entertainer.

The second discourse of violence spoken by black men is their powerful, incisive, and painful social critique, as discussed in chapters 2 and 4. When African American men speak of violence, their analyses move directly to economic and state violence. What we encounter through these interviews is a group of men deeply concerned about the fate of their community. Surrounded by street-based violence and drugs, as well as the violence perpetrated by police in their communities, African American men voice a deep systemic critique targeting the lack of jobs, racism, and police harassment.

Thus, for instance, when asked about violence in his community, Jon, an African American gay man, poses a caustic analysis of political violence.

The top people that control the society, they're the most angry, violent people in the world. They drop bombs. They spread diseases. They burn. They set up armies to do all kinds of things. I don't know all the violence that you talkin' about. Frankly, I don't see it. People stab each other. They always have. You know, so I see it, but it's just magnified on the television, but they don't show the real violence that they perpetrate, the economic violence.

In marked contrast to the white men we interviewed, the African American men do not (with one exception, a man whose father is a police sergeant) describe police as friends or relatives. For the most part, they do not trust the police. In fact, 75 percent relay stories of corruption. Most think that police brutality has worsened in the past decade, and almost all see a primary reason for the increase in proportion of men in jail as attributable to both the economy and intensified state violence (see chap. 4). Almost every African American man interviewed reported a story in which he was stopped by police, pulled over and frisked for no apparent reason. Some of the stories were told with fiery anger; others with a bitter sense of disgust and resignation. Carl, a "church-going man," recalls one incident:

In regards to police, we hear about police brutality and I really don't allow for police brutality when it comes to me. I remember one experience when I had my car stolen and I had gotten the car back. And over a year my car was never taken off [the list] as stolen. So I would call the police or whatever, trying to get it taken off. No one would help me. So I had gotten pulled over because I made a wrong turn one time, and I think you get a ticket for that [laughs]. I was pulled over. I gave him my license and registration. He was going to arrest me because he said my license was suspended. I said no. My license, well, there was something on my, whatever they said, whatever code they use, there was something on my record in regards to my driving. And I said, "No, my

*car was stolen and it has not been taken off." That can be the only
thing on my driving record. Alright. And so it took him a long time,
you know. And he threatened me about taking and impounding my
car and, you know, this other stuff. And then all of a sudden three
other cop cars pull up, stop, surround me basically, alright. Then they
push me, one guy, one cop tries to put me into the cop car and I'm telling them, "I'm not." I said, "I'm not going in this cop car because I've
done nothing wrong."*

Demetrius, another church-going civil servant, recalls this car-
related incident with the police.

*I told her [friend] to stay in the car and take the keys out of my igni-
tion. So she stayed in the car, and the next thing I know I'm walking
back across the highway. I went to the grass and sidewalk, and the
next thing I know a car came out of nowhere, all right? And he didn't
have his headlights on. So all I hear is the engine, and it's pitch black
out there, and I got another fifty yards to go before I get up under a
streetlight. And I'm on a sidewalk, and the car's on the sidewalk. The
car brushes by my leg, and we're on grass, and if he would have slightly
lost control of that car, he would have took my leg out, okay? The car
just slid right past me. I was actually running across the street to get to
the sidewalk, and that's when it happened. He jumps out of the car and
he came to me . . . and asked me if I wanted to fight. And my question
was, "Why?" And he started cursing and everything, calling me all
kinds of names, and so by then I'm getting mad. And so he approached
me and he pushed me, he pushed me in the chest. So I backed up, and
he's like, "What, you want to fight, black boy, you want a fight?" And I
backed up and, well, I guess there's no alternative, you know? So he
took a swing at me, right, and I blocked it, and I was going to hit him
back, and he reached in his pocket and pulled out a gun. That was my
first experience of actually seeing a gun up close, and he pointed it
right at my head. And I didn't know what to do, all right? So I just put
my hands up nice and slow. I said, "What's going on?" Just like that.
And he was like, "I'm a police officer," like that, right, "I should run
your big behind in," all this stuff. I'm like, "What are you talking*

about?" He was like, he's carrying on and carrying on, but he wasn't telling me what he was doing. All of a sudden, you know, he's a man with a gun. That what I see him as. I don't see him as a police officer. He didn't show me no badge. It's Halloween night. I don't know who's out here perpetrating that they were a cop.

Even Paul, whose father was a police sergeant, who explains that the "police have a job to do," notes that "if I go into a white neighborhood, I get stopped." These men repeat story after story of being suspect, and narrate the toll that it takes. Vincent explains: "White women are scared of black men. It makes you feel cheap." Vincent is asked what he tells his children about the police. He thinks, hesitates, and then remarks:

VINCENT: Well, [my] son, he loves policemen and cops and all this stuff. So, I'll let him see when he gets older, but now, I'll tell him the cops are good and when you are in trouble, call the police or an ambulance.
MICHELLE: So you do tell him?
VINCENT: I don't shatter his dreams. 'Cause he says he wants to get to be a cop when he grows older.
MICHELLE: Do you think it would shatter him?
VINCENT: If they're still going where they're going now, yeah, it will be shattered. Or if he have a struggle, I'll just focus on the other people [when we discuss it], and [I'll tell him] don't be like the other cops, like the way they are now.

Black men are not only far more structural in their explanations of the root causes of crime and corruption, but they are far more devastated and hard pressed than other groups to imagine how to turn things around. Many note, with regret, the absence of community-based programs and the slashing of budgets for after-school programs. John remembers, fondly, that his community used to care for all the children, and now he's scared. "The neighbors used to be so nosey," but now "I don't know what to do to stop the violence." The black men whom we interviewed were critical of the "system," concerned about state and street violence, and beleaguered in their attempts to help the "young ones, still comin' up."

STUART: *The neighborhood isn't as close as it used to be. Everybody used to be nosey, as a way of saying it in street talk. You know, if something's happening, you would hear windows going up throughout the neighborhood, and now you don't hear it, everybody is keeping to themselves. And if somebody's getting beat up or something outside, or if there is a crime taking place, they're sheltered. They don't open windows as much as, you know, because they're scared they might get a bullet, you know, or something like that. As when, back when I was growing up, my mother, if she seen somebody next door or around the corner, one of my friends doing something like that, they weren't supposed to do, she had the permission to get involved and, you know, chastise the person if they were doing wrong, and that's the same as me. Like, if I was around in somebody else's neighborhood, and they knew my parents, I knew not to do anything wrong because I knew that they were watching over me.*

JUDI: *So if you see something wrong now, are you likely to get involved, or are you not likely to get involved?*

STUART: *I just recently got involved with something. I wasn't able to stop what happened. A guy in my neighborhood that's my sister's friend, he was literally beat down with baseball bats and, you know, I just helped him out as far as getting him towels and ice and stuff like that, calling the police and ambulance. But I think that if I would have seen him actually doing it, I probably would have gotten involved. You know, I hate to see my neighborhood get, you know, get to total destruction like a lot of other neighborhoods that I've seen.*

JUDI: *So you feel partly responsible for it?*

STUART: *Partly responsible, exactly.*

African American Women

The black women we interviewed, like the black men, don't much trust police. While 25 percent think the police are corrupt and 25 percent report dealings with police in scenes of domestic violence, they are, overall, tired of picking up the pieces for white society and, they will add, for African American men. These women narrate stories of exhaustion, few resources, fewer supports. In locating the sources of violence, they cast the widest net around their dealings with the law – noting landlord-tenant cases, child support, restraining orders, and run-ins with case workers. Genette's fatigue with all parts of the system is clear in the following:

> So I said, "All right, you can see the baby, you want to come see him, you can come see him, but just know, me and you, we have no business with each other except for this child. Don't touch me, don't act like you want me," I said, " 'cause I don't want you." I don't know, he came like for three times, he came like every other day, he would come for like three visits. So the last day, he talkin' about, oh, "I don't want you on welfare." I said, "well, wait a minute, you don't have a job," and then at the time he was about to go to jail and I said, so, "How is my baby gonna get taken care of, how my baby gonna go to the doctor and everything," I said, "unless the system help me until I could get back to work?" "No, no, I don't want my baby on welfare," and this and that. I said, "Well, it's too late, because he's on it," so he gets mad at me. I said, "Well, you're the man, you go get a job now before you go to jail and you take him." I said and then you talk about the rest later, you know what I'm sayin', because the only reason why he didn't want me dealing with welfare because he knew the system would say, who the father is, and they would take him to court, so he didn't want to go to the process of having to pay child support.

Stories of male violence are not as frequent as they are for white and Latina women, but they are dramatic and devastating in consequence.

> TARA: Yeah. The time he was trying to hurt me, and I knew that he didn't want to hurt me, you know, to try to kill me. And when the judge asked me that, he didn't ask me that personally, he just said, "Tara, do you have anything to say about the situation?" And I didn't talk. I was scared. It was like [John] took over me. I didn't, I had just talked my piece. He wasn't a ruler over me. I just took it like I didn't have nothing to say.
> SARAH: Let's go back, okay. You pressed charges . . .

TARA: *This was years ago. Like five, maybe six years ago. He burnt my door and wouldn't let me out the door. And my brother and them came and moved the chair, and I got out.*
SARAH: *I understand that. Why did he do that?*
TARA: *To scare me. Remember I told you he been trying to scare me.*
SARAH: *Did you call anybody? What did you do, cry?*
TARA: *Cry. I panicked.*
SARAH: *And what happened?*
TARA: *I just got down on all fours . . . [laughs]*
SARAH: *And prayed?*
TARA: *Yeah. And woke up my kids.*
SARAH: *Your kids were inside too?*
TARA: *Yeah, all of us. And we all got down on all fours and sat in the house for fifteen minutes before the fire department came.*

The African American women with whom we spoke – even before "welfare reform" – were typically holding together their own families while at the same time caring for the children/parents of kin, and doing so with meager resources. Their anger at the police is matched by their anger at African American men, case workers, African American women who "make us look bad," and those in the younger generation who are committing crimes, rendering their neighborhoods terrifying for women and children (see chap. 8). These women speak through a dual discourse of responsibility and blame. More than one quoted, "You do the crime, you do the time." More than one alluded to a domestic cycle of drugs, violence, *his* doing time . . . and then *his* not paying child support.

Women experience brutality in their own homes, witness it in neighbors' homes, and worry that their primary obligation is to their children. "I don't get involved," they say again and again with little regret. They know that if they do "get involved," that is, if they do call the cops on a neighbor's domestic violence, that they are vulnerable to retaliation. Violence keeps them in their homes, scared for themselves and for their children's safety.

Latino Men

Again parting ways with the white men, and sounding more like their African American brothers, 100 percent of the Latinos in Jersey City remarked on high levels of police corruption in the city. This is in contrast with Latinos in Buffalo, where a critique of police does not surface as forcefully (see chap. 5).[2] One has a friend on the police force. One says he trusts the cops. Two cited incidents of domestic violence, involving mothers and sisters. Latinos, like the Latinas, see family problems as the primary predictor of men going to jail. They see police brutality everywhere, with the "police thinking they are above the law."

> ANDY: *Do you see any police brutality?*
> PABLO: *Yes. Some of the police get me angry because, in [the supermarket] we have a police officer there and they're there from five to eleven. I've finally, over the past five years or so, started to get to know them, and they know me by first name basis or give me a Police Benevolent Association card or, you know, now we talk to them. But what gets you mad is now that they know me, they let down their guard, and . . .*
> ANDY: *What kind of conversations do you have?*
> PABLO: *And they'll just have, you know, all types of conversations, you know, this scum was doing this, and the way they term people, that you already know they already have a bad outlook towards someone to begin with. And you'll have like two officers in front of me talking and he goes, "Yeah, I went to a Flores house, and he was talking about this and I told him to shut up, and he didn't say nothing. I stand on the floor and kicked him, and this and that, 'Are you gonna shut up now?'" And you're looking at the, and you just say to yourself, you know, I feel like I'm gonna report this guy or whatever, but what can I get done because then I've seen so many officers that have something reported on them and there's like a system. You're not gonna, unless you get something like a Rodney King that's on video tape, the possibility of a police officer getting in trouble for doing something like that is rare.*

Luis resonated to the desire to be useful amidst violence in a war zone. He sounds like the African American men when he says,

Oh, the police. They really think they're above the law. And they do what they want, and they get away with it. They really do. There's no way you can say it. The guy who got hung, they beat this guy when he had handcuffs, at the County jail? There were too many riots, protests going, so they closed the jail down and moved [the jail] to Kearney. All the prisoners. Those police officers, don't do that again. That's all they got. There was a trial, the family was suing them. It got thrown out of court. Those cops are going to turn around and do the same thing to somebody else. The police, definitely less police brutality now than before. I think in part because they're scared. Because if they hit somebody, that person might have a gun, or their friend might have a gun that will shoot them. So there's more like, this noncaring attitude, it's like, do what you want, do what you want. That's why I personally went and got a gun, but it's registered. And it sits right by my window. At night, if anything happens, the cars are parked right there, I won't hesitate to shoot. Because I'm sick of this place basically. The way it's going. I want to save it, but I don't know what to do.

Latina Women

By far the most pronounced critique of the police comes from the Latinas who are, like African American women, profoundly disappointed in both the police and in their men. In both instances they expect a lot and get little. Their disappointment with the police is much like their experience with domestic violence. Despite the violence – repeated and severe – they maintain a faith in family, heterosexuality, and marriage that is sacred and unwavering. A full 75 percent of the Latinas believe the police are corrupt and violent, and an equal percent have come into contact with police because of incidents of domestic violence. These women often know how to get the police to do what they need to do; they are aware of the racial politics that must be maneuvered in order to get the cops to respond.

MARTA: *Like I see the cops go by, and they see the kids in the corner, and sometimes they'll say something and sometimes they won't. You know, like they look the other way. You call 911 and say, "Okay. I'm*

*calling from such and such a building. There's kids hanging outside.
It's 3 o'clock in the morning. I can't sleep." The cops won't come. They
won't come. They will never show up. Or, "There's a domestic fight in
apartment such and such." You'll sit there and die before they come. I
mean the wife will be dead, and he'll beat her to death, before the cops
ever come.*

MUN: *Because they don't want, because they don't care? Or because
they don't want to walk in that neighborhood?*

MARTA: *I think it's both of them. I think it's just like, this society, I think
the way they see it is, let them kill themselves. They'll take care of themselves. You know, black people killing black people. The Hispanics are
killing each other. They're killing, they both take care of finishing, of
terminating each other. I guess the cops just let them do it, you know.
If they see two, if they see a white person and a black person fighting,
they'll stop it. But if they see a Hispanic and a black person going at it
they'll, you know, they'll let it happen. If you call because there's a robbery, they'll let it happen. If you call because it's a domestic fight,
they'll let it happen. . . . The cops, they are a joke, the cops. And most
of the cops know the kids, and most of the cops, how can I tell you?
The cops will tell them, "Look, I'm going to let you go this time. But
next time I'm going to do something to you." And they really don't do
anything. And some of the times, the cops are the ones who are dealing
with them. You know, so it's inside jobs. And sometimes you see the
cops talking to the kids outside. And the kids will tell you, "No, man,
he's with us. He's with us." So you have no type of police protection at
all, at all. I mean, if you, if you would live where I live and you order a
Blimpie, they will not take it to your apartment. You have to come outside and get it. Because they will not go in there. If you order a pizza,
they'll give you a hard time going into my neighborhood. "Where on
Jewett?" "Bergen Avenue." "Well, can you come and meet us outside?" Because they will not, they won't go up. They won't go up. You
have to go outside and get your food and then go upstairs.*

Latinas, like white women, come into contact with cops, crime, and
violence around issues of domestic violence.

CARMEN: *Yeah, that's why I would like to be a cop. Because, like, my brother is so terrible, I could, you know, just . . . just control him and whoever gets, my sister's husband hit her, I'd get in and, you know, control them, too. So I would like to be a cop. I like, let me see what kind of cop. I would like to be the ones that go when there's problems. They go to an apartment . . .*

MUN: *Domestic violence and stuff?*

CARMEN: *Yeah. That's what I would like.*

MUN: *If somebody, some husband is beating some wife, you would go in there?*

CARMEN: *Yeah. I want them to feel how she'll feel.*

———

TAMAR: *Because he was doing all the screaming and punching and she was the one doing all the crying, so you could tell. And I called the cops and said bring, you know, can you send me a car, there are kids involved, the man is hitting, and I said please hurry up, and I was polite. She was telling me, she was a black lady, and I'm like, but there are kids involved, you know, and I gave the information, so she wanted to have my name, and I told her, "I'm not gonna give you my name," and she's like, "Well, if you don't give me the name, I'm not gonna send the cops." So I told her, "If you don't send the cops, somehow there's gonna be a recording that I did call you and you didn't do anything about it," so, you know, and I hung up.*

MUN: *Did the police come?*

TAMAR: *Yeah, they came. They came in less than three minutes. If it wouldn't have been for me, forget it.*

MUN: *How did that make you feel?*

TAMAR: *It gave me flashbacks of me. And I wish that when they heard me screaming, somebody would have called the cops or knock on my door and tell me if I'm alright, they don't do that.*

Leaving a violent home is, then, no guarantee that the violence will stop.

MUN: *Why do you think some men are beating up women? We hear a lot about this.*

MARGARITA: *Excuse me, why do they beat their wives? I guess because that makes them in control. That's the only person they can control, maybe, you know, because, that's why I say sometimes, like, to the baby's father, don't be yelling at me, why don't you go and do that to a man outside and see what happens. You'll get punched right in the face. You know, 'cause sometimes it's true, you haven't done nothing to that person and they come and they, you know, treating you bad, and you say, "Wait a minute, what happened?" And I say like that, "Don't talk to me like that, or treat me like that. You have an apart-ment, go to whoever gave you the problem, see, and do that face to face," you know, cause they'll slap the shit out of you, or whatever, you know. But I think it's that, it's that they, control, that they can control you. I think he [her sister's boyfriend] went to jail for a couple of . . . a week or two days, something like that. She, she has no say in that and instead of getting, what is it these things?*

MUN: *Injunction?*

MARGARITA: *Injunctions to, those things don't work. It just doesn't work.*

MUN: *Why?*

MARGARITA: *Because I guess when a man sets his mind to do something, a little piece of paper is not gonna stop him, and I don't think even the police is gonna stop him. I think when they set their minds to, they're [men] gonna do this, they're gonna hurt you or they're gonna do this, they're gonna do it.*

Restraining orders have little effect, according to the women we talked with, and many women think the police are prejudiced by virtue of race/ethnicity and gender. And yet, with all the violence Latinas re-port in their families of origin and families of procreation and their fears of escape and retaliation, their commitments to *familia* run very deep.

Violence in Poor Communities

From our data, we hear poor and working-class young adults in the grips of violence. But we also hear the profound influence of their rela-tive position in analyzing this violence. So, for instance, we understand that all residents whom we interviewed carry around fears of violence and see police as very powerful players. For most white men, however, police are *protectors* of community. For most people of color, and some of the white women, police are *perpetrators* of personal and community abuse. This, too, speaks clearly to questions of policy. If police are not trusted broadly, if they do not represent multiple voices, do not come from and represent the demographic and neighborhood groups and interests of all community members, if they appear to be and/or are unconcerned with violence within neighborhoods of color while far more responsive when the caller is white, we need ways to reimagine and redesign community policing so that the level of responsiveness and the time of arrival are not calculated through racism and institutional neglect.

We began our data analysis committed to an analytic strategy that would cut across these demographic groups. We intended to look for any apparent "differences" evident in demographic contrasts, but were determined *not* to organize our analyses around these "differences." And yet our data surprised us, as powerful data often do, forcing us to recognize the material and experiential consequences of particular race/ethnic and gender positions in the United States. While the women and men we interviewed pledged the irrelevance of race/ethnicity and gender, "I don't think about it much," their stories are saturated with such evidence. Race, class, and gender *are* socially constructed – *and* deeply engraved.

So we conclude this chapter with a set of chilling reflections on cops, crime, and violence. After analyzing our narratives we must admit that the public policies and institutions we perhaps naively assumed were clear-cut ended up being much more fluid, interpretable, multiple, and transitory than we expected. So, for instance, notions of community, cops, violence, and crime were revealed as *not at all concrete entities* with clear referents. Instead these turned out to be highly negotiated and personally interpreted relationships, developed over history, within racial and gendered politics, in quite local and specific contexts. These policies and institutions perform quite differently for different groups. In contrast to our initial sense that demography was fleeting but social institutions concrete, our data suggest just the reverse. In poor communities, demography is more biographically engraved that we would wish. And social institutions are quite "discriminating" in daily experience.

Every interviewee was aware of and frightened by violence and crime. But the commonality stops here. For African American men, their most pronounced fears involve state violence. And, indeed, Jersey City and Buffalo Criminal Index data show a dramatic "spike" in drug arrests from 1985 forward, particularly for African Americans, which is perplexing given national surveys which indicate equal levels of drug *use* for whites and African Americans.[3] The vigilance for arrests, and black arrests in particular, has peaked as have the imprisonment rates. So while 13 percent of monthly drug users are African American, 35 percent, 55 percent, and 74 percent of drug-related arrests, convictions, and prison sentences, respectively, involve African Americans. For white men, their worries focus specifically on racially choreographed street violence. And, indeed, the Criminal Index indicates a rise in robbery, rape, assault, burglary, and larceny from 1975 to 1990 in both Jersey City and Buffalo. For women across racial/ethnic groups, their terrors surround domestic violence; national data suggest that women across racial/ethnic groups suffer roughly equivalent rates of violence, with low-income women far more susceptible to intimate violence than middle-class or upper-class women. We assert, then, in terms of policy recommendations, that a federal, state, or local crime policy must address simultaneously all three kinds of violence – state violence, community violence, and domestic violence. These three work as a set, a triplet, a collection of interrelated and embodied experiences of social life in poor and working-class communities. And as a set, they affect children and youth – the next generation – with devastating predictability, whether these children witness, are victims, or, for some, perpetrators of the violence.

A Note on Blame

As a chapter epilogue we offer some commentary about the discourses that community members deploy when they talk about crime, violence, and responsibility. We do this in order to right a set of publicly advertised misconceptions. While the popular media continue to paint degenerated pictures of poor communities of color, our data paint a very different picture.

Indeed the *only* group committed to an analysis of violence in which they take no responsibility for the growth of violence is white men. With some exceptions, white men, as a group, identified the source of the "problem" to be boys/men of color. The "solution," for white men is the containment/confinement of these same boys/men. In contrast, the most pronounced discourse of responsibility could be heard from the African American women, who are most likely to see criminal behavior as an outcome of bad personal choices and irresponsibility and *least* likely to offer up macro-structural explanations for why young black boys/men are so heavily over represented in jails/prisons today. That is, African American women tended not to assert that the absence of jobs, the presence of racism, or hard economic times contribute to high rates of imprisonment. Because these women see entire communities as vulnerable to these conditions, they are unwilling, with any regularity, to attribute criminal behavior to these structural conditions. They assert, instead, with remarkable consistency that "if you commit the crime, you do the time." No fancy explanations or justifications. "If my children can struggle out here and stay out of jail—so can the others." A discourse of responsibility, perhaps even blame, is articulated most unambivalently from these women, who sound a bit like the Republicans who demonize them.

In analytic contrast with their African American sisters, African American men in both cities, and Latinos in Jersey City, assert broad-based structural explanations for why their boys/men are overpopulating jails these days. Offering theories of "conspiracy," the "system," corruption, recession, no jobs, and racism, these men are *not*, however, shirking responsibility. Quite a few end their discussions of crime and violence with a sobering sense of personal powerlessness. Filled with a desire to create change, they voice frustration that few avenues for change are available. We remember the words of Luis who sits by his window with gun in hand, wanting to do something, but not knowing what.

Concluding

The mid-1990s have marked a painful moment in racial history. We are reminded often and sharply of the enormous racial and class divides that continue to define community life in America. We watch helplessly as Congress passes legislation which demonizes people of color and people in poverty. We listen in relative silence, if not collusion, as these women and men are blamed for their own conditions.

Our data suggest a picture of social, racial, and class relations quite distinct from those drawn by Congress. We hear women and men of the poor and working-class, white, black, and Latino, who are disappointed by public and personal institutions ranging from welfare to the family to public schools and in pain about personal and collective tragedies, but who are also searching for ways to hold families together, protect communities, and take back their streets. While white men are filled disproportionately with a discursive venom that is difficult to hear (see especially chaps. 2 and 3), we read even their words as evidence of the pain of losing ground in an economy that has assaulted *all* members of the poor and working class with only moderate benefits accruing to once protected whites.

We hear further that crime bills that would simply arrest, prosecute, and incarcerate, build more jails, cut school budgets, and deny job training will satisfy or assist no one. Not even poor and working-class white men. The depth and consequence of social violence is enormous and multifaceted. Street violence is a concern for white men, indeed, and it endangers even more profoundly the mobility and public life of poor and working-class women and men of color. But for women and men of color, state violence, police brutality, false arrests, the planting of evidence, exaggerated charges, and differential sentencing policies also figure prominently in their narrations of violence. And for many of the women, there is no respite from street violence. Going home is no safer, and perhaps even more terrifying, than walking the streets at night. And leaving a violent home is no assurance of peace.

The news is not good. Our communities are fractured, and we come together frequently in fear, sometimes in finger pointing. But, we would assert, public policies that speak largely from a privileged standpoint as if race/gender neutral – incarcerating men and women from oppressed racial groups, at unprecedented rates – contribute to the fracturing. There are policy answers for reinventing community and safety among our differences. Some of our respondents spoke of coalitions, petition drives, and local organization across race and ethnicity, within class, between genders. The question, today, is not what to do, but who is going to listen?

"I've Slept in Clothes Long Enough"
Domestic Violence among Women in the White Working Class

*I didn't have the luxury of sleeping in pajamas as a kid. I always slept in my pants
and in my shirt because you never knew what time of the night the fight was going
to break out and what you had to do. Because you might have to run out of the
house and go call the cops because they [her parents] ripped the phone out of the
wall and are choking each other to death. You never knew. So I never had that re-
laxing point of crawling into bed, which is part of my other phobia now. I don't
sleep with any clothes on.*

> —SUZANNE, a thirty-one-year-old white mother of four, in Buffalo.

IN THIS CHAPTER WE EXTEND THE ANALYSIS OFFERED IN CHAPTER 6 AND EX-
amine the lives of twenty-seven white working-class women, focusing
specifically on the violence in their domestic lives. Drawing from qualitative narratives gathered from individual and group interviews, we listen to and analyze the experiences of violence and despair, and resistance and hope, as articulated by the women in this race and class
fraction.

In chapters 2 and 3 we focused on white men in the urban northeast,
arguing that they are feeling squeezed economically, in their neighborhoods and in the domestic sphere. Assuming deserved dominance, they
sense that their "rightful place" is being unraveled, by an economy
which they argue privileges people of color over white men in the form
of affirmative action, and by pressure from blacks and Latinos in their
neighborhoods wherein they feel that their physical space is being com-
promised. Even in their homes, their power wanes, as women no longer

listen, according to men, and the man is no longer totally in control. Lacking economic power, they attempt, we argue, to reassert power in the home/family sphere. As white men enact border-patrolling strategies, all in the name of "protecting the family," the question arises, where does this leave the women? What does their existence look like?

At least part of the answer lies in the secret of domestic violence as it seeped through our interviews. This is a story that is just beginning to be told, as studies of white working-class women and girls have almost entirely neglected domestic violence. We will argue in chapters 8 and 10 that domestic violence is a distinct theme in black and Latina women's lives as well, and it is no understatement to suggest that poor and working-class women's lives, across racial and ethnic groups, are saturated with domestic terror.

We recognize that domestic violence is not limited to the poor and working class. It permeates society, from the very poor to the very rich. Stories of abuse surface with great regularity in classes taught by our women's studies colleagues at universities serving a relatively affluent population, and we know that much violence goes on behind closed doors in even the most privileged sectors of America. However, we do want to stress that the reported *rates* of such violence, and particularly the intergenerational character of violence in the home, are far greater among the poor and working class than among the economically privileged. So while we do not deny the ways in which patriarchy may lead to brutality against women in the home *across* social classes, we also do not want to minimize the striking *concentration* of such violence in poor and working-class families.

Amidst our two-city sample it was, initially, quite easy to distinguish between women living in two presumably distinct domestic scenes. Borrowing Howell's (1973) categories, women with "settled lives" survive within what seem to be stable, intact family structures. In deceptively simple contrast, "hard living" women float between different types of households, move in and out of welfare, have less education and more (low-paying) employment. Despite these apparent differences, however, our analysis leads us to conclude that almost all of the poor and working-class white women and their families are negotiating lives disrupted by an inhospitable economy, and many of these women are also surviving within scenes of domestic violence that span across generations. The distinction between the "settled lives" women and the "hard-living" women may, sadly, only be determined by whether or not the woman has *exited* from her violent home. While current political debates romanticize the "settled lives" woman – the good woman who stays home, cares for her children and husband, and "plays by the rules" – and demonize the "hard-living" woman – who leaves her home, lives in poverty, flees her husband/boyfriend, and relies intermittently upon social services – our data suggest that both of these groups of women come from the same communities, have endured equivalent levels of violence, and differ only to the extent to which they expose their "private troubles" to public view (Mills 1959).

That these two groups of women are actually living within very similar domestic contexts is particularly disturbing as welfare "reform" debates contend that "hard living" women are lazy, irresponsible, and unwilling to commit to family life. Our data contest these claims and suggest, instead, that poor and working-class white women, whether they "stick it out" or "exit," are faced with high levels of domestic violence, and that those women who leave the "ideal" (if violent) married domestic space for a "safer" public sphere on welfare, are today being disparaged in part because they expose the fundamental *fallacies* of the family wage and domestic ideologies – ideologies which have been so sacredly coveted in the United States. Because of the "hard living" women, the image of the comfortable and stable white working-class family is beginning to shatter.

Contemporary White Working-Class Women and Domestic Violence
While the white women whom we interviewed do not see themselves living in an "ideal" family structure – that is, they admit that they work too much, that their partners earn too little, and that "home work" is still theirs – they also report, with far less critique, extraordinarily high rates of domestic violence. Across both cities and both types of "living," we documented abuse in 92 percent of the interviews. These women had either witnessed the abuse of their mother, or had been severely, and in many cases repeatedly, abused by a parent, early lover, current husband/boyfriend, and/or had a sister that was presently be-

ing abused. These poor and working-class white women, however, seldom raise a critique of men or the family, and all discuss abuse as if it were only experienced in the past. Although "hard living" and "settled lives" women negotiate the secret of male violence in different ways, the data suggest that women from both groups learn to arrange their lives around the violence that erupts behind closed doors.

A review of current studies on domestic violence indicates large gaps in our understanding of it. While it is widely argued that violence in the home appears across social classes, it is now generally acknowledged that there is more such violence among poor and working-class families. Alcohol abuse is linked to violence, but the removal of alcohol does not necessarily guarantee that violence will end (Downs, Miller, and Panek 1993). Rare in the literature are portraits of male violence against women drawn from *within* communities, across race/ethnicity groups and social classes. In addition, there is very little literature that explicitly explores the relationship between gendered violence and race, especially among those who are white, and it is noteworthy that our white respondents report markedly more domestic violence than our black respondents. Although rates of reported domestic violence within white and Latino communities are somewhat comparable, very few studies focus specifically on the experience of violence in the home *within* racial groupings and the ways in which racially distinct life experiences may be linked to expressions of violence and reactions to such violence (White 1985; Marsh 1993; Coley and Beckett 1988). In taking up the topic of domestic violence throughout the book, we hope to pry open necessary discussions both within and across community. Indeed, our data forced us to open up this discussion, even though we did not anticipate either the power of domestic violence in the womens' lives or the power the data would have over us. Without question, domestic violence is the most pervasive theme among the white working-class women we interviewed.

One study which does attend closely to dynamics of class and race, within gender, was conducted by Kurz (1995), who randomly sampled divorced women from Philadelphia (N = 129) and found that *across classes and races* a full 70 percent of these 129 women had experienced violence at the hands of their husbands at least once. Kurz's sample is strikingly similar in narrations and demographics to our sample, in which we find that an overwhelming majority of the white women we interviewed report experiences of childhood abuse (physical or sexual) and/or adult domestic abuse at the hands of a father, or mother's boyfriend, or husband or boyfriend. In our work, however, the conditions of "hard living" span across the seeming "stability" of families, whether the woman is currently married or not. In order to advance the debate over the need for public services to serve women and children in flight from violence, we are in need of more in-depth studies of the ways in which communities of women within class and race groupings narrate their experiences with violence in the home as well as their responses to this violence. Spaces ultimately need to be opened in which women can participate in collective critique of the violence that emanates from gender arrangements inside some poor and working-class white families.

Family Wage Literature

As the white women from across these sites narrate their experiences, they reveal that they have historic relationships to working-class life, most having had fathers and grandfathers who worked in factories and plants, and mothers who stayed home to raise children. Dorothy Smith (1987b) and others have argued that the working-class family historically has been characterized by a marked subordination of women to men, although, as we point out in chapter 3, working-class men today feel their dominance waning. An implicit contract between husband and wife stipulates that she provides household and personal services demanded, in return for which he provides for her and her children whatever he deems appropriate. Thus, the household is organized in relation to his needs and wishes; mealtimes are when he wants; he eats with the children or alone, as he chooses; sex is when he desires; the children are to be kept quiet when he does not want to hear them. The wife knows at the back of her mind that he could take his wage-earning capacity and make a similar "contract" with another woman.

Over the past two decades, numerous scholars interested in class and gender have attested to the conditions of white working-class women's lives, focusing on the notion of the "family wage" as a contributing factor to their experience. Martha May (1987) suggests on the basis of a study of the Ford Motor Company, that the family wage as ideology became and remained important because it appeared advantageous to *all* family members. To achieve this goal, however, this ideology rigidly deployed and maintained existing gender distinctions in work/domestic roles. For employers, the ideology of the family wage held out the possibility of lowered wages for some workers (mainly women) and a stable workforce whereby industry could amass long-term profits. By linking gender roles and subsistence for the working-class, the family wage ideology successfully reinforced the notion that women should receive lower wages than men or stay at home. Woodcock Tentler (1979) contends that although many white working-class women historically were in the wage labor force before marriage, their wage work experiences failed to alter their dependence on the family since nearly all jobs available to women offered less security and status than did the role of wife and mother, and many jobs were no longer available to women once they became married or pregnant. Thus, for white working-class women, life outside the family offered little economic protection and was not seen as respectable, as compared with life within the home.

While the family wage presumes a situation in which the man works full-time with benefits, and the wife stays at home with the children, our data reveal this is not the case for our sample of contemporary poor and working-class white women. Most of the women in this sample are employed, with jobs that are mostly clerical and not well-paying, to be sure. At present, almost all the married/attached women have husbands/boyfriends who are currently employed in blue-collar jobs or civil service blue-collar work such as security and other city employment. The prospects for employment for these men, however, seem to be dwindling, and many have experienced long periods of being out of work. In Buffalo, for example, 21 percent have, at one time or another, received welfare benefits, although that is not the case currently. Dwindling also, are the women's expectations that men will support their wives and children. Some of these women and their families, in fact, continually fall in and out of working-class and poor modes of existence. Donna, the oldest woman in our sample, narrates what she has seen as a decline in gender role expectations devolving since she was growing up:

> I was taught to . . . stay home . . . cook, clean, take care of my children. These [young] girls . . . nah, they're taught to . . . just go out . . . dress up . . . leave their kids with other people. They're not taught anything. Well, I'm glad my daughter doesn't do that. I mean, we take . . . my granddaughter at times, and keep her with us, but there's times that she . . . ya know, she'll take her and spend a couple of weeks with her, and then we'll . . . she'll come back with us for a couple of days. So we help her out a lot. . . . They worked [men in the past]. They had jobs. I mean, they didn't stay in school. They quit as soon as they were of age and they worked. The men today don't work. Teenagers, rather. They don't work. They just bum off their girlfriends, or their mothers. There's . . . there's mothers that are goin' to school with me, that have their seventeen-year-old sons . . . livin' with them, 'cause they have to. But they don't work, and their mother's givin' them money, buying their clothes, and . . . they don't go to school, they play hookey from school. The one girl [in the other class], she quit . . . because her son was hangin' out on the street corner, all night. . . . She said her son . . . was tellin' her, I'll punch the shit out of you; you can't tell me what to do. I said . . . if my son ever . . . and she said, well he's big; I'm afraid of him. . . . As soon as you show you're afraid, he's gonna . . . come at you. . . . I just said, take a baseball bat and crack him with it, you know.

For Donna the ideal male still provides for his family, but lived reality falls far short of this ideal. Young men, she describes, are no longer fulfilling their obligations to their families. Joan, another white woman from Jersey City, expects only the minimum from any man in a relationship. That is, he must "contribute:"

> First of all, I would never accept any man into my home who is not going to contribute. Physically we can contribute to each other; that

has nothing to do with it. Material, yes, has a whole lot to do with it. You know how they say material does not? It does. They also say "money doesn't buy you love," well, but I'm sorry to say, money buys everything else . . . [laughs]. . . . Money is a necessity, no matter how you look at it. Without it, where are you? Where could you even begin, you know. Love is not going to bring you bread to eat.

In these poor and working-class white families, women work and men are employed, but their family contributions are neither steady nor reliable. The romance of the family wage is fading fast. Many of these women, in their interviews, are critical of the inadequate money brought in by the men in their lives and the inequitable division of labor within the household. They complain that while they (the women) work, the men do little around the house. Katlin explains the difference between the attitudes of her abusive former boyfriend/father of her children (George) and Mack, her current boyfriend:

George felt that I was supposed to take care of him. My job was to take care of him. My job was to take care of the house. His job was to go to work. Mack doesn't feel that way. You know, Mack is like, if he comes here and there is food there, I be like "Mack, you hungry?" he be like, "Yeah." I be like, "Well, go serve yourself." George, on the other hand, if I said "George, you hungry?" he be like, "Yeah, serve me." Yeah, George was taught . . . that that's what a woman was supposed to do; a woman was supposed to serve you.

With the rapid decline of the U.S. steel industry and other areas of manufacturing and production over the last few decades (Bluestone and Harrison 1982), in the span of a few years, white working-class males have been left without the means of securing a steady family wage. Although symbolic forms of the family wage ideology remain intact within homes—for example, George upholds the marked subordination of women to men—today, both women and men struggle in the public world of work to make material ends meet in a circumspect economy.

Whole Cloth: Women's Lives of Violence

We now take you into the private worlds of three of our narrators – Suzanne, Kathy, and Anna – in order to open up the pain, passion, and violence which fester beneath the surface of these women's lives. Suzanne is a thirty-one-year-old white female. She might be considered among the "settled lives" women. Married, she is currently a volunteer in a local school, is unemployed and has four children. She and her husband have applied for public assistance but were denied funds because they fell over the designated income line for qualification. Her story of growing up with two alcoholic parents highlights the ways in which alcohol abuse and violence saturate her family of origin and all who were associated with this family:

> I grew up in an alcoholic family. Both parents were alcoholics, so we basically were left alone a lot. We were raised, basically, in the back room of a bar. We didn't have a good home life as far as that goes. That's probably why I'm the opposite. There was always degrading things said to us . . . there was none of the self-esteem stuff, or anything else like that. We were always called dumb and stupid and told we weren't going to amount to anything. I have two, well, I had three sisters and one brother. One sister died of SIDS [Sudden Infant Death Syndrome] when she was three months old. And my brother committed suicide when he was twenty-seven because he just couldn't handle, he, he was one of those kids that never felt like he fit in. So, he did everything, what everybody dared him to. When he was twenty-one, somebody dared him to jump into the creek, in the middle of winter. And he did. And he became paralyzed . . . so, when he was twenty-seven he killed himself because he couldn't handle the fact of being paralyzed and not getting married and not, you know, having anything else. My other sister turned out to be an alcoholic because she followed my parents' steps. And my other sister is an oddity. Because they usually say if you come from an alcoholic family, you're either an alcoholic or you're totally against it. I'm totally against it [drinking]. My sister turned out to be an alcoholic, and my other sister is a social drinker [laughs]. Which they say doesn't happen.

Suzanne draws attention to the ways in which alcohol and violence were, for her, linked. According to Suzanne, many of her siblings were, in hindsight, unaware of the family's dysfunctions while growing up, and today, are living lives filled with the same forms of abuse:

She [her nonalcoholic sister] lived in la la land. I always tell her, I don't know where she lived, because she didn't live in our house. You know, she's so condemning of my [alcoholic] sister. And I told her, but look at what we were raised in. And that's the first thing my other sister [the alcoholic] will say is, "Well, Mom and Dad did it and we're all here." But we're not all here. You know, my brother killed himself because of it. And, she actually lost her life because of it, because she's so busy drinking. She's not raising her kids either. So her kids are going through the same thing, basically, all over again. And she also, my mother was abused by my father all the time. And my sister let men beat her up too. She used to get beat up terrible all the time. So, her kids have seen that already too. And they say that's another trend . . . the abuse. You try to find somebody like your father and you end up in that type of situation. And just like my brother, my brother hated to see my father beat up my mother. But at the same time, he beat the hell out of his girlfriends. So . . . it's a thing, after you see it, you think it's normal even though it's not. I'm against it [alcohol] because I saw my mother [who also was an alcoholic]. My father used to tell my mother, "Who would take you with four kids? What would you do?" [if you left me or I left you]. And he used to call her fat and ugly, and she was beautiful and thin. You know, but it's a game they play to keep you in your place.

Suzanne comments further on how she used to defend herself from the outbreaks at home and the ways in which she is affected today by those experiences:

And with me, with my father, he tried once. He used to try to, used to fondle me. And that was about it. So, and then one time he grabbed me and I smacked him. It was the only time I ever hit my father, because I don't believe that you should ever hit your parents, but I swore that he was not going to do to me what he did to the rest of that family. And since that time, he never touched me because I'm bigger than him . . . and my mother [is the same size]. I used to tell my mother, why didn't you sit on him? He was so thin and so little, you could have just sat on him instead of getting beat up all the time. But my mother wouldn't. She was afraid of him. Yeah, I used to get to the point where I stood in between the two of them, praying that neither one of them would hurt each other, and I'd end up getting punched in the middle because I couldn't stop them and get them parted. My father would come home drunk. He would go out on the couch and go to sleep, and my mother would wake him up and drag him off the couch. Well, you're asking for a fight, you know. I don't want him hitting her. Just like I don't want her hitting him. I mean, there was blood in our house just about every day. Somebody was always whacked with something. And dinner time, to this day, I still don't sit at the dinner table with my kids. We eat in the parlor in front of the TV, or whatever. I can't sit at a table and eat with my kids. Because every time we sat and ate, we had to sit there. And you weren't allowed to leave, and just as you're getting ready to eat, a fight broke out and you couldn't leave the kitchen. So you had to sit there and listen to it. So I can't sit at the table.

Contrary to the Norman Rockwell images of the nuclear family sitting down to eat dinner, Suzanne, as a child, is entangled within a set of family relations that drown in alcoholism and, according to her, violence associated with that drinking. As she states, "the scariest thing is never knowing if you were going to wake up and have a mother and father," or facing what would be going on when she awoke.

Kathy is a twenty-four-year-old white female. She is currently unemployed, having worked previously in a church-sponsored residential home as an aide to profoundly physically and mentally handicapped adolescents. Kathy is not married but is in a relationship. She has an infant son and a five-year-old daughter, neither of whom are the children of the man whom she currently sees. Kathy received WIC benefits but has not applied for welfare. Her savings amount to $1500, and this is what she is living off of at the moment. Kathy's life has been filled with violence from every direction. A prototype of the "hard living" women, she was raised by an abusive father, raped when she was twelve, and brutally assaulted by the father of her first child when she was eighteen. Kathy remembers the things that frightened her while growing up:

> My father terrified me . . . he had a very bad temper . . . and my mother's drinking. My father would never physically hurt my mother because she would have packed us up in a heartbeat [she later contradicts this]. But he mentally abused her. Nothing was ever good enough, nothing was ever right. She wanted to go back to work. He kept telling her, "No, no, no. Your place is here." No matter which way she turned, he was there with a blockade, trying to stop her from being her own person, developing her own will. She started drinking . . . I don't remember when she started, but I do remember one instance very vividly. My brothers don't remember this. I was ten. We were down in Georgia, visiting my father's sister and her husband. My mother had a glass and it was half full of wine, and what she kept doing was drinking it and filling it back up to half when my father was gone. And I saw this, like, well, my father caught on to her. And my father was a big man, he was probably about six foot one or six foot two. He grabbed all three of us, picked us up and threw us in the Winnebago and took off. And he was going to leave her there. And I remember screaming. We must have gone about four or five miles out, and maybe even more than that. We were screaming, screaming, "We don't want to leave mama; we don't want to leave mama." He was just going to leave her down there and take us with him. At that point, I didn't care if he hit me or not. I just kept screaming and screaming and screaming. And if he hit me, I was going to scream even louder. I wanted to go back, and I didn't care what he did. You know, if he slapped me for screaming, I was going to scream louder. I screamed myself hoarse and he finally turned around.

In Kathy's case, it was her mother who was the alcoholic. The scenario of violence, however, is similar to that of Suzanne. Both Kathy and Suzanne narrate lives filled with shock and shame, surrounded by hitting, crying, verbal abuse, and insecurity.

Anna is a twenty-six-year-old white female. A single mother, she has one son, age eight. She is on public assistance and is unemployed at the present time. She has been in and out of abusive relationships throughout much of her young life. A member of the "hard living" group, Anna has sought out therapy for the past year and says that she has found it helpful for understanding her tendency to pursue and stay in abusive alcoholic relationships. She is forced to confront her past:

> *My father worked at a place called J. H. Williams, and they made tools. He was making pretty good money. The only problem was, my father was a miser . . . actually I really couldn't say he was a miser because he would spend money, but he would spend money on himself. . . . He would order things out of these magazines that were junklike. I used to get one from Spencer, one from, I don't even remember the names of these places. One thing I can remember was a calendar, where it was like a lifetime calendar. You could just change the months on it and the days. When my father passed away, I think we had about thirty of them, all the same. Coasters. There were tons of them, just stupid little things, he would buy by quantities. He would save everything from twist ties to bags to the Styrofoam packages from meats, and I can understand saving some of it, I save certain things like that . . . but my father, they [all the collected "junk"] were in the upstairs apartment which, we could have been renting it if we could have fixed it or cleaned it up, because when I was young, probably about one, we had a fire, and he started fixing the downstairs, but he never finished the upstairs, and all of his stuff was just up there. It was in my bedroom [she never had a bedroom because there was too much "garbage" in it—she slept in her parents' room]; it was in the pantry; it was in the . . . kitchen. There was just stuff everywhere, on the kitchen table, in the bathtub, just junk that he would buy or save. And he used to buy himself lots of clothes. He never bought me any clothes, or my mother any clothes. My uncle used to go and get me clothes from the Goodwill.*

At a later point, Anna describes her family as follows:

> *My father's an alcoholic, and my mom is mentally ill. She's schizophrenic and it was tough. My father was also abusive in some ways. He*

wasn't real abusive compared to what you hear about some kids going through, but he was abusive . . . he had a big belief that the man runs everything and the woman belongs home barefoot and pregnant. I was kind of the caretaker. I did the cooking from, I can remember seven years old, making dinner and cleaning. It was more or less, I was to take care of my mother instead of her taking care of me.

At school, Anna explains that she was picked on by the other children due to her lack of hygiene. This lack of cleanliness was a result of her father's obsessive control over the household. Anna also remembers a few instances of sexual abuse, while perhaps dismissing others from memory:

[The teacher] would call me "piggy," "smelly," "dirty," names like that, and the kids started following along with it. And I'd say by the fourth grade, I started cleaning myself out; I didn't care anymore, but my father had this thing that you were allowed to take a bath once a week. He would measure the shampoo, he would measure the soap, and if he thought somebody was using the shampoo when he said you shouldn't, you'd get a beating [this contradicts her earlier statement that he didn't hit her, only verbally abused her]. But I got sick of it, and the beatings almost became to be painless when hit with a belt or punched. It almost didn't faze me anymore. I figured I'd rather be clean and go to school and have friends, because it hurt more to not have friends than to be hit by my father. I know that we all slept in the same bed, which was another thing. I didn't have my own bedroom. My bedroom was filled with garbage, and I remember when I started developing, my father would put his arm around me and touch me on my breasts, and I always wondered; he would make it look like he was sleeping, but sometimes I thought that he was awake, because I would move his hand, and it would go back up. But I don't remember anything more than that. I suspect that things had happened when I was in foster homes, and that I blocked it out, because I do have a hard time with any intimate relationships.

Suzanne, Kathy, and Anna describe sexual, verbal, and physical abuse. Kathy, the daughter of an abusive man who attempted to abandon his wife in Georgia, recounts how she is beginning to suspect that her father killed his first wife. Through self-reflection, she is piecing together the emotional fragments of abuse in her own life and that of her half-sister and is coming to believe that her father could have shoved his first wife down a flight of stairs, from which she suffered an aneurysm the next morning and died. Apparently she did die from an aneurysm; the only question is the extent to which his beating precipitated it. Kathy can, though, imagine that it is true – that her father was such a violent man that it is conceivable to her that he did, in fact, do this. As she approached her teens, she used to run by the railroad tracks to get away from home. There, one day, she met another sixth-grader – a boy – who raped her in her secret hiding place, that private space by the tracks to which she would run to escape her abusive father. He left her with a "surprise package" – she was pregnant at the age of twelve and her friend's mother arranged for her to have an abortion. Her own parents never found out. Kathy has been lurched from one violent encounter to another, as have many of the women we have interviewed.

The hand of the male is not soft and supportive for Suzanne, Kathy, and Anna, but is instead large, violent, and brutal – a force to be feared. Given this, one would expect that poor and working-class white women would voice some critique of men and family. The most striking point here is that they do so only rarely. As we will argue below, the intimacies shared in an interview do not translate into collective sharing, nor do they spur a critical analysis of the role of family, heterosexuality, and/or men in ways that begin to break the cyclical patterns of violence that have programmed and continue to regulate gender relations inside some poor and working-class white families. While white women were willing to tell us a great deal in the secret space of our interviews, they left relatively unaltered their tone of reconciled contentment in which they wrapped narratives of the family as loving and supporting, and little scratches the surface as these women attempt to raise the next generation.

These three women come from very similar childhood spaces and live in very different adult worlds, and yet all carry biographies and endure the pains of domestic violence. As we reviewed the narratives of all twenty-seven women, we noted a set of recurring themes emerging as the poor and working-class white women manage the "shared secret" of male violence. While "hard living" and "settled lives" women negotiate the secret differently, many (and the vast majority of our sample) are managing lives around male violence and impending poverty.

"Hard Living" Women

Very much like their presumably "settled lives" sisters, "hard living" women report long histories of violence at the hands of men – from childhood forward. Whether describing fathers, step-fathers, or "neighborhood boys" who molested them as children, these "hard living" women, as girls, often turned to their mothers, seeking care, attention, and resolution. Many women note with disappointment that their mothers, caught in the ideology and finances of the family wage, "didn't want to" or "couldn't" talk about it. Stranded in a world in which family life is assumed to be private and sexual violence is assumed to be a woman's problem, many of these mothers tried to be as responsive as they could be – within the fixed space of heterosexual domestic life amidst poverty. This meant, typically, attending to their daughters' needs while ignoring the guilt of the boys/men involved. In many instances, mothers tried to maintain "stable" homes amidst a gendered violence which was crushing their daughters.

Sherile, a twenty-two-year-old white woman who was sexually molested by a neighborhood boy when she was just a child, sought comfort and conversation from her mother. Sherile reports, as many did, "My mom, I tried to find out what really happened, but she doesn't. It's like everybody feels uncomfortable talking about it to me, and that bothers me, because they were old enough to know and could tell me. Whereas my memory is kind of foggy about it." Lorraine shares a similar story: "One of my mother's boyfriends' friends molested me. And another man that my mother had babysit me, he had molested me when I was a kid. When I was a kid I tried to tell my mother, but she didn't believe at the time. So then I just like, didn't say anything . . . I, I never did anything about it; I just accepted it. When I went to college I went to counseling for it and stuff. I'm still going."

Rose's account differs slightly but has a similar theme. She also could not turn to her mother for help. Rose also explains how her neighbors chose to ignore the abuse:

> Like I said, my mother's boyfriend used to beat us. And then my mother was, on and off, she'd be violent too. . . . I was silent about it . . . I guess at the time I just didn't feel like there was anything I could do . . . like I remember, as a kid, trying to tell my mother to leave him . . . he was violent towards her too. And she never did. So, like I said, I guess I just felt like there was nothing I could do. When I was young, it was kind of like everybody knew. Like, everybody on the block knew, well, he hits those kids, or whatever. But . . . nobody ever did anything. Actually I remember . . . one time family services . . . had come to our house. I don't remember who called or why they had come, but I remember . . . they had to talk to me, to ask me how I was getting along with my mother's boyfriend. And I remember before that, they [her mother and boyfriend] were threatening me, saying, "Oh, we'll beat you if, you know, if you say anything. Pretend like we get along fine." And so that's what I did.

Most women tried, in vain, to talk to their mothers. And most mothers, caught in the web of threatened poverty and domestic ideology, chose not to hear. It is well documented that children in homes where mothers are battered are at great risk for physical harm and are also likely to be adversely affected by some of the ways in which the mother struggles to cope (Steinmetz and Strauss 1974; Jaffe, Wolfe, and Wilson 1990). In two cases in our study, young girls turned to mothers who were, indeed, helpful. But even here the girls worked with their mothers *around* the accused man, never confronting or holding him accountable for his actions. Susan, now age twenty-seven, describes her family as, "Great family life. Me and my brothers and sisters. We were close." Further into the interview, however, she explains what happened when she learned she was pregnant as a teenager:

> I guess I was too young to really know. I'd . . . skip my period and I said . . . I think I'm pregnant and I said there's one way to find out, I'll

*talk to my mother. So it was me and my best friend, two very good
friends of mine. We went, and my mother's very open about sex, you
know, if you ask any questions, she'll explain it to you point blank. So
we was like, we're having a problem with somebody . . . I didn't tell my
mother I was pregnant though. But afterwards, my father hit me and
he had punched me on the side and I peed blood, and I went and told
my mother I was peeing blood, and when I went to the hospital they
kept me for observation for twenty-four hours or whatever . . . and
they did blood work and everything. Then the doctor told my mother I
was pregnant, and she came into the room, she told me. And I was
like, I knew that Mom; I just didn't know how to tell you. She was like,
why were you hiding it? I was like because I didn't want Daddy to kill
me, and we hid it from my father. My mother took me and got the abortion; my father never knew.*

Susan's story is an attempt to tell and be heard by Mom. But even
here, father's abuse, horrific as it was, was overlooked. Mom did double
duty, working "around" him and his temper, and saving her daughter.

Moving into adult domestic abuse among "hard living" women, we
find similar patterns of attempts to speak, amidst fear of reprisals and/
or the absence of audience. Yet, while very few "settled lives" white
women actually tell family members or friends about their abuse, we
do see a number of the "hard living" women speaking aloud – be it to
friends, neighbors or kin, through religion, psychotherapy, or the justice system. These women are, for the most part, not married, on their
own, and have fled violence and teeter on the unreliable edge of pov-
erty/homelessness. These women appear to feel more *free* to speak
about domestic violence. In comparison, "settled lives" women – living
in what appear to be intact, stable marriages – are relentlessly silent
about their own stories. "Hard living" Gena describes how when her
boyfriend beat her, he would find her to blame:

*[He would say] it was my fault. I made him do that, because I yelled at
him and he couldn't handle it . . . I threw him out. I'd block the door,
he'd kick the door right in. And when I would call the cops . . . he
would hide in the building; they couldn't find him and they would*

leave . . . and then, he'd stay away for a couple hours or all night . . . go to his friend's or his mother's. Then come the next day, "I'm sorry . . . I . . . messed up again. I won't let it happen again." And this went on for a year. I told him the next time you hit me, don't go to sleep here, 'cause I will chop you up. I sat in my chair with an axe in my hand . . . and said I was gonna chop him up that night . . . he wasn't gonna touch . . . hurt me again. He wasn't gonna steal anything. He wasn't ever gonna hit me. And he wasn't gonna ever tell me what to do. Then I, I'd just sit. Who were you to hit me and then tell me you wanna make love to me? Please. And it's my fault [he would say that]. That's sick . . . every time he fought or stole somethin', the cops never did nothin'. They would say, "We can't do nothin' 'cause we can't find him." So what are you gonna do? Press a complaint to . . . he ain't gonna show up in court.

Gena also explains that when she gets pregnant, his violence erupts. Among this sample there were a number of women for whom the onset of pregnancy and the reassertion of violence co-occurred. During pregnancy and the first few years after the birth of a child can be a time of heightened financial, physical, and emotional stress, all which has been linked to an increase in the potential for violence (Schechter and Jones 1992; Gelles 1988; Parker and McFarlane 1991; Campbell et al. 1992; Helton, McFarlane, Anderson 1987). As Gena describes, a restraining order helped at first, but it did not stop the violence from continuing:

That helped. He went and stayed with his mother. And he wouldn't come near me, because he was afraid to go to jail . . . that was like [lasted] for three months . . . because when he came back . . . it was good. And that's when he was doin' really good . . . and then I got pregnant with Jessica. And then when Jessica was born . . . it started all over again. The same cycle. With the . . . drugs, him stayin' out. But then he started . . . instead of takin' things from the house, he started just usin' his whole pay. You know, borrowin' all week, and then come payday, he didn't have a full pay. I'd have to go down and meet him at the job just to get the money . . . or else, if he got his pay, he'd be done [laughs].

For other "hard living" women, the courts offer other forms of temporary salvation. Julia remembers that pregnancy also brought out violence in her child's father:

> See, with my second son . . . their father used to . . . beat me up. And
> he broke my ribs and I was two months pregnant with my second one
> and I had gone to the hospital. I didn't know I was pregnant. I put crim-
> inal charges against him. He went to jail because what they did was
> they arranged for him to remain in jail until I had the baby, because
> they didn't know whether I would survive, or something would hap-
> pen with the baby during the pregnancy, whatever, and indeed if any-
> thing happened to either one of us, he was going to be charged with
> first degree murder because it was inflicted on me. . . . He was incarcer-
> ated for, I think it was . . . which time? 'Cause I had him locked up sev-
> eral times for no child support. Oh, when he hit me, he served three
> years.

A few women turned to counseling, although the costs typically exceed their resources. Quite a few testified that God was their salvation. Jana, a woman of white and Puerto Rican parentage, now gives full credit for her escape from her abusive relationship with Mike to her reliance upon God:

> Mike would beat me; he beat me up all the time. Take sex, and I didn't
> want to give it to him . . . I was scared of him. He said if I fought back,
> he would kill me. Look, I'm not talking about a slap. It came to a point
> where he hit me like I was a man. Plenty of times I would call police.
> There were lots of times I did. Mike was the type of man that he would
> tell the cop to mind his own fucking business. . . . Mike was the kind
> of guy, he would play you off, he would have you on his side. Any male
> species he would have on his side. Oh yeah, he used to say, "She's a
> bitch. You know what she did to me." He would make up stories. Oh,
> Mike was good, he was a good actor. He was a good con artist. My
> mom didn't know for years. I was ashamed. "Oh, Mom, I got some-
> thing to tell you. I'm getting beat up now." It was something that I
> didn't say. I had nothin' good to say. He was a drug addict. Mike was
> into heroin. . . .

As for her children, she describes how she would do all she could to protect them from his rage:

I loved them. They were mine. Regardless if I planned them, I took care of them. I did everything in the several years relationship with Mike. Getting beat up, protecting them, crying, telling them it's okay, Mommy is all right. I would get better. I was my kid's savior. I protected them from it. [He] never hit them. Never yelled at them. I would get beat up for them. They did something wrong, I took their beatings. . . . I was in a shelter with nuns, St. Francis in downtown Jersey City. I overheard a conversation he was having with a friend. Mike was a car thief. He would steal car radios. I heard he [Mike] was going to New York to steal a car, hijack a car and bring it to New York and sell it. So I dropped the dime on him . . . it was like God told me to. I don't know. I think God saved me. I think God put him in jail. I think God wanted me to hear the conversation. God dared me into doing this . . . God knows everything. He knows everything about me, inside and out.

Through extensive bouts of violence, from childhood through adulthood, these "hard living" women seek audience, find few who will listen, and end up with therapy, the police, or, occasionally, God. Given the depth and pain of violence in these women's lives, it is curious that even these women, willing to seek remedy outside their homes, *do not talk about violence in current relationships.* This is a noticeable absence, considering that these women are at various stages in their lives, with and without children, in and out of work.[1] Indeed, we begin to notice that many of these women describe current relationships as "good," and then elaborate by explaining that their current partners do *not* beat on them. The absence of reported current violence is presumably evidence of a "good" relationship. For example, Sandra reports:

It's good; I mean, he's there for me. It's good. I don't know what to say . . . [laughs]. He listens to me. He's a friend. I don't know, I guess I got all the conveniences of a nice relationship . . . I don't get beat up;

*I don't get put down. He listens to me. He gives me advice. He's a
friend and he doesn't do drugs; he doesn't drink, so that's good, you
know. He is a good father. He's just got to pay a little more attention to
his son, but in overall, he's good.*

Sandra, a twenty-one-year-old woman, describes the "good" aspects of her relationship in the negative; her fiancé doesn't beat her and,
therefore, the relationship must be good. The absence of a definition of
a good relationship suggests that these women have expectations for relationships that are abusive and that any partner who does not abuse
them seems like a "good" partner. "Hard living" women are on the
move, but never free – for long – from violence.

"Settled Lives" Women

Unlike the "hard living" women, the women living in what appear to
be "settled lives" are far more reluctant to reveal evidence of violence to
anyone. While we opened a relatively silenced space in the private interviews, information about domestic violence, by their own admission, is
rarely shared. Abuse remains a *well-known shared family secret* in its
worst form. One has to protect oneself and one's children, in so far as
one can. When things get too bad, of course, there are shelters which
can take these women in, but most "settled lives" white women do not
avail themselves of these services unless absolutely necessary. Given
that the woman's role is to sustain family life, with stories of abuse
come embarrassment, and, ironically, evidence of *her* failure. Silence
cloaks abuse in the hope that its biting reality will soften and eventually
fade away. Keep it private, keep it private, and then maybe it will go
away. Maybe today will be different. Maybe he (or she) will not come
home drunk and set off a series of encounters that will result in beatings, in violence, in our sleeping in clothes, in our thrown plates of food,
in our blood, in our screams, in our terror. Will my sister have a knife?
Will she be drunk? Will she set dad off? Will mom leave? Can I use soap?
Why don't the "settled" women, white and working-class, scream in
rage about the family that allows this to go on? Why is this all so
guarded an event in the discourse of this class fraction? For whom,
among poor and working-class whites, does the myth of the harmoni-

ous family survive? Living in violence may be better than living on the streets, or losing custody of one's children. If she speaks, the "settled" woman could pay the price of becoming "hard living."

For "settled lives" white women, like Suzanne earlier, domestic violence is a domain of muted critique that has difficulty breaking through. We offer some observations and speculations as to why this is the case. We argue here that this silence about abuse is tied to the ideology of the family and the way in which this ideology has historically worked through married white working-class women's lives, as well as the ways in which family, as an ideal, is cross-valorized with the construction of race through the marking or nonmarking of white as a race marker that intersects with the ideology of the family. For both white men and women, then, whiteness is symbolically linked with maintaining a "good" intact family. For men, as we argue in chapters 2 and 3, it is about border-patrolling strategies that keep family and community "safe" from encroaching others. It is also about materially sustaining family, and, in the absence of the ability to do that, being symbolically dominant in the home. For women, whiteness is linked with "settled living," thus encouraging the silencing of what really goes on behind closed doors in white working-class families. It can be speculated that part of the anger of black men toward black women is that black women refuse to participate in the dance of silence as do their "settled lives" white working-class sisters. (See chapters 4 and 8.)

As noted earlier, white working-class women's lives have been largely defined and contained by the family. The struggle for the [white] family wage was a struggle that solidified men as breadwinners, as individuals who were responsible for the support of dependent women and children. While this is certainly true in every white class fraction, white working-class women had virtually no means of escape from this position in that they could not acceptably obtain employment outside the secondary labor sector whose income levels conventionally frustrated possibilities for financial independence and autonomy. Thus their existence was almost totally dependent upon the male wage (father and/or husband) and the way in which this male wage established patterns of male dominance in the home. There has not been, then, any historically based critique from *within* the white working class of the nuclear family or of male dominance, as has been the case for white middle-class women, for example. In other words, these women have not had available to them the structural conditions in which to articulate a vocabulary of critique.

Certainly feminist language and analysis has reached deeply within the white working class in some ways (Weis 1990; Sidel 1990), but the sense of a collective movement has not been lodged within this class fraction. Thus there is nothing internal to the class which would lead white working-class women to critique and challenge male dominance and its potential link to violence. (Indeed, it can be argued that its very "middle classness" caused working-class white women to reject the women's movement in the same way that some black women rejected elements of the women's movement which were seen as white.) White working-class women who rejected the ideology of domestic life and its attendant violence sacrificed their "respectable" place in the class fraction. They became seen as, that is, painted as, "hard living" women who experience within-class violence and expulsion from the standards of gendered life. By so doing, gender/class/race ideology remains intact, as dissenters exit – and are punished.

Since the "settled lives" women evidence that, at all costs, they perpetuate the myth of stable and agreeable home life, it is here where we can see the possible ways in which ideology of family and the production and maintenance of whiteness as a racial identity marker work together. At this juncture, we find total silence in the literature on violence in the home.

As Frankenburg (1993), Spivak (1990), Morrison (1992), and others have argued, and as we have pointed out in chapter 3 in our discussion of white masculinity, the construction of the dominant white self cannot be understood except in relation to the construction of the "other." Frankenburg (1993) suggests that it is the legacy of colonial discourse that generated a sense of whiteness as an "empty" space, but one that is simultaneously normative. Whiteness is appropriated as the norm, as that against which all others should be judged. It is, then, an unmarked signifier – a marker only full in relation to the constructed other. Its fullness, then, inscribes, at one and the same time, its emptiness and presumed innocence. It is here, then, that the co-construction of the African American becomes so important. The African American, according to our white informants, is largely lazy, prone to violence, and does not want to work. While this is a largely male critique (see chaps. 2 and 3), white women express similar sentiments. Certainly, as we point out in chapters 2 and 3, this construction of African Americans circulates throughout racist America, and is not limited to the poor and working class. But, as we show earlier, much of the identity work of the white working class involves continuously distancing self from "other," in this case, from African Americans. More affluent whites do not need to labor at this as intensely, since they are more spatially/psychologically distant from poor African Americans to begin with. Among the white women in this study, negative images of those of African and Puerto Rican descent circulate throughout descriptions of the "other," as Carol narrates:

> *Like I said, I'm sure there's quite a few out there that are pretty decent. It's just a lot of people won't give themselves a chance to know them because they're afraid, or just so sure that they're bad because they're black or Puerto Rican. What can you do? It's hard to say, but sometimes that's all you see in the paper, is they're black or Puerto Rican. Granted, there are white ones that are white trash too. But the majority of the time, the ones that are causing trouble are them [black and Puerto Rican]. And I can understand why people feel that way. And it's too bad that not everyone can get along, but that's just the way it is.*

Although Carol recognizes that there is "white trash too," she adds that "the majority of the time, the ones that are causing trouble are them [black and Puerto Rican]." This line of thinking is sustained in conversation with Judy, whose ready association of black folks with criminal activity undermines any possible space for a notion of the black family as a "good family." Such families are seen only as white: "I guess we think of black people as . . . more involved in crime [than white people are], people who are going to hurt you . . . not couples who are the same as you [white] . . . with families, trying to make ends meet like you are."

These projections of the social deviant coupled with that of the "nonworking" African American enable white women, like white men, to draw the boundaries of what signifies acceptable nonworking at the borders of their own community. Many white working-class men and women whom we interviewed received welfare benefits and/or food stamps at one time or are receiving them now (19 percent of white women in Buffalo at one time received welfare benefits), but, as they articulate, this is somehow "different" than when African Americans receive such benefits. There is a material dimension here as well. White women, if they are married, have husbands who have had a better chance to obtain a white male wage, thus offering the possibility of securing greater financial stability. For those women living with male wage earners, the steady family income that their husbands have brought home draws, for them, the line between them and African American women, for whom this possibility is all too often ruled out in the face of stark levels of unemployment among poor black males.[2] Although many white women work outside of the home, and white men do not earn (or share) the kind of wage that they (or their fathers) may have had in days of heavy industry, it is still the case that a white male wage can mean the difference between being working class or destitute (Oliver and Shapiro 1995).

Note, then, that the "settled lives" women, who endure domestic violence in smarting secrecy and belittle African American women-headed families, may be voicing their anxieties about falling into the "hard living" pit. For the "settled lives" white women, the black family becomes her discursive trash bin, but the white "hard living" woman may be her embodied terror. Given what we have heard from the women who are "hard living," we see that exit from the traditional family is no escape from violence, just temporary respite, and almost assuredly leads to poverty—at least in the short run.[3] Many of the "hard living" women have had to reinvite once violent men, fathers of their children, back into their homes, even if they are on welfare, in order to make financial ends meet. And yet just as poignant, the "settled lives" women have no escape and no recourse. Justifying their decision to stay, they disparage the black "other" in terror of their white counterparts' life.

Concluding

The "hard living" white women whom we interviewed may merely be the front-runners of a generation of white women suffering, as women of color have long suffered, in the context of an economy that is crushing and punishing to the working-class and poor. These women may be the archetypes of a world yet to come for many poor and working-class white women. Merely an admission of violence away from those women who appear to be thriving amidst "intact" families, the "hard living" white women live and speak more like the African American women in our sample. Although still privileged by whiteness, the "value" of a white working-class man has been diminished in both the economy and in the domestic sphere, just as the "value" of an African American man has always been circumscribed in the United States by a racist labor market (Oliver and Shapiro 1995). And so white family forms, like African American and Latino, reshape in political response to the economy, the rise of jails, the dwindled presence of men, diminished resources for children and women – married or not.

As the public sphere collapses, or more aptly is collapsed, by a Congress eager to universalize cutbacks for the poor and abatements for the rich, and a president who recently signed a "welfare reform" act, women of the poor and working classes are being squeezed into tighter and tighter domestic corners and pushed out of the public world of work, welfare, and battered women's shelters. While escape from violence appears easy to those onlookers who ask, "Why doesn't she just leave?" we hear from these women that they can barely *afford* to exit, especially if they have children, and that male violence often follows them, whether they exit or not. They need "safe havens" to exit to – havens which are being taken away as monies for battered women's shelters wither. As the public sphere shrinks, women will get beaten with more regularity with fewer options, and more muzzled critiques. They will be swept into the corners of a reinstitutionalized "private" sphere, secured in its violence by the hollowing of the economy and the retreat of public sector services for women and children.

Today, Suzanne makes it a point not to sleep in any clothes as a form of resistance to those many years when she kept her clothes on day and night in fear that she would have to flee unexpected outbursts of family violence. Held hostage to the difficulties of critique and escape, she and these other women are left to defer desire in dreams for the next generation.

8

"Food in Our Stomachs and a Roof Overhead"
African American Women Crossing Borders

> Our African American sister knows oppression because of the race problem, the
> woman question, and the poverty predicament. But we dare not speak of her in
> exclusive terms here, for in sharing the first jeopardy with Black men, the second
> with women, and the third with the poor of the world, there is a universality
> which connects her with others.
>
> —JOHNNETTA COLE, "Jesus Is a Sister"

IN *THE SALT EATERS*, TONI CADE BAMBARA DESCRIBES THE DAILY NEGOTIA-
tions performed by African American women as aspects of the art of
being a "borderguard"—the person who keeps landlords, bill collec-
tors, and other would-be intruders from getting past the front door. In
chapters 2 and 3 we saw men patrolling the borders of community; here
our interviews with African American women reveal the ways in which
women both patrol the borders of home/family life, and, at the same
time, constantly carry themselves and their children across those borders. In this chapter we'll see the multifaceted ways in which this meta-
phor plays out in the lives of poor and working-class African American
women: at home, in neighborhoods, in jobs, and with the state. We'll
also see the distinctive ways that themes of spirituality saturate the
stories these women tell.[1]

Despite all the evidence that these women occupy economic and representational space at the bottom of contemporary U.S. society, despite
all the evidence that they give to others far more than they receive, these
women stand strong, voice outrage, love kin, and "will not be dimin-

ished" (Belle 1989, Wade-Gayles 1995). Surviving in an intergenerational journey, struggling to have a "roof over our heads and food in our stomachs"—a cliché repeated so often by so many as to seem a mantra—these women tell their part of the American story.

The background against which this borderguard work goes on is one where women are, more so than in any other community examined here, independent from men. This does not mean that men are not around, or that fathers do not contribute to the household economy, whether living with their children or not. What it does mean is that women support and raise their children on a day-to-day basis, with some monetary help from men, the state, or other women. As Stack (1974) pointed out twenty years ago, and more recently Stack and Burton (1994) have demonstrated, African American women in poor communities share resources, food, and child care in order to raise the next generation. Stack's most recent book demonstrates the ways in which this cooperative tradition works cross-generationally, North to South, and relates how African American children are often sent home, "down South," to be raised by kin when the North does not fulfill its promise or when children wander too far astray (Stack 1996). While many African American women living in poor northern communities are critical of men, they also understand the system as having denied these men jobs and broken their spirit. The passion with which many African American women want men to assume their "rightful place as head of the family" cannot be missed. Though strong themselves, these women want that strength to be shared with African American men; they want men to step up and take their place as head of the family and leaders within the community. Presently, though, in these interviews, there is much disappointment and accompanying criticism of African American men, both within and outside of the community, as the accumulated tides of joblessness and racism take their toll. So these women work the borders, carrying babies, elders, and self from home to streets to the public sphere of school and "downtown," journeying between "what is" and "what could be."

Borders between Home and the Streets

One set of borders African American women must negotiate is that which divides the home from the street. Women must keep children safe in the midst of street-based violence and, at the same time, prevent children from falling prey to the lure of its money as they grow older. Most of the women we interviewed talked in great detail about how violence has swelled around them and overtaken their community. With fears for their own safety and that of their children, they are vigilant about keeping the kids "locked in the house after school."

The caring and shouldering of burden is not new to African American women, who, as has been fully explored by hooks (1990), have traditionally created the "homeplace" as a dual site of love and resistance. What is relatively new, however, at least in the urban North, is the narration of the constant search for "safe spaces" in which to live and raise the next generation. And it is, without question, the drug economy of the 1980s and 1990s that is fingered in the demise of community, family, and self.

TRACEY: Can you tell me about the neighborhood that you live in now? How is it the same or different from the neighborhood that you grew up in?

CAROLYN: It's a lot different. I live in an environment with a lot of drugs. It's hard to keep your kids in the yard when there's a lot of activity going out in front. And they want to go out and watch it. It's a lot different. Where I grew up, it was peaceful. And now it's, like, rough. Real rough.

————————

LOIS: Talk to me a little more about your neighborhood. You say that it's so different from when you grew up. What's going on now? Can you describe it?

AYISHA: In this particular neighborhood, they're selling drugs. They [young people] think that that's the only way they can get the things they want, and what really upsets me about it, is that their parents know and they're not trying to do anything about it. I know when we were growing up, if we came in the house with something, we better have an explanation as to how we got it, where we got it. And they'll tell their parents anything and they'll believe it. I mean a hundred and fifty dollar sneakers and things like that. And the parents don't say anything. It's like they don't even care. Everybody is so wrapped up into doing their own thing, and that bothers me. There's a lot of young kids in the neighborhood, and what if these guys [who] think that they know everything about selling drugs ever run in with somebody somewhere else, and they come over and start shooting; there's so many young kids around here. Maybe the oldest one out of a group of the young kids is maybe seven or eight. It's not fair that they can't live and enjoy their life the way that we were given a chance. There's been many times where we would be sitting out on the porch and somebody may pull up in a car and jump out with a gun. You know that this is what they have in their hand is a gun. Now what they're getting ready to do with it, you don't know. The bullets don't have no name on them. And you're just scared.

Ayisha and Carolyn narrate being "under siege." For Ayisha, movements are further and further restricted. She and her son can only go certain places. She cannot go safely to the store. Her son cannot play safely on the streets. She cannot sit safely on her own porch, or her mother's. Her space is being taken over by young people, many of whom are involved with drugs, who have "no respect" for themselves or others. The guns that accompany the drug trade make space in the inner city perilous. Kathy concurs:

As some say, it's definitely not a good neighborhood to bring your kids up in, especially if you're a person like I am with any morals. I protect my kids. I like to protect them. Sometimes I may be a little too overprotective, but there is a lot of shooting over here, possibly drive-by shooting. There's a lot of drugs, you know, being sold over here. It's just not a safe neighborhood. A lot of times there is a lot of places, basically now, that you can't be safe anywhere, but I'm pretty sure that somewhere there is a much quieter neighborhood for our children to grow up in. Parents not having to worry about keeping their kids either in your house or in the backyard, being able to let them go out on the sidewalks and ride their bikes or play with other children, you know, but in this neighborhood, I can't do it. I have to keep them, in the summer-

*time and wintertime when they want to go outside and play, I have to
keep them in the backyard, you know. I, I don't feel comfortable letting them out in the front to play.*

Most residents in the neighborhoods where we interviewed stated
they had nothing to do with drugs. The majority are law-abiding
people who are not involved in the drug economy at all. The problem,
however, as Bourgois (1995) points out, is that the law-abiding majority has lost control of public space. In his work in El Barrio in East
Harlem, regardless of their absolute numbers, or relative proportions,
hardworking, drug-free Harlemites have been pushed onto the defen-
sive. Most of them live in fear, or even have contempt, for their neighborhood. Worried mothers and fathers maintain their children locked
inside their apartments in determined attempts to keep street culture
out. They hope someday to be able to move out of the neighborhood.

The drug dealers that residents in Jersey City and Buffalo describe
are, likewise, only a small fraction of the neighborhood population.
But, like those in East Harlem, they unfortunately set the tone of public
life. Residents fear getting caught in the cross fire as anger swells over
bad drug deals, as the well-known "craziness" associated with the
lethal crack overtakes their streets, as young people turn increasingly
disrespectful with dreams of big money, money made by participating
in the crack economy. Again, these are the few, but they control public
space; they set the tone for lives that law-abiding residents have to live.
Mothers have to protect their children—from drug deals gone bad,
from the lure of making large amounts of money on the streets. For
dealers want young runners—they are only prosecuted as youthful
offenders—and mothers want to save their kids from possible death.
The constant struggle between the inside of the house and the outside streets is played out throughout the community, as children grow
older.

There is a tremendous sense of hopelessness surrounding the narrations of neighborhood, community, and drugs. There seems to be no
way out since neighbors, men, police, and government are all impli-
cated in the selling of the inner city and its residents. It has become a

space in which there is almost no place to hide from drug dealings gone bad. The most painful aspect of this, according to the interviewees, is the effect on children. Virginia talks passionately about what has changed since she was a child. The biracial daughter of artists, she grew up associated with a neighborhood art center, where she now works. Virginia is an artist who works forty hours a week, earns little money, and receives food stamps. She lives with her husband and two young children. Her infant sits on her lap as we talk, she, reminiscing about the past:

> VIRGINIA: *I grew up on Dodge and Rollers . . . in that neighborhood. There was always a gang around, but the difference that I noticed, in that same neighborhood today, is the gangs — when we were growing up — had a tendency to take care of their turf, or their neighborhood, and now the gangs don't. They have a tendency to just milk it for what it's worth.*
> LOIS: *Can you say more about that? What do you mean that the gangs took care of their neighborhood?*
> VIRGINIA: *Well, I know it will sound strange to somebody, but they don't — as opposed to robbing the people who live in your own neighborhood — they robbed the outside people [laugh]. You know what I mean. They don't, they didn't let another gang come in and bother nobody.*
> LOIS: *They sort of protected the place?*
> VIRGINIA: *Yeah, they didn't — you know, how little kids will pester the old people sometimes and get on their nerves; they [gang members] pick them up and tell them not to do that, take them home to their mother. Or, if their mother wasn't home they'd say, "You shouldn't be doing that." You know, "Leave that old guy alone."*
> LOIS: *And that's not the case now?*
> VIRGINIA: *No. They just milk it for all it's worth. It's like, I can walk through the same neighborhood, and I'm older than most of the gang members, you know, and I've been there a lot longer than they've been, and normally there would be a certain amount of respect, that they wouldn't bother me. And now, you know, they don't do anything but,*

you know, they sit there and they bother you when you walk by, and this and that, you know. In all the years my parents lived there, in the past, they've never been robbed. In the past year and a half they've been robbed three times. And the people who have been there for a long time, it's all the same, they've all been robbed at least once, but it's all been in recent history. Before, if anybody was bothered, it was never by anybody within the neighborhood.

LOIS: *Why do you think this is the case?*

VIRGINIA: It was just a given, you know. You didn't want to rob, you know, your best friend's parents, which is what it boils down to, you know, or their grandparents, or their friends, or, you know what I mean. It's like everybody who lives in the neighborhood has got parents and they live there too. So if you're going to rob one of the houses, you know, likely, the likeliness of it, that it's, you know, gonna be somebody who is related to a friend of yours.

LOIS: *You're saying there was just a certain amount of respect.*

VIRGINIA: Yeah. You know, there wasn't as much pressure to be in the gang. You know, you could exist in the neighborhood without being harassed by the gang. Now the gangs don't have any respect for the neighborhood. They want to get what they can from anywhere they can. Their turf is sort of considered [to be the] section that they get to, you know, rob and pillage, this sort of thing. Rather than, this is the section we're protecting, you know.

LOIS: *Why do you think that's changed?*

VIRGINIA: I think the drugs are a lot harder. That's a part of it. It makes people a lot crazier than they used to be. The drugs used to sort of mellow people out. Now it makes them crazy. And they'll do anything, and they don't know who you are, they don't, you know. It's like somebody could look at you now and they might be fine when they're straight. But if they're high they'll do anything to anybody because they don't, you know, they care less and less. Probably because, at least when I was little, there wasn't much in the neighborhood, but there was a Boys Club where you could go do stuff. There's nothing else for them to do, you know. The system's taken everything away from them. Nothing for them to do. It's like when we were little, we could

*go to the Science Museum, 'cause it was free. Now the Science
Museum isn't free anymore, so it's not available to anyone in the
neighborhood.*

Virginia has an expansive critique of what is happening in the neighborhood – her community, the community in which she works and
where her parents still live. For her, the plight of the inner city is due to
a structural dismantling of services available to the urban poor (the Science Museum now charges; there is nothing for these kids to do) as well
as a pillaging on the part of gangs of the very neighborhood they used
to protect. Hers is not a romantic understanding of the past. Her
brother was in a gang for many years and she recognizes the problems
associated with her youth. However, the gangs of her past were an inte-
gral part of the community in which gang members lived. They did not
prey on friends. They did not try to get young kids addicted to drugs in
order to make a better buck. They had some respect for the community
to which they were tied. This is no longer the case. Crack has "made
people crazy." Gang members plunder the community from which they
come. They no longer feel any need to give back. In fact, the community is just a marketplace – a place from which to find young kids to be
drug runners. A place from which to sell, and to which to sell, irrespective of the consequences for the space within which one lives. According
to Virginia, no one is really safe anymore. As she notes, when she was
little the gangs were

*not into trying to get the kids hooked so young. A gang member would
not come up to me at the age of ten and try to sell me something, you
know, or try to get me to run something. Not saying that maybe a little
brother or somebody might not get into running because they're, you
know, the little brother, is right in the house with him. But they
wouldn't try to come up and sell anything to me if they knew I wasn't
doing any drugs. They'd be like, "She don't do it. Don't bother her."
Now they're trying to get kids hooked as young as possible. Everybody's trying to hook in these younger kids because then it's more
money coming in.*

And yet, at the same time, of course, these women, like all women, also live the "mundane." They get up each morning, those with children walk their children to school, deal with public schools or other public institutions, cook dinner, struggle through homework, and put their children to bed. In between morning and night TV is watched, newspapers are read, a beer is drunk, and friends come to visit. (Grand)mothers, in particular, play a large role in the rearing of their grandchildren, and daughters are often ambivalently dependent on their mothers. While one child is being walked to school, the other two are "with my mom." When money gets short, the whole family eats at "my mom's." Many mothers and daughters see each other virtually every day, and the family economy is absolutely dependent on shared resources. It is these shared resources which allow poor women to make it. While many get money from the father of their children, such money is not a stable part of the household economy. It is the women's networks that enable survival.

Women are trying to set up safe space in their homes as ways of protecting against the outside streets. These "safe spaces," these places of homesteading are, however, not always safe, or as under the control of women as they might like. There are other "borders" of threatened violence.

Crossing Family Borders: Women Speaking Out on Domestic Violence

Poor and working-class women today face terror from two directions: on the streets and inside the homes. While it is arguably the case that all residents in America's inner-city neighborhoods face the kind of terror described above, particularly as it swirls around issues of drug dealing and that associated with the drug economy, women face the threat of domestic violence as well. Thus African American women exemplify an "intersectionality" of terror, to use a term from Crenshaw (1989), in that they are terrorized by violence in the home just as white and Latina women are, and they are terrorized by violence in the community, just like African American men are. A focus group discussion led by Lois Weis raises these issues among a group of African American women whose children attend an early childhood program in Buffalo.

LOIS: Has anyone experienced domestic abuse?

AYISHA: If there is anybody in a relationship, somewhere down the line there is some type of violence or domestic violence.

GLORIA: It's not a pretty picture. I went through it twice. One time I was lucky. Two, it was to the point where the violence was so strong, at the point where you had to wait for this person to go to work to escape from your home. So I was like, my safety for my kids had to come first. He would want to be the controller. He wanted me to listen to him. He wanted me to bow down by his rules. He used to tell me, he used to make me believe that I was nothing. He lowered my self-esteem, make me feel like a little bit of nothing instead of built it [self-esteem] up. When I felt good, like, say I got up in the morning and I felt good about myself, he would tear that wall back down where he'd have the control. Then he would be the force giving the abuse, and I didn't have no choice but to accept it, because at the time, it was like, well, I had to make up my mind, and the choice, well, I can't live with this man. I can't keep putting up with abuse. I have a child, my child sees that, so then one time he said he [boyfriend] was going to stop it [abuse], and I said, okay. Next thing you know, my son walked into the room and he seen me get abused real bad, to the point where I went to the hospital and I was abused from the thigh down, from the back down, and he [the son] was like, "Well, are you still going to let that man abuse you, Mommy?"

There is a great deal of domestic violence in the lives of poor and working-class women – white, black, Latina. In chapter 7 we demonstrated that 92 percent of white women in our two-city study report violence in their immediate family environment. Either they were abused as children, their mothers were abused by their fathers/step-fathers, they were abused by former boyfriends/spouses, and/or their sisters are currently being abused. What is striking in the white women's stories, however, is the extent to which the violence is a well-kept secret which comes leaking out through cracks in our interviews.

This is not the case for African American women. While the incidence of narrated violence is less than that reported for the white community, it is talked about much more. Violence is far less hidden below the surface than is the case with white women. Witness the focus group interview above. Whereas white women are deeply involved in protecting the images, and wage worlds of their spouses, fathers, brothers, and so forth, and, more importantly, protecting the image of the domestic unit as a whole, there is little comparable cover among poor African American women. This is not to say that these women do not deeply respect and desire the domestic unit nor to say that they do not worry about protecting African American men from police and public scrutiny (Ritchie 1996), but rather to suggest that there is open and honest discussion of these issues among poor and working-class African American women in a way that seems more taboo within the working-class white community. White women spend a good deal of time propping up the image of the nuclear family and hiding the abuse, while poor and working-class African American women are openly suspect of the institution.

Among African Americans, women reach out to other women – *crossing* family borders – to discuss aspects of their lives, breaking the silence . To begin with, there may be less to be gained historically or today by hanging on to the ideology of the nuclear family among African American women given that black men have not had access to a "family wage" in the same way that white men have. White women have, therefore, more of an economically based reason for preserving the image of the nuclear family. It has worked for them in economic terms better than it has for black women. Also, it is arguably the case that the ghetto is the "new tenement" of old, and that the interdependence of people within these sites encourages more sharing of information regarding all aspects of life than the more individuated living situations characteristic of the current white working class (Rubin 1976, Howell 1973) Gordon's (1993) historical work on battered immigrant women suggests that the information regarding battering was shared historically, much as is the case today among African American women. In today's white working-class communities, far more presumably autonomous families exist than in former white immigrant communities where people were packed together in tighter spaces. Turning inward as a result of the "freedom" that less crowded housing affords, becoming less interdependent, white working-class women buy into the secret of domestic violence in a way that poor black women in the 1990s have not and cannot.

Both Gloria and Ayisha discuss what happened when domestic violence arose in their respective homes and, in so doing, reveal the very public nature of domestic violence events among poor African American women. We pick up the conversation with Gloria and Ayisha where we concluded the discussion above.

> GLORIA: *I don't think God put me on this earth to take abuse from any man. So I figured, well, hey, I love myself, I can't live without myself, I can do bad by myself and I can do good by myself. I don't have to live by man, or be with man. So it took a lot for me to make that step. My family, they knew, but it was to the point where, yeah, we knew, we can't make you [leave], we can suggest [that you should leave him]. So I had made my decision for myself, on my own. I got rid of him; I left him. He went to work one day, and I had the, it was like a prayer, I swear I was so broke, down to my last nickel, and I said I don't got no money to try to get this stuff out of this house, and it was like, oh God, please help me. I went, put my numbers in [played the lottery], next thing I knew my number was in, and they said okay. Then I went in and called U-Haul and got everything out of my house. When he got off work he came home to an empty house. What I hated was that I had to run, and I had called the cops, and they told me they could not do anything, for the simple fact that he was with me in my household. So what I had to do was take everything that I had in my house and my kids, and I left.*
>
> AYISHA: *If you do something to protect your own self, you get in more trouble with the law than, it's easier for you to take actions into your own hand [than trust the cops and/or courts], but then you're in trouble with the law. It takes longer to settle it through the law. And to me it causes too many problems for the law to be able to take care of it. You have to go through so much. You have to get a restraining order. You have to go through being put on the calendar in the court system. You have to go through trials, where this person might show*

up and this person might not show up. So that it keeps happening
[abuse]. Then they just throw it out of court. [All the women in the
focus group shake their heads in strong agreement.]

No doubt the police and court systems are highly unresponsive for this group. Central to poor African American women's collective wisdom is a deep suspicion of these systems (Jones 1992). Police do not come. Restraining orders expire. Court appointments are not kept. So women, their families, and their friends take things into their own hands. They leave. They fight back. The whole affair becomes highly public. Ayisha, below, describes the highly public nature of a beating she suffered at the hands of her boyfriend:

The police were called. I didn't call the police. What happened was, my
son was there and he was so upset and crying, and he went to sleep. I
was bleeding. I think he [boyfriend] was trying to stop me from calling
anybody because he had ripped the phone apart. And I put the phone
back together and I called his [boyfriend's] mother and told her that
she need to find him because something was wrong with him. I didn't
know what was wrong with him. And I told her, you know, that we
had been fighting. So I needed somebody to be with my son while I
went to the hospital to make sure that I was okay. And I called my
mother and she came over, her and my sisters came over, and she called
my aunt. And it turned into a big nasty fight because my aunt had her
phone calls forwarded to my house. And her son called, and I
answered the phone. And I didn't know that my aunt was on the way.
Well, she had transferred her calls, and he [her son] could tell that I was
upset. And he [my cousin] asked me what happened. And I told him
and he went to look for him [her boyfriend]. You know, he wanted to
know why he put his hands on me? Why did he hit me? And he went to
my boyfriend's mother's house, but he [boyfriend] wasn't there. So he
[my cousin] had upset his mother, and his mother called the police. She
called the police and she found out where he [boyfriend] was at and
asked him to come home because my cousin had made threats against
his life, to his [boyfriend's] mother. And I didn't want it to go that far,
you know. But I was so upset at the time, and scared. I didn't know

what was really going on as far as my health went. And my mother
went back home, and his mother [boyfriend's] lives down the street
from my mother. So, you know, you can look out my mother's house
and see down to his mother's house, and the police had stopped my
brother and them, my mother and my sisters, they were in two separate
cars. The police stopped both cars because his mother said that my
cousin had guns, and there was a whole bunch of people looking for
her son, and she was scared.

In the above conversation it is apparent that while the original incident involved a woman and her boyfriend, it quickly involved a large number of people; her mother, the boyfriend's mother and son, her sisters, brother, and an aunt. This all took place within less than an hour. Part of this, of course, is the proximity within which poor and working-class African Americans often live to one another in a medium-size city like Buffalo. Ayisha's mother and the boyfriend's mother, for instance, were neighbors. African Americans were squeezed onto one side of town, and family interconnections are apparent. It is also the case that mothers, daughters, sisters, aunts, and so forth are in and out of one another's houses repeatedly as goods and services, particularly as related to children, are traded. Thus the conditions exist for these events to become highly public in a matter of minutes. The police and courts are not trusted to do the right thing – they have not done so historically and they won't do so now. But they are called. In addition, however, family members and friends take it upon themselves to take care of what needs to be taken care of.

Borders of the Public and Private Sectors

Poor African American women are not only negotiating their relations with local violent communities and homes, but they are also balancing the public sphere of education, welfare, jobs, and job training, and the private sphere of home and family life.

While many of the women we spoke to are on welfare now (in Buffalo, 73 percent have been on welfare at one time; 53 percent receive welfare currently), it wasn't always so. Most of them worked outside the home before they had children. Some worked as assistant managers, fast food servers, and salespersons at local retail stores. Their notion of "taking care of oneself" meant juggling schoolwork and one or more part-time jobs. Here, some of the women describe their early work experiences:

AMIRA: *Did you work while you were in high school?*
RACHELLE: *Yes. I started working when I was fourteen years old, and I worked at a fast food restaurant. Then I had a job at State Hospital . . .*
AMIRA: *You always went to work?*
RACHELLE: *Always. Because I worked at both of them, Henry's and the State Hospital.*
AMIRA: *Did you work while you were in college?*
RACHELLE: *Yes. I worked at Jenss [retail store]. I worked at Hens and Kellys [retail store] before starting college.*
AMIRA: *You had a child?*
RACHELLE: *No. I didn't have a child until 1986. I worked both [jobs] until I got pregnant with my first son.*

———————

JACKIE: *I said, I'm going out and find me a job, you know, trying to help our family.*
TRACEY: *How old were you?*
JACKIE: *Sixteen.*
TRACEY: *Did they [parents] insist on you getting a job, your first job?*
JACKIE: *No. No. It was my choice.*

———————

KATHY: *No, at that time, I did not have kids. I didn't have my son until I was twenty-two. But in between that time, I worked; I started working when I was fifteen, and I worked and went to school.*
AMIRA: *Did you work by choice or out of necessity?*
KATHY: *No, by choice. It was something that I wanted to do, in my spare time. . . .*
AMIRA: *What did you do at your job?*
KATHY: *At that time, I was working at Red Barn Restaurant, that was on Kensington, before it closed down.*

The African American women we interviewed worked as early as fourteen years of age. They worked while still in high school and/or college either to help out the family or to have something to do in their spare time. They juggled part-time jobs and schoolwork. If one job did not work out as planned, because the business closed, for example, these women set out to find another job. Here, for example, is Tia's early work history:

Let's see, my first job, I was a cashier at Tops when I was maybe a sophomore in high school . . . fourteen years old. I worked there for a little while, and, let's see, why did I leave there? I think we moved. From there, I worked for L. L. Berger. I worked there, in fact, like two or three years in a row, when I was in school. Worked there, like, during Christmas . . . and it was like, you know, something [the store] that had been in existence like forty, fifty years, and recently closed in the last three or four years. I worked when I went to Bryant and Stratton. I worked in . . . they had a print shop, I worked there. Okay, the reason why I left there was I was graduating and the job was for students only. I worked at a telemarketing . . . [laughs] . . . the reason why I left there, it closed down; it got raided by the FBI.

Once these women had children, their "spare time" no longer existed. Work became a necessity as well as more stressful. They worked long hours at various jobs during high school and after. Not only did they have to take care of themselves, they also had to make sure their children were safe while they were out working. Many of the women had to quit their jobs because they did not have anyone to watch their children, too much time was spent away from the children, and/or employers were unbending in their scheduling of shifts. The borders between home and the public sphere of work became more difficult to negotiate once children were born.

LOIS: *Did you ever have a job?*
ALLISON: *Yes, I had a job at McDonald's. Well, actually several McDonald's. But I always had to quit 'cause I didn't have a babysitter. So that was one of the reasons. One time I worked out at McDonald's for almost a year, and I was going up for assistant manager, but I had to quit because I didn't have a babysitter, and welfare wouldn't pay for one.*

KATHY: Because of the hassle that I was getting from the Unemployment Division, the hassle that I was getting from my former employers, you know, I called them, and I knew that my position was open. But they wouldn't give it back to me. [I] explained to them. I was there [at the former work place]; I was giving you twelve hours a day, six days a week. And no one was available to watch my kids for sixteen hours a day six days a week, you know. And I said, had there been someone available, you know, if there was someone available, which it wasn't, I couldn't work that much, you know. There was no way, because I am the type of parent where I have to put aside quality time for my kids. You know, there was no way possible I could work sixteen hours a day, six days a week, and only have eight hours off in a twenty-four hour period. You know, where does the time come in to make sure that my kids, you know, get at least four hours of that time? But it got kind of frustrating for me and my family, because I became a very irritable person.

The stress described by these women is linked to their desire to work in the face of scheduling conflicts and the lack of available child care. Perched at the bottom of the wage labor structure, these African American women present employers as insensitive to the needs of their children. Some women, as a consequence, decide not to work outside of the home at all while the children are still fairly young, thus entering the welfare system. For Kathy, working outside of the home meant that she did not have "time to spend with the kids, and it made it hard for me." As a result, "I became a very irritable person; I became very bitchy, you know."

Still, what is most stressful is looking for employment and not being qualified (or sometimes, being overqualified) for any of the available positions in a tight economy:

KATHY: It seems tough, it seems too tough, you know. When I went to the bulletin board and read. There were so many job openings, but there was nothing that I was qualified for.
AMIRA: What kind of job openings did you see?

KATHY: *Oh, nursing this, and pharmacy assistant and so forth. I said well, that's okay, be patient because you already know what you want to do. Eventually, when the time is right, you'll be ready to do it, and you will be qualified to step into that job or this job. So, like I said, a lot of things now, that where there are job openings, you have to have one or two years, or maybe plus years, of experience and so forth, you know, so it's just dealing with it, trying to stay calm.*

JACKIE: *I mean there's a lot of things that's bothering me. I'm having a difficult time trying to get a job. No one seems to wants to hire anyone. You know, I've always been the working type of person. And I'm having a hard time trying to find what I want. So, even these little, little, little, small places, you know I've been, some of everywhere. Small places, drug stores and so forth, tells me, well, you're overqualified, or you don't have the experience.*

TIA: *First of all, the economy right now is just really tight for everybody. And so that means that competition is even more fierce. . . . Economics tend to have a great effect on family structures. Of course unemployment is the highest in the black community. Because the economic situation is as [it is] it's hard to, to really realistically pursue the American Dream. You know, I'm not saying that it's not achievable, but on a whole, I think it's very difficult.*

As they have gotten older, the rules for negotiating the borders between home and the employment sphere have changed considerably. The act of trying to "stay calm" becomes more difficult in an economy that has gotten tighter. Some of the women also discussed unfair treatment as a result of prejudice and/or discriminatory actions from others in the workplace. Some of the unfair treatment resulted in job termination or denial of a promotion, as with Tia:

[I was denied promotion on the basis of a negative review.] I was again evaluated five or six months later by my present supervisor, who said she had read the previous review and thought that it was simply B.S., that everything that this person said was contrary to what she had

observed within her six months of dealing with me, and I didn't even change. So you know, it was very, you know, very traumatic. But again, it said to me, as a young, you know, African American woman, you know, what . . . not what my place is, but how people view me, or how I must try to handle myself, or what strategies I have to think of to move myself forward, because if I'm talking about fairness, it's not going to happen, okay? It's not going to happen. It's not going to happen, so you know. That's basically it. It just made my . . . perspective a little clearer.

Negotiating the borders of home, jobs, welfare, and the streets, African American women in poor and working-class communities have substantial analysis and critique of the local institutions and relations they juggle. While African American men exhibit an expansive systemic critique which blankets the economy, racism, and the social representation of their race, African American women narrate a more specific set of critiques than any other group. They center directly on those people they know who can (and do) provide or withhold resources.

In so doing, in addition to critiquing specific individuals in the wage labor world, African American women critique African American men (Dyson 1996) and caseworkers, both of whom are experienced as having resources which could be available to women as they struggle to raise their children. Caseworkers are seen as withholding resources and treating their clients poorly, as engaging in inappropriate surveillance. The site of welfare can never be totally trusted, and caseworkers, as gatekeepers in this process, cannot be trusted either. This is, though, not so terribly different from the other groups we have examined, as we have seen. Allison, Ayisha, and Diane, in discussion with Lois, explain:

LOIS: *So, how many years have you been on welfare?*
ALLISON: *Oh, I've been on welfare since I had my first baby when I was fourteen [she is twenty-five now].*
LOIS: *How would you describe the experience of applying for welfare and then being on welfare?*
ALLISON: *Applying, everything was hectic, and you have to wait like hours and hours and hours before they call you. You have to fill out all*

these papers, and then when they finally do get you on welfare, you have to wait so long to get any type of money. I mean, landlords don't wanna wait two or three months to get any money, and you're trying to apply for welfare, and you're dragging the babies back and forth with you to get to the welfare building to try to fill out these applications and bring in all . . . you have to bring so many papers and stuff like that. And they talk to you really nasty. It's as if they're using their own money to give to you. They talk to you really, really nasty.

LOIS: *Can you give me an example? Are the majority of them white?*

ALLISON: *Yes, the majority of them are white. One time they told me, when the kids' father [who is a cocaine addict] was living with me, I said "Well, I didn't get my money this month." She said, "Well, tell Donald [children's father]," she said, "Tell Donald to go out and get a job and maybe you can get your money." It's little smart remarks, "Why do you keep having all these kids? [Allison has has three children.]*

––––––––

AYISHA: *Now recently, I had another problem [with welfare]. I had just moved into a new apartment that didn't have a refrigerator, and I had two young children, and the baby, he was constantly sick. And his medicine needed refrigerating, you know, amoxicillin [for ear infections], anything with penicillin. And so, I kept calling down there talking with the caseworker, the supervisor. The supervisor called me an idiot and told me that, "Why don't I talk to the caseworker." I told him that I did that. He told me, why I don't get off my behind and do something besides sitting around, hanging . . . sitting next to the phone and everything. And I didn't think that was right because if it had been . . . I believe it was a family member of theirs, or if it was his child, I know he would want to see some kind of satisfaction done for them. And so it took me three months to get a refrigerator. So all that time, I was resorting to pantries and friends, you know, to deliver me things and what not.*

––––––––

DENISE: *They [welfare workers] would just be so nasty when they asked you the different questions. One was a woman and she asked me a question about my son's father. Did I know where he lived at, and I told her yes. And she was like, "Well, how could you get pregnant by somebody like that, you know, who wasn't going to be willing to take care of their son?" And I looked at her, you know. And then I said, "Is it any of your business?" You know, and it was like the money was coming out of her pocket.*

"It was like the money was coming out of her pocket"; "it was like the money they was giving me was their own"; these were statements that we heard again and again. "Downtown" means standing in long lines, being asked inappropriate questions, dealing with nasty case-workers, dragging the babies back and forth day after day in order to get a refrigerator. These are the labors of being an African American female and poor in urban America. None of these women like this system—all would like to have a consistent source of income they could count on, and all struggle to get off welfare. Chancing it off the welfare rolls in a minimum wage paying job which could disappear at any moment is not a particularly good alternative, though. A job usually means no medical benefits or pension. And losing the job, which happens all the time, means that one has to wait in long lines again, dragging the babies back and forth, to reopen the case which won't be reopened for another three months. Only a more real set of economic opportunities can change this pattern. The "public patriarchy" of welfare is an institution that women desperately rely upon, fundamentally mistrust, yearn to leave, and fear its slated disappearance.

On Hope

Against this backdrop, in marked contrast to other groups, and in unparalleled commitment, African American women speak about pain, struggle, and violence through deep and intimate connections to God. Indeed, substantial numbers of African American women we interviewed talked not only about God, but with God, through God, and never separated from God. Making a way out of no way, they see light and possibility in life's trials. They struggle with all the borders in their life; with men, with caseworkers, with jobs, with the police, with the streets. But they make it because God is with them.

MUN: *What is good about the church, though?*
SARA: *It helps you understand that you're not alone and it's, if you happen to be approached by a problem or situation, that God is here for you.*

Gloria explains that God gave her strength to hit her number so she could leave her abusive boyfriend. God keeps people off crack, and God renders children safe. As Diane said, "There is almost an invisible wall around my son. A wall that keeps him from getting shot while walking to school, a wall that keeps my son safe." For without police and courts that work, all the violence both in and outside the home, what does one have? It is the same spirituality that kept the community safe during times of slavery and Jim Crow legislation. It is this sense of God that allows women to survive. Prayer and meditation become a space within which one can find comfort and solace.

LOIS: *When you feel kind of low, or like things aren't going your way, what do you do?*
CAROLYN: *I usually call up my godmother and I talk with her about it, or I sit down and I just start praying about it. And ask the Lord to help me.*

———

LOIS: *Okay, when you feel low, how do you cope?*
AYISHA: *Sometimes I cry. But then, I don't like crying all the time because I don't want my son to know how insecure I am about things. So a lot of times I'll go and wait until he's asleep or something, and then I just cry, and I pray.*

———

KATHY: *I will just be glad when things do get better, if it can, changes like this. The life that we live, we make it truly hard for ourselves and for those who can make it easier for themselves, make it easy and, I guess, in my life I'm not making anything hard for myself. I'm trying to make everything easy but, like I told Rasheed [boyfriend] the other day, last night, there's always somebody in the back of you is going to kick you, you know. There's always somebody at the top of the ladder whenever you try to take a step up the ladder. There's always some-*

*body right there. Somebody's foot in your face to kick you back down
two or three steps.*

AMIRA: *Do you feel like there's going to be a way to get out of that cycle?*

KATHY: *Oh, eventually, eventually. I don't know how or when or where,
but I know eventually. Like with myself, I have to keep faith in God.
I have to keep the faith, like my mom always told me, "He will help
those who help themselves." I mean, like me, I've always been one for
always helping myself and I would do more for another person before
I do for myself. And then, like I ask my mom all the time, "When is my
blessing going to come?" I mean, she says, "There is no time on a blessing. It will come, it will come."*

African American women practice a variety of different religions.
Some, like Kathy, are Seventh Day Adventists. Some are Baptist. Some
are Catholic, or, like Toni, Moslem. Some attend church or mosque on
a regular basis. Some rarely go. But all the women interviewed expressed strong spiritual sentiments. God is a source that can be tapped
into when and if needed in order to keep them strong, to enable survival. White working-class women may or may not attend church, but
the wellspring of spirituality expressed here is, by and large, not expressed by white women.

TRACEY: *In what ways do you feel like you've changed since high
school?*

LAVONNE: *I changed a lot. I'm not a hot-tempered person. You can't push
me to that point no more where I just go off real quick. It takes a lot to
push me, and I'll sit back and act just reserved. And I take it one day at
a time.*

TRACEY: *What do you think brought you to that point where you don't
get as hot-tempered as when you were younger?*

LAVONNE: *Praying about it.*

TRACEY: *What are you praying for?*

LAVONNE: *Praying that I get a better understanding about people and
understand my own self, because I feel that you have to love yourself in
order for you to love anything else.*

TRACEY: *Did it take you a while to learn to love yourself?*

LAVONNE: Yes, it took me a while.

TRACEY: Do you feel that praying has been helpful in helping you to love yourself, or helping you to change some behaviors that you didn't like in yourself?

LAVONNE: Yes. A prayer brought me a long ways, and that it's a daily thing, and if I didn't believe that my father kept me in his prayers, I wouldn't be here today. Because I could have went in another direction, but I chose to stay in this direction, the right direction.

Allison also credits God and prayer with allowing her to stay on the right path. Donald, the father of her children is a crack addict, who tears though her apartment on a regular basis, stealing even the clothing from her childrens' dresser drawers. In the wake of his destruction, she reflects upon her ability to stay off the drug which is shredding the fabric of her community:

Well, I never tried it. I never tried cocaine before. Well, [Donald] offered it to me three times. My aunt was living with me and she was doing cocaine, too, and I really think it was God [who kept me off], because they [Donald and her aunt] were bringing their drug friends around. I could have easily [done it]; I had access to it. I could have did it. I don't know what made me, maybe it was the way I was brought up because, really, until I got out of high school I didn't know anything about cocaine and drugs and stuff like that. It's just, I always think what would my kids do without me, and they wouldn't have me if I was on drugs. When I was younger, I was very spiritual. I went to church constantly. I went to Mount Zion Holiness church. I went to church a lot and, to this day, I think only, the only thing that can keep you away from cocaine is God.

Two aspects of our interviews with black women are especially striking. First, these women, particularly in their narrations of personal tragedy, see themselves as deeply lonely but *never alone*. They live in a line of women and God is with them—for better or worse. He (and it was consistently "He") watches over, cares for them, intervenes when necessary. These women credit God when they have managed to cope actively and effectively with incredibly trying circumstances. For these women, God is a source of agency and strength, not a figure of dependence or a prompt to passivity.

As well, these African American women, poor and working-class, speak in a discourse punctuated by sentiments of both responsibility and redemption. Conservatives who demonize these women would, ironically, be impressed. Sharp in their accusations of others – for irresponsibility, immorality, bad mothering, cheating – poor African American women are, however, also generous in their willingness to redeem. They believe that in God's hands, people can turn their lives around. Evil can become good; greed can become generosity.

It is God who cradles women as they try, in the midst of poverty, to live their lives and raise their children. Bordered by an inhospitable economy, community violence, domestic violence, crack, and structural decay of all forms, God represents at times, for many, the only solace, the only space in which real homesteading takes place. At the end of the twentieth century, there is no vibrant social movement which suggests that life can and will get better for poor blacks. In spite of this, poor black women, in particular, hold together to raise the next generation, retaining connectedness through sharing resources and by many individually leaning on God in the midst of private and public assault.

9

Working Without a Net
Poor Mothers Raising Their Families

Poor Mother (def.)

1. A woman who is rearing children without adequate financial resources.

2. A woman who is rearing children without adequate parenting skills.

3. A woman who deserves our sympathy.

POOR, POOR MOTHER. THIS CHAPTER SETS OUT TO ANALYZE THE MICRO-politics of child rearing amidst poverty. The story we tell comes from interviews with over seventy-five women, black, white, Latina, across two cities, trying to raise up the next generation with insufficient financial resources, often surrounded by violence on their streets and in their homes. As Ruddick (1989) Scheper-Hughes (1992), Ladner (1971), and others have shown a number of years ago, rearing children under any conditions is tough work. Alone, very difficult. Without money, excruciating. Within violence, near impossible.

We write this chapter amidst our own balance of work, children, babysitters, soccer, dance lessons, reading tutors, and activism within our children's schools. Our class status, our living with men, our race, allow us the privilege of privacy, of bad parenting in the closet. Our material and cultural resources assure the presumption of "good mothering."

We have been well educated by scholars, most particularly Nancy Scheper-Hughes and Patricia Hill-Collins, who recognize that "good mothering," or what passes for good mothering, happens in a particular context; a context of money, time, and excess. And that in the absence of these, it is far too easy to "discover" bad mothering. As a society, we scrutinize the least equipped and least resourced women, holding them to standards of mothering that most of us could not and do not achieve.

One of the great contemporary illusions is the belief that mothering is, indeed, natural; that care of children is wired in; that "good mothering" is anything but work that needs social support to be possible. And yet that is our social belief. Women who have birthed or reared a child who fall short of our always-inching-up-standard slip rapidly into the category of "bad mother"; if she is poor, she may risk having her child taken from her.

This is not to say that we write entirely above judgments about what's good for other people's children. And yet this chapter is written to understand the work of mothering in poverty; to understand that all mothers are vulnerable to critical watch; to recognize that the features of "good mothering" which appear natural are indeed cushioned by material resources, people and relationships, flexibility, time, and the other creature comforts of sitting within and above the middle class.

There is a literature on mothering, moving from the romantic to the terrifying, focusing largely on the practice of (white, middle to upper-class) mothering as it is "supposed" to work, noting that these practices are never always engaged by women cross race, class, geography, circumstance. This literature typically falls in one of two categories: the close, sweet look at a mother and her child, or the bleaker side of life in the midst of maternal ambivalence.

In contrast to the splitting that characterizes much of the literature on mothering, Sidel, in *Urban Survival* (1978), provides rich testimony from working-class women, given the "opportunity to describe their lives, their daily reality, their hopes and their fears without an intermediary, an interpreter who is invariably from a very different social class" (2). Sidel notes that the literature on mothering has fetishized the "lives and concerns of middle class, the upper middle class and of superstars," neglecting stories drawn from the working class and poor. She notes, further, that when poor and working-class mothers are the sub/ob/jects of social research, *we* typically get to learn about *their* deficiencies, aspects of "poor mothering," what *their* children don't get that *our* children presumably do.

Yet, there is a growing literature that marks the lives of poor and working-class women, and their children, as intellectually and politically important territory. Polakow, in *Lives on the Edge* (1993), has produced an important monograph analyzing the ways in which structural conditions have produced mothers barely scraping by, with children who enjoy few of the freedoms of childhood at home and are forced to endure a "pedagogy for the poor" at school. Polakow traces, through history and contemporary analysis, the ways in which poverty has become a "private affair" to be endured by women and their children, as public responsibility for children recedes. Her words could not be more timely: "Mothers without husbands are cheap; they deserve less and if deserted, divorced or unmarried constitute a gray and dubious category of the undeserving poor. . . . It is not scarlet letters that we now affix to the bosoms of errant women; rather it is the discourse of 'benefits' – food stamps that brand her, visibly humiliate her, in the supermarket, welfare offices that regulate her sexual relationships and judge her mothering as at risk."

Polakow argues cogently that "the poorer and less patriarchal the household, the more imperative the need for state-sanctioned parents patriae intervention to judge the moral rectitude of the home and the correct upbringing of the family."

In our analysis of poor and working-class mothers in Jersey City and Buffalo, we hear the desire to mother for protection and care, the delicate steps women take to avoid public scrutiny, and the excruciating surveillance endured from the state. These are the tasks of mothering in poverty. We come to this analysis with an appreciation of what Ruddick (1990) calls "maternal thinking." That is, we agree that "mothers are people who see children as 'demanding' protection, nurturance and training; they attempt to respond to children's demands with care and respect . . ." (xi). We further agree that mothering must be construed as work, with forms of thought and practice derivative of that labor. At the same time, we are seduced by the stories that mothers tell, repulsed by the conditions within which they must mother, and convinced, therefore, that what we consider mothering, particularly good mothering, is so dependent on material and social wealth that women who must contend with children in far more financially and socially impoverished circumstances can't easily fill the shoes of "good mothers." Good mothering might entail giving your children opportunities to run free, go to the park, smile at strangers, assume the world loves them. And yet the mothers with whom we speak, living in poverty, must constantly guard their sons and daughters, typically indoors, caution them never to talk with strangers, anticipate the world to be a dangerous place. White mothers presumably don't have to counsel their (white) children about racism, warning them about the racist social land mines, diminished expectations, and heightened accusations that await them; African American mothers do (Ward 1996). Women with resources can "afford" to ask for help or purchase the assistance we need; women without resources are typically frightened to admit the need for help, lest the agency involved read this "need" as evidence of an inadequate home. Money and race/ethnicity matter; context produces discrete tasks of mothering. We seek then, in this chapter, to shift how we look at these mothers and to notice that context affects, enables, and shapes what is produced as mothering—good and bad. And we note that as economic conditions worsen, policy talk increasingly targets "bad mothers," and threats to remove children heighten. The gaze fixes on poor mothers. Economic and structural decay vaporize.

These women are, and describe themselves as, very much alone. By this we mean not that they are utterly disconnected from public institutions, relatives, neighbors, lovers, partners, and social service or educational workers. Of course, their lives are deeply enmeshed with institutions and persons—by choice and by coercion. And yet, most claim to have few to rely upon. The women fear each time they touch a public institution—particularly African American and Latinas—for the security of their children remaining under their roof. In the language of contemporary debates about "concentrated poverty" and "isolation," we acknowledge that the isolation is not total, but there is much devastation in their lives (Wilson 1996; Gregory, forthcoming).

TABLE 9.1

Employment Status	White				Black				Latino			
	1980		1990		1980		1990		1980		1990	
	M	F	M	F	M	F	M	F	M	F	M	F
In Labor Force	71.0	45.4	74.5	53.1	68.1	54.3	72.0	60.7	78.8	44.9	81.6	55.7
Unemployed	8.0	9.1	8.6	9.8	12.0	11.3	16.1	13.6	10.6	15.1	12.2	16.9

Source: Mishel and Bernstein (1994).

On Context

The context for the women whom we interviewed is typically one in which money is tight, flexibility minimal, space crowded, safety illusory, and networks constrained. The state hovers, in the guise of welfare and/or child advocacy, ready to remove children or place them in more "appropriate" settings. The children are sicker and needier than most. Physical survival looms large as a need – often unfulfilled, always in jeopardy.

As we track, through the census data, the recent historic shifts in the

TABLE 9.2

COLLEGE ENROLLMENT AND PERCENTAGE OF HIGH SCHOOL GRADUATES
ENROLLED IN, OR WHO HAVE COMPLETED ONE YEAR OF, COLLEGE
BY SEX AND RACE: 1960 TO 1986

	Percentage of High School Graduates Enrolled				Percentage of High School Graduates Enrolled in or Completed 1 or More Years of College			
	Male		Female		Male		Female	
	White	Black	White	Black	White	Black	White	Black
1960	31.1	21.1*	18.1	16.9*	47.1	33.5*	35.6	31.8*
1970	42.9	29.5	26.3	24.7	60.8	41.2	47.1	39.0
1975	36.9	33.4	29.4	32.0	56.6	50.3	49.1	46.4
1980	34.3	27.0	30.9	29.2	51.8	44.4	51.0	47.5
1985	36.6	28.2	33.6	25.1	55.5	43.5	55.2	43.9
1986	36.1	28.2	33.3	29.4	55.0	43.7	55.6	50.2

*Black and other races.
Source: U.S. Bureau of the Census, *Statistical Abstract of the United States: 1988*
(108th ed.; Washington, D.C.: Government Printing Office, 1988), table 233.

TABLE 9.3

FEMALE-HEADED HOUSEHOLDS AND ETHNICITY

FOR 1970, 1980, AND 1990 FOR JERSEY CITY AND BUFFALO

Population Group	Percent of families with children under 18 years old that are headed by single females	
	Jersey City	Buffalo
1970 General	19.1	19.4
1980 General	36.9	36.6
1990 General	35.6	44.5
1970 Black	35.6	...
1980 Black	55.1	58.6
1990 Black	56.0	65.6
1980 White	25.5	23.9
1990 White	26.8	30.1
1980 Asian or Pacific Islander	...	19.4
1990 Asian or Pacific Islander	9.3	16.8
1980 Spanish Origin	...	42.4
1990 Hispanic*	37.9	52.7

Source: U.S. Bureau of the Census, *Statistical Abstract of the United States: 1988*
(108th ed.; Washington, D.C.: Government Printing Office, 1988), table 233.
*For Puerto Rican women (younger than other Latinas), the percentage escalates to
43.3 percent for 1990. U.S. Census, 1990.

economy, for women and men, and their effects on household arrangements and, therefore, on the labors of mothering, we see (in tables 9.1, 9.2, and 9.3) that from 1980 to 1990, there was a substantial increase particularly in the percentage of white, black, and Latina women in the labor force, a small rise in their unemployment rates, and dramatic increases by whites, blacks, and Latinas in pursuit of higher education, in most cases a *fourfold* jump during the decade.

And, most profoundly, we witness an extreme rise in female-headed households from just 1980 to 1990; a threefold rise for blacks and Latinas, and a doubling for whites. During the Reagan-Bush years, poor and working-class women worked harder, went to school more, and ended up alone in numbers far outdistancing generations of women before them. For Latinas and African Americans, the shifts are striking.

It is in this context of an engagement with paid work for women, a motivated search for education, a rise in unemployment, a loss in "real" wages, and a dramatic increase in female-headed households (see tables 9.1, 9.2, and 9.3), that we now turn to the labors of mothering in poverty.

In the Beginning: Getting Pregnant

While many conservatives are eager to argue that having a baby "too early" is a death knell to the otherwise productive trajectories presumably available to poor girls and women, data to refute this mythology are mounting. As Frank Furstenberg has written, paraphrasing Arthur Campbell: "The girl who grows up in an impoverished family has 75 percent of her life's script written for her whether or not she has a child early in life" (Furstenberg 1996).

Recent writings, for example by Luker (1996), suggest that class and race better determine the outcomes for poor girls than does early childbearing. And yet early childbearing can induce, and be used to induce, a sense of personal shame and regret. A large number of the women whom we interviewed became pregnant sometime between ages fifteen and twenty. From the white women, we often heard regrets: "It was too early." For most of these women, having a baby propelled them into marriage and dropping out of school. Clare, a white woman responds: "Yeah, getting pregnant [laughs]. It changed my life dramatically, because there were a lot of things that I wanted to do that I couldn't do. You know, I couldn't go out anymore. I couldn't, well, I wasn't allowed out anyways."

The retrospective reviews of getting pregnant "too early" dramatically vary, however, by race/ethnicity. In contrast to the white women interviewed, many of the African American women, pregnant at the same age and moment in their development, speak with reflective delight about their childbearing. "It was the turning point in my life. I got myself together then."

Paula, an African American woman, explained: "Yeah, so I looked at him [baby] and I said, 'Now I got to give him a better life.' You know what I'm sayin'? I said for me, I've been scraping and make this deal . . . you know what I'm sayin'? I said but now I got to make sure that he has something. So now I'm goin' back to school. Tryin' to get a job and get off the system and everything so that I can give him a better life." Diane, also African American, offers: "It was good for me in more ways than one, because it made me get more responsible and it made me get more mature. And I had something that I really had to do. Because it was, if I was by myself, I'd say, well, I want this. There's a certain item. Because, you know, not for survival. You know, I could do without. I don't need it. With my kids, I can't say that. They had to have it. *So it made me go out there and do for them*, you know. It made me stronger too, much stronger."

For many of the African American women, having a baby meant becoming responsible, although many had held wage-paying jobs before (see chap. 8), and for these women having a baby typically did *not* precipitate getting married. Most ultimately returned to school and/or got a job, although as we argue in chapter 8, having a child also made it that much more difficult to participate in waged labor given the responsibilities of child care.

For Latinas, more like the white women, getting pregnant almost always meant getting married or moving in with the father, often getting abused and, for some, leaving him, after "spending years isolated, captured in my home." Marta reflects: "I just got out of a marriage a year ago. I was married for five years and we had the type of relationship that nobody comes to the house and I was just home having babies, like they say, cooking and cleaning is the best thing I know how to do, and he was just . . . come from work and stay home and go to sleep, like that."

From most of the poor and working-class women whom we interviewed, we heard a common story line, although interpretations varied widely by race/ethnicity. Most got pregnant a bit "too early," by her own retrospective moral account; the white women and some of the Latinas and a few of the African American women got married, or moved in with the father.

Life with Babies . . . and Beyond

Once their babies are born, the women we interviewed often end up connected to a man who shares some of the child rearing with them. Sometimes this is the father of the baby, but often not. A few in our sample described the grueling process of losing, or "giving up," their children to strangers, mothers, or mothers-in-law after thoughtful consideration or painful coercion.

Sherry, a white woman, talks about placing her child with her mother during a period of drug addiction:

SHERRY: *I used to tell them, I was not an everyday drug user. It's something I got caught up in. And that was it. It's over. It's past. You's are tellin' me, put the past behind me, in counseling, and then you're bringin' up the past to me. How the hell am I gonna forget, if ya keep tellin' me . . . this is what you did. You did this to your children. I used to cry myself to sleep at nights. Thinkin', what am I gonna do? Then they started threatenin' me that after a year, then they could put your children up for adoption. This is what they hit you with, too. I was able to go to my mother, say Ma, do this for me. Take them in temporary custody. I'm gonna go to school. I'm gonna do the right thing. Whenever I work, I'll give you the money. And she did. My mother took them in September of '92, and then I got custody January of '93. Four months later.*

MUN: *Then, were you allowed to see your kids then?*

SHERRY: *Oh, yeah. I lived with my mother. And it wasn't my house. I did all of that. And it wasn't enough. It was not enough. Then they wanted drug screening.*

MUN: *What does it mean, though . . . for you?*

SHERRY: *Oh God. It tore . . . it put me and my children through a lot of . . . lot of strains. Psychological . . . damage, because we were separated. I mean, I . . . there was time where I just wanted to say, forget it. And commit suicide. There was like, nothin'.*

MUN: *Nothing left.*

SHERRY: *Yeah. I went through that, thinkin' about that. Maybe they'll be better off where they are. Maybe I can never be a good mother.*

MUN: *So you blame yourself.*

SHERRY: *Yeah, I always . . . I blame myself. It was . . . well . . . it was my fault. It was my decision. Nobody twisted my arm and said, you have to snort this line or go cop the drugs, ya know. But I never thought that just walkin' into a drug . . . and coppin' drugs, was going' to take my children away from me. You know. I wasn't an abusive parent. He*

[Sherry's son] was in the shelter . . . in a foster shelter with other children. He was separated from his sister. See that, I think, made it hard for him, you know. But when I took him to therapy, it . . . only a few sessions we had'a go . . . he knew. I told him. I talked to him. I told him mommy was . . . doin' drugs and . . . it wasn't right. I hung out with bad people, and it . . . I didn't think, and me and Daddy used to fight . . . I had'a explain everything to him . . . he doesn't like him [his daddy] at all. I try to talk to him and tell him, well, he's changed. He's not bad no more. 'Cause I don't want him to hate his father, you know. So, things are . . . things are startin' to fall into place now, you know. And I tell him I'm goin' to school now because I wanna be a nurse, and take care of sick children. I said, then I can buy a house soon, and we can have our own. And I'll get a car.

As you can hear, Sherry negotiated her children, the Division for Youth and Family Services, her mother, and a formerly abusive husband – all while trying to stay off drugs. She has managed this scene better than many. While few of the women we interviewed are in the midst of serious and nasty custody battles, *many*, across race/ethnicity, are consumed with fear over their own powerlessness and are troubled by questions about how to raise children while subjected to public surveillance, struggling with custody contests, and with few of the material resources necessary for contemporary parenting. And often, as noted throughout, they must contend with violence in the streets and sometimes at home. Responsibility for children means negotiating lives and "the system" while trying to help children imagine futures worth investing in.

The Labors of Mothering
Ruddick (1989) has analyzed in exquisite detail what it takes to notice and respond to the demands voiced by children, in their innocence, their incompetence, and their vulnerability. While Ruddick has been criticized for universalizing and essentializing the work of motherhood, we applaud her for extracting those aspects of care taking, the work and relations of mothering, which women (and some men) strive to accomplish in very diverse and very unequal settings.

A critical component of mother work coming through from these working-class and poor women concerns protection from violence of all sorts. In the midst of strategic protection from street violence, home violence, unsafe and unsavory child care, these women want to *model for their children how to notice and how to respond* to social injustice, based on race/ethnicity, sex, and/or class. Sitting at the bottom of a social telescope focused on poor women and their children, these women have to dance for their dinner, socializing their children to both resist and accommodate. Ruddick writes:

> Even more important than her attitude towards children's battles is a nonviolent mother's commitment to resist authorities and policies that are unjust or harmful. Like anyone else, in the face of superior power, mothers often succumb to fearfulness and despair. But they also often name and encourage, in themselves and their children, the *duty to resist*, and they recognize their lack of resistance [as] failure. Most striking is the courageous resistance, in the face of danger, against enormous odds, by mothers who live in poverty, tyranny and slavery. . . . When they identify resistance as a virtue, mothers try to teach children to stand up for themselves and others, knowing that mothers themselves may be the first authority a child resists and that those around them, including their mothers, may criticize the spiritedness they have fostered.

Nina, a white woman, offers:

> *My children's lives, their future. That's what I worry about. I said I have no problems, you know. I don't let nothing bother me. I just worry about my daughters and the way the world's going, and, you know, what is it gonna be like when they grow up, you know? I kind of like worry about that. Because the way it's going now, it's like pathetic. Everybody's killing everybody, and all the drugs, and like you got nine-year-olds shootin' ten-year-olds, and . . . I worry about how is it gonna be when they get older, you know? I actually tell them, don't have any kids, because the way the world's going. I tell them when you get older, don't have any kids. Wait to see if it gets any better, you know, because*

why bring a child into life? I mean, if I knew the world was gonna be like this, I don't think I woulda' had my daughters. For what? So I can keep 'em prisoner in the house? You know?

No longer are playgrounds, open parks, and family walks the standard fare of childhood. Instead, repeatedly we heard about maternal maneuvers of what we might consider *strategic agoraphobia*; mothers incubating babies and children within their apartments and homes much more intensively than in the past. Much television, many arguments about freedoms and independence, high levels of tension within the home can be found. Maria, a Latina, offers:

MARIA: *Let's say I would send my son to the store for a gallon of milk, there would be fourteen and fifteen-year-old kids that carry guns, and they would run up to my son to steal his bike.*
SARAH: *It happened once?*
MARIA: *A couple of times, and that's when I went out and confronted the kids, and these other parents told me don't do that because they have guns. That scared the hell out of me.*
SARAH: *Because you don't know what they're gonna do.*
MARIA: *So I told my brothers and my sisters I gotta move. You gotta help me get an apartment out there. My sister said we'll look and I'll help you out. If you can't find an affordable apartment that you could afford by yourself, I'll help you with your rent. But I did, I found one that I could afford. I didn't sleep nights and I didn't eat during the day. I cooked for my kids, I fed my kids, and I was sitting at the table with the newspaper.*

What these mothers describe as "good mothering," many observers might consider overprotective. And yet violent communities warrant exactly such high levels of concern. Many comment that they wouldn't trust any child-care facilities, even home day care, lest someone harm their children. Eager to have "the best for my children," these women are convinced that they can trust few outside themselves and, perhaps, their mothers, sisters, the children's father, or their current boyfriends, to care for the children. And they fear for their children's future. Pam says,

Okay, but it's the people. It's the environment. Broad daylight, you gotta . . . if your children is outside playin' in the front . . . you gotta keep a eye on them because there's people out there shooting, you know . . . shooting out there. There's drugs in the hallway. The only reason why I'm there now because . . . housing is very expensive . . . okay. And . . . I felt that having two children, and I wasn't getting any younger, I felt that, I should be on my own . . . okay. And I had applied for housing when I first was pregnant at the age of fifteen. But it took me ten years. And I wouldn't have even got in there, because they told me I was not qualified because I was not on the street. And I told them if I was on the street, I wouldn't need it. I'm doin' this for my children . . . ya know. So . . . I finally got in there. . . . I basically keep to myself. Because you live in a bad environment doesn't mean you have to become like everyone else, ya know.

Lila worries: "I'm afraid, since I'm always sick, maybe if I pass away . . . they [my kids] don't have anybody. So Division for Youth and Family Services will take care of them. No one will take care of them, [they] would take them away from me, because my mother drinks. My other brother's in jail."

When parents are split, tensions around child care rage across generations. Sometimes, particularly among Latinas, fathers of the children move to the shadows as mothers-in-law insert themselves or are inserted as the "good mother" alternative, standing ready to rescue the child from the "bad mother" — that is, the survivor of domestic abuse who, indeed, probably doesn't have the financial resources, "home," nor an abundance of time. While there may be significant, rich cultural traditions by which many mother each child (Collins 1992), this needs to be distinguished from coercive loss of children.

When fathers (or, sometimes in poor homes, when grandmothers or grandmothers-in-law) fight for custody of the children, those who contest have been more likely to "win" because they (the men) have jobs or "other women" to care for the children, and/or a "comfortable" home (Polikoff 1978). In contrast, biological mothers, often left behind in the ashes of poverty and oftentimes domestic violence, may not have jobs (if they do, they can't be "good" — that is, full-time — mothers), usually do not have "other women" to watch the children, and rarely have "comfortable homes." Sara, a Latina, related her struggle for custody of her daughter:

SARA: *I'm close with my boys. My daughter's not close to me. . . .*
Because her [paternal] grandmother, since she goes there every week-
end, her grandmother talks. I guess puts things in her mind and she's
very confused. She don't know what to do. They're taking me to court
now; she wants custody. She wants to take her away.
MUN: *Are you fighting her?*
SARA: *I am fighting her for my daughter. [She] wants to be with her*
grandmother more, but it's because they have everything, you know
what I'm saying, toys, money, she got her own room, TV, VCR, what-
ever she wants.
MUN: *How come they have so much money?*
SARA: *Well they're old people, and I guess they don't have all the kids to*
support, and they work all their lives, so they have everything they
want. But she has a low-income apartment; she don't pay much, so all
that money goes to the bank.
MUN: *What happens if they win? Are you concerned about that?*
SARA: *I'll be very hurt. And I told my daughter . . . she told me she*
wants . . . I want the best for her; she's happy.
MUN: *You're trying your best?*
SARA: *Right. I'll be hurt, but if that's what she wants and the judge*
decides like that, well, I guess it's gonna be like that.
MUN: *What are their chances of winning?*
SARA: *I don't know, 'cause I've never been through this. I mean I know I*
don't use drugs. I'm a good mother. My house is clean. My kids are fed.
That's about it, and I'm going to school, but on the other hand, she has
everything over there. I don't know what the judge is going to decide.

Joann, a white woman, solved her problems of insufficient resources by relying on her mother, rather than her former husband:

JOANN: *Yeah, the only reason Crystal is with them is 'cause her father*
tried to take her from me. And he could have gave her a better home so
I took her to my parents.

SARAH: How old did you give her up?

JOANN: She was like nine months old, eight months old.

SARAH: So you kind of relinquished your responsibility?

JOANN: Yeah. When I found out that her father was trying to take her from me, 'cause I had a friend in the house and he [the friend] heard and he came and told me what they were up to, so I took her to my parents, my father took me to a judge that he knew. My father gave the judge $5,000 cash up front. The judge signed papers stating that my parents had custody of the baby since she was born, so we went to court.

The *chances* or *possibilities* of losing their children are *ever* present in the minds of many of these women, especially women of color. In courts and in family disputes, the "best interests" of the child are yanked from the historical and political contexts in which women's and children's lives are lodged. The context for childrearing in poverty is oxymoronic; it is perverse and cruel to compare settings of privilege and settings of poverty and then tear children thoughtlessly from their mothers in the latter contexts. Women living in U.S. poverty often lose their children, or risk losing their children, because of *policies* and *contexts* of deprivation, not necessarily *relations* of deprivation.

One consequence of their vulnerability to accusations by the state of poor mothering is that many poor and working-class mothers *refuse* to trust or only with ambivalence rely upon social services for the much-needed resources of childrearing. Getting "help" has become a danger zone. According to many, such help is better off avoided.

Sites of "help" for families in poverty – social agencies, social workers, schools, and welfare offices – in fact usually double, today, as sites of scrutiny and surveillance. As a consequence, women (and men) in need of help, who may want or need to speak through the troubling times of parenting in poverty, for instance, refuse in good conscience to trust, and, therefore, to present anything short of perfection to their caseworkers. In such contexts, those most desperately in need are those least likely to receive assistance. We believe, ironically, that this is why so many spoke so candidly to us – as strangers we were privileged as academic ventriloquists. We could tell their stories and maybe even get a hearing. And they could keep their children.

Sherry comments on the stress of self-presentation amidst surveillance:

> Oh, I had two or three sessions with group sessions, but psychiatric care, I didn't really get none of that. They ran tests on me. But, he said I showed no emotional love; I didn't show this. I was like, you go into there crying and everything, they say you're unstable because you're crying; you go in there trying to act normal, you know, hold back the tears, oh you're a cold-hearted bitch. You know, so you lose either way, so I went to apply for small city welfare, what I'm doing now is I'm waiting for them to give me my Medicaid. Once I get the Medicaid I'm goin' to see a therapist, a psychiatrist on my own.

To the extent that these women *do* rely on anyone but themselves for help with childrearing, two early childhood related programs stand out as offering sites for much appreciated help: Head Start and EPIC.

Head Start, both in Jersey City and Buffalo, has a rich array of programs for poor and working-class mothers. It provides opportunities for women, and men, to come together to discuss the problems and delights of childrearing, to gain nonjudgmental support, and to ask the questions we all harbor but few dare to speak. EPIC, Effective Parenting Information for Children (also called Every Person Influences Children), in Jersey City and Buffalo, has emerged nationally as a network of parent educators, trained and ready to collaborate with community-based groups, inviting talk of childrearing from infancy through adolescence. Particularly accessible within African American communities, EPIC is also a resource in which lateral sharing, nonjudgmental listening, and advice-giving can happen within a context which does not double as surveillance; one does not risk losing one's children as the price for honesty. (We will address the power of these sites more fully in chapters 11 and 12.)

A third site from which help was sought was Medicaid and, at times, public assistance. Without Medicaid, that is health insurance, many of these women claim they would have had to give up custody of their children to kin and/or foster care. Further, for many women, African Americans in particular, welfare was seen as the only alternative to brutalizing domestic violence. This is particularly important to remember in times when Congress is debating cutbacks in the area of publicly subsidized health care and welfare, and is refusing consideration of national health insurance. Poor children are sicker than most; mothers trying to raise children in poverty are without the resources that most enjoy; prolonged exposure to violence suffered by mothers and children is deadly (Ritchie 1996). That the state has successfully converted most sources of help into sites of surveillance and mandatory reporting, bodes poorly for getting help to mothers in need.

> CARLA: *Because, it's [welfare is] good and it's bad. They have their good points and they have their bad points. Bad points, why? Because when mothers are trying to get on their feet, and they're doing it, they're proving it, Division of Youth and Family Services still is there. And it's not fair. You've got so many kids out here who were put on this earth and their mother or their father, or both parents did not know. They're no good. And Division of Youth and Family Services don't even do nothing to them. And those are the ones they should investigate. But they don't do that. They always bother the ones who just made one mistake. And you can't get rid of them. They follow you everywhere you go.*
> MUN: *They follow them?*
> CARLA: *Yeah. They started doing that two years ago. They follow you and they watch everything you do. And* how *can you live comfortably like* that, *knowing that someone is actually* watching *you?*

The simultaneous disappearance of the safety net for poor mothers, increased surveillance by the state, and media assaults on poor women's "inability" to mother are not, of course, coincidental. The dismantling of welfare and the prior scathing discursive critique of welfare mothers are all a perverse fit (Piven 1996).

It is at this spot – in the "poor" mother and child relation – where social attention is now focused, and focused with scorn. Frigga Haug, a German theorist, helps us see historically and critically, that societies scapegoat poor mothers as culprits when, in fact, it is societies which refuse to provide: "Individual responsibility always appears when general rules stop working . . . female responsibility is a mistake, a social deprivation which points to a general disorder in society. What is being neglected here are the basic elements of physical well-being. This disorder consumes human energies."

So we point our social fingers at poor mothers when we as a society have relinquished social responsibility and abandoned moral accountability for the lives of poor children.

The Joys of Motherhood

Despite the financial stretch, the social difficulties, and the personal pain they experience, these women take great pride in their children and great pleasure in their moments with "the kids." We heard about cautious, windy, and wonderful trips to the park, watching always for hypodermic needles and vials; books read to children; stories passed on across generations; doing homework together; giggly conversations with early adolescents about sex, passions, and dangers; weepy talks about last nights' overheard violence and why Daddy doesn't live here anymore.

When asked, "Do you think Miguel would come back, for the kids?" Patricia explains: "Maybe some day. I tell my other son, my son Miguel, maybe he'll come back when you're getting married. Let him into your house. Not into mine, no more."

Like all mothers, these women are deeply ambivalent about how they are raising their children in a world hostile to their children, whether the "kids" get "enough" of what is needed to make their lives successful, and what awaits them. But they are also very proud. Carmita explains:

And I guess it shows a little . . . because they have beautiful hair, you know, and the way they speak. Now when we first moved up in Duncan . . . the kids used to call my oldest daughter "white girl." Not

because she . . . her color, because the way she spoke, the way she car-
ried herself, you know. She speaks intelligently, you know. Now she's
startin' to talk like, you know . . . the street talk, the slang. And I told
her, I said, "Sweetheart, when you around your friends, fine, you can
talk like them, okay. But when you're in school or somewhere, you
speak the way you're supposed to be." You know. And apparently,
she's doin' fine because she went for a job interview, and the man was
so impressed by her. He complimented her and he told her to tell me I
did an excellent job in raising her.

As sociologist Beth Ritchie has written about poor African American women: "These women's stories . . . show the extent to which our society has set up this situation . . . they quite simply cannot succeed in the current social arrangements . . . left with no good, safe way to avoid the problematic social circumstances that they find themselves in, unable to change their social position and ultimately blamed for both." (Ritchie 1996).

Trying to instill in their children a sense of pride and, at the same time, caution about racism, drugs, violence, and abuse, these women are negotiating the urban damage of the twentieth century every morning over breakfast. And yet, in the end, when we ask, "In hard times, what keeps you going?" the most popular response is "My children." Paula, an African American woman beams: "Yeah, that's why I want to get my G.E.D. . . . because I want my kids to feel proud and instead of when they tell you in your school, what's your mother . . . they go no, my mother's a cop, my mother is something, you know, that's why I want to study something."

These mothers, poor in finances, rich in survival skills, and deserving of our collective respect and social struggles, are indeed doing the best they can, without a net. Wanda, a white woman ends her interview: "Oh, yeah. You know, I'd consider moving. I'm on welfare . . . I work at night, and my sister babysits for me during the day, and I save all my money under somebody else's name so I can take my daughters and move out of this area. Because I want to live in the suburbs. I think it's a better environment for them."

Sandra, an African American mother describes her source of hope:

Because of my children. If they see me weak, then they become weak. It takes children no time to follow behind what their parents is doing. And nowadays kids pick up quicker than what you expect. So far I'm proud of my children, both of them. They love to learn. They love school. And they're happy. They're happy kids. If my children are not laughing in my house, something is wrong. And a lot of times they laugh so much and they talk so much that it gets on my nerves. But I don't stop. Because if you don't have laughter in the home, something is wrong.

10

Refusing the Betrayal
Latinas Redefining Gender, Sexuality, Family, and Home

IN CHAPTER 5, WE HEARD POOR AND WORKING-CLASS LATINOS WORKING HARD
to re-instate cultural citizenship on the mainland. In the face of anti-
immigrant policies and practices and elite control of an economy to
which Latinos in the United States have little access, these men have embraced a culture, history, and tradition which demands cultural pride
but often presupposes gendered subordination.[1] In concert with chapter 5, the data presented here suggest that Latinas, too, are reworking
cultural citizenship. But these women are producing a version of "living
Latina" in which gender as traditionally lived is being rewritten with
neither economic nor domestic subordination of women assumed. As
these women stretch the borders of gender *within Latino culture*, and
dare to raise their sons and daughters within revisionist definitions of
culture, gendered relations *within* Latino homes and communities
grow more and more contested.

White, African American, and Latina women are, indeed, in this
generation, rethinking and redesigning the borders of gender and sexuality. As we read in chapter 7, white women whisper their troubles and
act rarely. In chapter 8, we heard African American women testifying
more boldly and acting more often. Here, in chapter 10, we witness Latinas protesting quietly but maneuvering quickly to get themselves and
their children out of the way of danger.

Throughout this chapter you will hear a story of gender, culture,
and generation as told by the largely Puerto Rican sample of first-
generation women whom we interviewed. These women detail the very

traditional worlds of gender in which they were raised; relay biographies in which they witnessed and/or experienced a fair amount of abuse at the hands of men they knew intimately; and they describe childhoods – and adulthoods – filled with prayer to gods and spirits. And now, in a swirling historic time just post–civil rights, just post-feminism, and just precisely at the moment when their men aren't making much money, these women are instigating a quiet revolution. Returning to school in record numbers and entering the labor force with equal strength, Latina women are rebuilding family, spirituality, and community. Refusing the betrayal of a life they were promised and denied.

We interviewed more than twenty Latinas from Puerto Rico, Cuba, Ecuador, and Colombia, with the vast majority being from Puerto Rico. Each woman, each nationality, brought with her a strong sense of what gender means within her cultural context. Approximately 70 percent of our Jersey City respondents identified themselves as Puerto Rican, and 100 percent so identified in Buffalo. On the one hand, we take seriously Juan Flores's (1996) proposition that Puerto Rican identities are deeply and particularly influenced by the colonial relationship between Puerto Rico and the United States and should not be masked with a broad Latina sweep. Thus, we analyze these data given the specificities of the Puerto Rican experience, most profoundly the impact of colonization and gendered identities. On the other hand, our interviews with women representing Central and South American ethnicities revealed a set of shared experiences that, at once, move across ethnic categories and stem from common histories of conquest and (im)migration. Domestic violence, joblessness among men and women, and the spirit of resistance embodied by Latinas in refusing the betrayal are among the experiences shared by the women we interviewed (Espin 1995). Of the Jersey City women, 61 percent have children, 33 percent live with a husband/partner, 92 percent have experienced or witnessed some domestic abuse.

Colorful, energetic, cup-half-full scrappers, the Latinas whom we interviewed sing a wonderful, optimistic, life-giving song, about their own biographies and the futures they envision for their children. As you will hear in their own words, these women believe deeply in family, religion, and culture, even as they raise significant and profound questions about violence at the hands of men, churches filled with more hypocrisy than spirit, and a culture built on the backs of their mothers and the subordination of women.

On Generations of Women

Listening to these narratives, we were struck by how deeply each woman wove her story with the stories of women of her family. Generations past, present, and future. With a soft but firm refusal of individualism, the stories told portray women connected, betrayed, catching each other, defending one another.

In Puerto Rican culture, as with African Americans, stories are often handed down from mother to daughter, and father to son. Some would argue that storytelling constitutes the heart of cultural survival. Benmayor et al. (1987), however, argue that for Puerto Ricans, family folklore is rarely romantic, always strategic:

> For Puerto Ricans, telling life stories is *not* a process of passing down treasured family lore or the experiences of the past to later generations, who no longer share the same class position as their immigrant forebears. The "rags to riches" stories of many older European immigrants are predicated not only on individual achievement but on the collective upward mobility and social access enjoyed by those groups as a whole. Life stories of working class Puerto Ricans who came to the U.S. decades ago do not reflect a significant difference between then and now. For young Puerto Ricans today, who typically occupy low paying service and clerical jobs – as bank teller, hospital workers, sales clerks or office workers – the stories of their parents and grandparents who eked out a modest living as factory or domestic workers contain strong and painful parallels with the present. They have strategic, immediate value, giving historical perspective to current struggles. (3)

We, too, heard stories of pain, understanding, talk, and wisdom passed on to generations, carrying politics, cultural memory, pain, loss, and connection.

CARMEN: *She [her mother] was thirty-nine. She was so beautiful at thirty-nine. She looked very young. A lot of the people could not believe that she passed away, friends, associates of hers.*

MUN: *How were your brother and sister affected?*

CARMEN: *They take it a lot better than I was; I'll be honest. They just . . . they hurt a lot, but I took it like, well, I was, like they say, I was like a gum to her. I stuck through my mother through everything. I stuck by her, yes, we did. In fact, oh, I don't even have the chain with me. My baby brother, I tell you he doesn't speak about it, but he'll react to it. He brought a heart, a gold heart, it's broken in three pieces, and that heart symbols my mother's heart. So at Christmas time we separated the heart in three pieces so each one of us has a piece of that heart.*

Placing oneself in a "line" of women, as Carmen describes her life, there is a loving unwillingness to see herself as separate, autonomous, or concerned merely with personal interests. Rather, as Lykes (1985) has described in her analysis of "social individuality," the self as narrated by Latinas swims between and among women within a family, a community, across generations. As we point out in chapter 8, this is similar to women in African American communities as well.

Most of the women we interviewed grew up in homes where both their mother and father were employed in factories:

DENISE: *My mother worked in the Coca-Cola factory, until it closed down, on her feet for ten hours a day.*

————

MARTA: *My mother, she had a job—you know, the Colgate-Palmolive clock? It used to be a factory. I waited for her at the back entrance.*

At some point, for most of those women we interviewed, *papi* left. He may have returned to Puerto Rico or Colombia, with his "American money," inviting a reluctant family to accompany him. Or, he may have left to create another family, with another woman. He may have drifted off, for a while, drunk or no longer wanted by his family. Regardless of how he left, more often than not, he left. Suddenly, the family of many, which had survived with two inadequate but combined incomes, was left without *papi*. The general interdependence of domestic roles collapsed as families grew impoverished. Marina describes how her father's departure affected her family:

No, it affected the whole family all together. Because it was my father, my mother, my sister, my grandmother, and me. My grandmother is my father's mother. So when he left, my mother expected him to take his mother with him. He didn't. He left my grandmother with us. So my mother was like, "Oh, on top of everything you did to me, now I have to take care of your mother too?" Then my grandmother said, "No. I raised Marina." She goes, "I can't leave her. She's like a daughter to me. She needs, you know, she still needs me. My son is a grown man. He has his own money, his own future. He could do with his life whatever he wants. But she's still young. I can't leave her." And I know my grandmother's here because of me. But it's a conflict between my grandmother and my mother. That is her son. And if my mother wants to go on with her life, she can't do it in front of my grandmother, because that's a lack of respect. So it's kind of hard. And then my father paid for everything in the house. My father paid for the rent, the phone bill, the light bill, the shopping. My father paid for everything. Once my father was gone, it was like we couldn't live on my mother's paycheck alone. We were so used to having it all [and then there] came a time when we didn't have it any more. We got so used to my father giving us money once a month to go shopping. If we needed a pair of sneakers, "Dad, I need a pair of sneakers." [He said,] "Here you go." "Dad, I need this." We were so used to that. Then it came to a point that we didn't have it any more. And we couldn't tell our mother, "Mom, can I have this?" because she didn't have it . . . so I started working, and then my mom took another job. So now she's working two jobs, and I'm working one job. So I help my mother out. My sister is graduating high school. So she needed a prom dress. She needed everything. So now in my house the money is very tight. You know, we have to save each and every penny and make sure that we don't misuse the money on stupid things. You know, my mother doesn't tell me what to do with the money I make. I help her out. Every week I give her fifty dollars, a hundred dollars. But she has to make sure that she has enough money for the rent, for the phone. If the phone goes up too high, she'll tell us, "Girls, stop making these phone calls. Don't, you know, the phone is pretty high this month. Don't turn on the air conditioner too much. When you turn on the iron, make sure you don't leave it on too long." Things we were never used to.

In poverty and hard times, as these women witnessed so often, "*Mami*" rose to the occasion. She worked extra hours, took in neighborhood children, skipped meals, did laundry. She kept the family together. And all the while, the daughters were watching, and trying to give a hand. Never wanting to burden *Mami* further. Consuela explains:

The reason we came here, my mother had a lot of problems, money situations. But again, my family was always there for us too. But she felt like kind of embarrassed to ask for help. But my family was always there for us anyway. And I'm very proud of her. Because she had it rough. She had it rough. And I'd try to help her as much as possible, you know, like taking care of my little sister while she was working. She had two jobs. She was working during morning and nights, to support us. And even though it was very hard, she wanted us to go to a private school. She always tried to give us the best, the excellent education for us.

Keeping the family together was *Mami*'s job. And she did it well. For more than a few young women, mothers were sick when they were young. Some died young. By the time our interviewees grew into adolescence, they too, were going to school and working. Until they got pregnant. Which most, but not all, did in their late teens or early twenties. More than a few were pregnant from an abusive boyfriend, scared/embarrassed to tell *Mami* or their father about the abuse or the baby. Our focus group says it best:

BEATRICE: *And it's always up to us. It's always up to a woman. Never . . . I don't trust no man to tell me. My ex-husband: "Yeah, baby, you won't get pregnant. O. K. I'll take it out." That's how I got my daugh-*

ter. Of course, I didn't know. I didn't know. He says, "Oh, don't worry.
You don't need that." I was young. I was fifteen, sixteen when I started
having intercourse with him. So I was so scared. Never mind that my
mother would find out that I was sleeping with this boy. But to go to
her and say, 'Ma, can I go to the doctors and get some birth control?'
Are you stupid? No, that would be the end of me right there. I could
not. So everything I did would have to be hidden. I had to do it behind
their back. I had to do stuff secretly.
MERCEDES: *That's what happened to me. When they found out that I*
was pregnant, they did not even want to know. But they kicked me out
of the house. He [her father] called me a puerca *[pig] and* puta *[whore]*
and, what else was it? And a perra *[dog]. Because only a* perra *would*
do what I did. So and then he started calling me names.

A few of these women "surrendered" these babies to adoption. One
had her baby taken from her by the state. The rest kept their babies,
while many families asked them, the daughters, to leave at least for a
while. Living with a boyfriend, his family and/or on her own, a young
woman had to contend with violence, protecting her boyfriend, negotiating his mother, and sheltering the children. Here, for example, are
Marina's and Yolanda's descriptions of the conflicts abuse created for
them:

So by this time, the neighbors saw everything. They called my mother
over. They go, "Your daughter's getting beat up by her boyfriend."
So of course my mother's like, "Oh, my God." So my sister and my
mother, they ran outside. And I wasn't there. So when I finally got
home, my mother was like "We can't keep going like this. Why is he
doing this to you?" At that time my father was in Colombia because
my grandfather had died. But when my father came back, the neigh-
bors talk a lot and they told him. So he confronted me and he was like,
"Did this really happen? Has he really abused you? How long has this
been going on?" And then I had no answers for him. Because in a way,
I was so in love with him that I protected him. And I always fabricated
excuses. "Well, I deserved it. It was my fault." And it really wasn't my

fault, you know. All along, it was his fault. And then my father was like, "I'll kill him." You know, and I was so scared for that. I was so afraid that my father was going to find him one day.

———

MUN: *Did you press charges?*
YOLANDA: *No. I had to go to the hospital and he had told me, you know, oh please . . . he'd . . . he told me please, please . . . and I'd get . . .*
MUN: *What?*
YOLANDA: *He told me, "Please, please don't say it, that I did it." And I did, you know, being stupid I . . . because the policeman did ask me what happened. And I said, "Oh no. I fell." But, you know, it's funny because . . . I guess maybe I believed it. I don't know why I didn't just say, "Yeah. He did it," you know, and let him go to jail. I don't know.*
MUN: *Did you go back home when he was being too abusive?*
YOLANDA: *Go back home?*
MUN: *Yeah, to your mom?*
YOLANDA: *To my mom? You've got to be kidding [laugh]. There was nowhere to run.*

These Latinas—across ethnicities—narrate a form of gender relations firmly embedded within rigid and relatively unchallenged assumptions of heterosexuality, machismo, and "traditional" formulations of family. While Latinos are being exported from the labor market and are thereby betrayed by economics, these women explain that, for many, patriarchy thrives at home. Here, for example, is Theresa on the preferential treatment of brothers over sisters:

THERESA: *Right, wash clothes, iron clothes, or wash dishes. My brother . . . my father wouldn't even let him throw the garbage out. Because my father said, "With all these girls, why he got to do it?" That's what my father used to say.*

Many of these Latinas explained that they grew up understanding that women's tasks swept across nurturance and feeding of young and old. They were socialized for subordination to men and learned that they had responsibility for controlling men's anger, for self-consciously "overprotecting" children (especially daughters), and for assuring that the next generation would be imbued with a sense of possibility, despite overwhelming evidence to the contrary. As Beatrice explains: "*I felt that was my job, yes. I was raised in the type where . . . I cooked everything. As a female, that was my job. This is why, this is like a trade school where I would be taught what to do for the future. So, now I had this man.*" Carmen concurs:

CARMEN: *He was the type that if things did not go his way, he was very dominant. He had to be served. He had to be obeyed like he was some father or God or something, and that's when the beating started. . . . He was hitting me when I was pregnant, but I never, never told my mother. Never told her, 'cause she was hurt by what I did, so I said I'm never gonna tell her that he's abusing me.*

MUN: *Who did you run to when he was hitting you?*

CARMEN: *To nobody.*

MUN: *You just took it?*

CARMEN: *Yeah.*

MUN: *How long did this happen?*

CARMEN: *How long was it going on? For a year. I was almost two years with him.*

MUN: *How was his relationship with his mother?*

CARMEN: *His mother, she felt what he was doing was right, yes. [She thought] If I wasn't a disciplined woman to him and if I had a bad mouth and talked back to him, I deserved to get hit. Oh yes, you just don't know [laugh]. Yeah, and being the way I was raised and how I have so much respect for older people, how I learned not to act like one of those wild crazy women. I was the type that . . . hey, when he hit me, I felt like I didn't deserve to get hit, but I didn't deserve either to make my mother feel the pain I was going through.*

MUN: *Did at any time, did you call the police?*

CARMEN: *I never called the police on him, only until . . . my daughter — well, my daughter was born and she was in the playpen in the kitchen and I had this . . . no, he never touched her until one day, he did touch*

her, and that's when I practically almost killed him. I picked up the
knife, and I said, "This is it."
MUN: *He slapped the girl?*
CARMEN: *He hit my daughter, not on her face, but he bent over because*
she started . . . she was teething. She had two baby front teeth and she
started biting on the kitchen chairs. He bent over and started hitting
her. He hit her hard, like [as if] she was three, four, five years old. Boy, I
climbed on him like a cat. I scratched his neck and everything, and he
threw me against the refrigerator. He took me, and he hit me, and I fell
to the floor. He kicked me in my stomach. I got up and picked up a
knife.
MUN: *Did you stab him?*
CARMEN: *No, I didn't get to stab him. I was swinging the knife. I said,*
"Please," I said, "Come over and hit me again. Please come and hit me
again."

The promise of *una familia Latina*, in all its tradition of gender roles, has been washed away by shifts in economic and state policy. As the daughters of this generation witnessed this betrayal, somewhere, quietly, they tucked away a plan to care for themselves and their children. And yet they kept watching and hoping for a change.

Witnessing
Perhaps most painful, for this generation of Latinas, is the work of *witnessing* the contradictions within culture. For some, this means witnessing violence that their mothers, sisters, and sisters-in-law endure within the family. For others, it means watching from their windows, witnessing other Latinas neglect their children or witnessing boys and young men turn against family. For all, it means witnessing the loss of lives in streets and neighborhoods infected with drugs and crime. Listen to Marina:

You'll be looking out the window like, "Come on. Let that lady go."
But they won't listen to you. If they really need the drugs or they really
need it, they're going to do whatever it takes. And you hear the fights

with other kids. And then they have their own little gangs. And then the other gangs come over. And then the shoot-outs. You know, that's the biggest problem, in between that line, because you know you'll get shot and you'll die over nothing. It's a very bad neighborhood. It's not a good neighborhood. I mean, you have to tell them [people in the neighborhood], "Listen. I've got a new boyfriend. He's such and such and such, so when you see him coming up the block, please don't mug him." And they go, "Alright, alright, we got you."

Despite the witnessing, this generation of Latinas carries a sense that things will work out; that family, church, and community will prevail. The more they witness, the more they claim it is *their responsibility* to set things right, to restore family, spirituality, and community. Through an ironic self-blame and sense of responsibility, they refuse the betrayal. Latinas, of all the women whom we interviewed, voiced the most profound and, for us, the most disturbingly high levels of self-blame and belief that it is women's responsibility to tame men, to care for mothers, and to protect children:

> CARMEN: *'Cause I'm afraid that if anything does happen to them [to her sisters], I feel like it will be my fault.*
> MUN: *Why?*
> CARMEN: *Because I would feel that I could have prevented them from doing, and, being my mother is not here, I feel that I should do it in my mother's place, and I should do it for them.*

If you listen closely you will hear that the women do not precisely blame themselves for the violence, although some do, but that they do blame themselves for not being able to protect and maintain peaceful, loving, and adequate homes for their children. They endorse the ideology of the safe, nurturing family as though it were real, and then hold themselves, and other women, accountable when they cannot achieve this goal.

> MERCEDES: *But I went through the same thing you did, since I was little. As soon as I turned eight, I learned how to cook. I learned how to do*

everything in the house. But what did my father always think: me and him could never get along, because he always wanted to be the little boy in the house. I could have a man, but I'm not gonna take the abuse. I know that's what they teach you and everything, but I don't play that way. I deserve respect just as much as you have respect. I really do. Right now, I have two kids from different guys, and maybe it's because I want respect, and they don't feel like that. They feel like I should be at home with the chankla *[slippers] and be like an old lady. No. It's not like that. I always wanna hold my own. I wanna do things. I wanna do them for me, not for anybody else.*

———

BEATRICE: *And that's something I will never lose, my self-esteem, for a man. I don't care how much I suffer, because I've suffered a lot for what he made me do. They made me go through hell. 'Cause [they] think they are the man, and you gotta do whatever they think.*

While the Latinas whom we interviewed could easily be seen as "traditional" or relatively "conservative" in their gender and sexuality arrangements and judgements, it would be misleading to presume that they are unconflicted about the dance of power/gender/sexuality that unfolds in their homes and on their streets. Indeed, this generation of young women knows all too well the torture of gendered role prescriptions. With the blended passions of Latina sisterhood and spirituality, the muted legacy of U.S. feminism, and the dismantling of the economy for their men (and themselves), they are fighting, at home and in public, with their men, their mothers and their mothers-in-law to loosen the hold.

As is evident in the spiked rates of Latina female-headed households (1980–90), Latina entry into the labor force (1980–90), and Latina enrollment in higher education (1980–90), this is perhaps the first generation of Latinas to pour their anger and disappointments out onto the streets, courts, and into welfare offices and to direct their energy toward jobs, college, and their own apartments (see tables 10.1 through 10.3). These women are "going public," with bad news and good.

For percentile *increases* in entrance into the labor force, pursuit of higher education, and rise in female-headed households, among white,

TABLE 10.1

EMPLOYMENT STATUS FOR WOMEN AGES 16+

	White		Black		Latina	
Employment Status	1980	1990	1980	1990	1980	1990
In Labor Force	45.4	53.1	54.3	60.7	44.9	55.7
Unemployed	9.1	9.8	11.3	13.6	15.1	16.9

Source: U.S. Census, Labor Department, 1990.

TABLE 10.2

YEARS OF SCHOOL COMPLETED FOR WOMEN AGES 25+

	White		Black		Latina	
Education	1980	1990	1980	1990	1980	1990
4 Years High School	33.7	31.9	34.4	30.6	24.4	26.2
1–5+ Years College	7.9	23.9	6.3	28.9	4.7	20.2

Source: U.S. Census, Labor Department, 1990.

TABLE 10.3

PERCENT OF FEMALE-HEADED HOUSEHOLDS BY RACE/ETHNICITY

Census	White	Black	Latina*
1980	6.1	12.3	9.3
1990	13.7	35.5	26.4

Source: U.S. Census, Labor Department, 1990.
*For Puerto Rican women (younger than other Latinas), the percentage escalates to
43.3 percent for 1990.

African American, and Latina women, Puerto Rican women have
taken the lead. These women have witnessed too much and are on the
move. Seeking independence, self-sufficiency, and physical safety, they
yearn to make good on "the promise" to their sons and daughters, all
the time looking back and forward, as they narrate identities embedded
in personal and social histories of violence, colonization, and survival.
Beatrice shares the lesson she will pass on to her daughter, a lesson
based on her own experience of abuse:

It's easier now to teach my daughter. Now, the relationship that I'm in now, I don't look at people and think well, do you regret your ten years with him. I think no, because life is experience. And I have three children that live . . . those are my kids. He was just there. But I won't ever trade . . . I don't regret those ten years because those ten years made me who I am today. Now he thinks I'm a bitch. "Yes. But you made me who I am." I don't teach my daughter anything bad. But I do teach my daughter in the house. In the situation that I'm in now. What you said, if a man respects you, you respect him right back. But you are nobody's, nobody's pillow. You are nobody's hitting toy.

We hear, then, in our interviews, gendered tensions rumbling within and tumbling outside these Latinas' homes. Luisa explains her maneuvering out of violence, even as she refuses to turn "him" into the police:

LUISA: *Yeah, my mother was really scared, because it got to the point that he would park in front of my house and sleep there all night, see what time I got home, who I came home with, who dropped me off.*
MUN: *Did you involve the courts at all?*
LUISA: *No, I threatened to, but I didn't have to. During this period in time, he had begged and begged, so I decided to go out and have a talk with him and explain to him that things have changed, what have you. During this time, he was trying to show me that he had changed so much. So I figured okay. I said, you know, "I care about you. What happened between us changed everything." I said, you know, "But I do care about you enough." I was like so reluctant to start a new relationship, and go through all that, so I figured, hey, I'm just going to try this again, you know. And I did, which was my mistake. Because I had a friend of mine who kept telling me, "Everyone deserves a second chance. He really might have changed. He must love you." So I kind of, you know, used that as an excuse to go back with him. Big mistake. During the time I was with him, he forgot to tell me that during the time he was stalking me, he had a relationship and was staying with someone who was staying in his house, which was a friend of mine. He also forgot to tell me that she was pregnant, okay. He forgot to tell me*

a lot *of things! So by this point, I was so rebellious toward him – I hated him – that I started, every time he was stalking me, or came around or anything, I would do something to his car. I carved his car. I slashed his tires. I beat the shit out of him in front of his parents, and I told him, "Now, I'm fighting back." I said, "I'm not scared of you. If you harass me again, you're going to live to regret it." I said, "If I ever see you crossing the street, I will run you over." I said, "That's how bad it's gotten." I said, "I don't want you in my life. I don't want to go to the police with this. No, I just want you to stay out of my life."*

MUN: *Well what was the reason that you didn't want to involve the police?*

LUISA: *Because he's now a senior in college, and he's going for law, and that's something he really, really wants. And I figured if I would press charges against him, if he did get near me, because I know he would have broken them, you know, tried to go against them, and stuff like, and that would ruin his career, you know, might, as a lawyer. So I thought about his best interest at that time, while he was making my life a living hell, I'm still thinking about his best interest. That's why I didn't do it.*

The quiet revolution is not, however, without its own ambivalence. The protectiveness that Luisa talks about can be understood in terms of the within-group solidarity Latinas experience and assure. As Hurtado (1996) has written about Chicanas, the women with whom we spoke view their world through a tunnel of cultural loyalty. Across multiple positions and allegiances, they embody a solidarity with Latino men which both binds and blinds them to the abuses they suffer. Keenly aware that economically, politically and socially, there is rarely an even playing field for themselves or Latinos, Hurtado explains that unequal power relations based on ethnicity make it difficult for Latinas to critique, in "productive ways, the internal functioning of the ethnic . . . group even on the issues that negatively affect women in these groups, such as sexism, incest and battery." She continues, "The awareness of the relativity of merit leads to anger and to intergroup conflict and almost simultaneously to extreme intragroup solidarity" (13). Women pay a price and often stay quiet.

The social component of this solidarity is articulated by the women through their experiences as gatekeepers of tradition, culture, and life. Sharff (1987), an anthropologist who writes on the extraordinary rate of death among young people (mostly males) in Latino families, concludes that sometimes young Latinas are socialized to be "young child reproducers," to provide replacement for lost members of the household. "A fourteen-year-old girl gave birth to a son within a year of her older brother's death. The child was named after the latter" (45). We see this example as yet another pressure on Latinas to preserve culture as they simultaneously embark on transforming gender relations.

Latinas witness the deaths, incarceration, and unfair treatment of Latino sons, brothers, fathers, uncles, boyfriends, and husbands. Understanding the nuances of gendered, heterosexual power in homes and on the streets, perhaps more astutely than many, these women are, at the moment, in the midst of a cultural shift. Trying to realign gendered relations within the Latino community, they seek to assure that domination, jealousy, and abuse are no longer constitutive of family life.

These women have not wholly internalized gender subordination, like so many of the white women we interviewed. Nor have they given up on the possibility of an "equal" relationship with men, as many of the African American women have. While they do not raise much of a critique of heterosexuality or marriage, they do insist on being treated with dignity and respect. This posture puts them at odds with men, sometimes with their mothers, often with their mothers-in-law, but very much in relation with sisters, daughters and, to their own delight, often with their sons who have witnessed too much violence. These are, then, mothers who embody what Collins (1991) and Ward (1996) describe as the "duty to resist." Even as they resist the traditional role of *wife*, they exit violence as *mothers* protecting their children.

In the focus group, Beatrice delights in her independence and reflects on her responsibilities as a mother after leaving her man:

BEATRICE: *I did [I left]. I loved it. Somebody, for one, is dependent on you. And that makes you stronger, I think. That makes me stronger. That means that I can't screw up. I can't screw up 'cause I got three other little lives depending on me. I can't go out and do things.*

MERCEDES: *Let me tell you. Don't you feel bad when you know your kid wants something and you can't give it to him?*
BEATRICE: *If you do it right, that's one of the lessons that had to be learned.*
MERCEDES: *That's why I don't want to be a mother.*
BEATRICE: *But if you do it right . . . I don't know. Being a mother, I have to be sober. I'm studying now. I'm a mother with three children, and I'm in my third year of college. I have to sit my butt up there till two, three in the morning. I don't mind. I don't mind. Me and my kids, we all do homework at the same time at home. The same time. I even take my kids to school with me when it's report card time, and it's time for me to get my grades at school. I take my kids with me. And I think in my situation it gets us closer. Me and my kids, we don't talk like, I don't talk to them like a mother. I'm more like you say, a friend. My daughter is actually got her menstrual cycle already. We have a good relationship. My boys, I don't call them. It's like, I don't know, it's different. I enjoy it. Some women don't like it, the responsibility. I enjoy it. I thoroughly enjoy it. Makes me happy.*

Carmen explains:

It [motherhood] makes me want better things. It makes me want to do better things. It makes me want to be careful and work hard like I'm doing now. I want to work and show my daughter so when she's a teenager, I don't want to have to tell what my mother did for me was, well, we're on welfare, or we got this man living with us because we don't have enough money. So I want to make it better for her. With the abuse and everything, anybody lays a hand on my daughter, they're dead. That helped me to be strong for her and she's the only daughter too.

Beatrice adds,

The turning point [for me] was that I thought in my mind that if he was gonna do that one more time, one of us was not gonna wake up. One of us was not going to wake up. And I knew, I had, I feared about how to do it. I had good ideas about how to do it. But then my kids would be left without a mother. Or without a father, not that they would have cared for him. But I wanted to see my kids grow up. And then I was thinking, my daughter was about four years old, she feels it [that I was beaten] throughout her whole life! And the thing that bothered me was that . . . he hit me that whole week . . . was that, [I thought] God, my daughter is seeing this and she's gonna grow up thinking a family is supposed to be like this. They say a cycle repeats itself. That's what happened in my home. That's what I saw. That's what I got into. I was just so angry at myself for letting that continue. Now my daughter is getting older. She's already had four years of this. She is already indoctrinated in a certain way because this is her home life. This is the norm for her. This was the norm. But I started thinking like that. I left and I said, "I'm gonna let her live like this?" It would be my fault if this happens to her. And I said, "Hell, no!" And while he was asleep, I just packed the kids. 'Cause it was, he had a little gun, he always kept at home. That was gonna be for me.

The duty to resist means doing whatever is necessary – even going on welfare – to protect the physical survival of your *mami* and your children. As Benmayor *et al.* (1987) have determined, we too found that poor and working-class Latinas were committed to the *strategic use of welfare*, and the appropriation of educational and employment opportunities, to the extent that such services enabled them to maintain and advance the standings of their families. Seeing these women as "resource strategists" rather than as "dependent poor," Benmayor et al. extend our social consciousness of the public safety net as a vehicle deployed by women, poor and working-class, to sustain self and children. Nestar explains:

It stinks! How do they expect you to live? I've been on welfare. My first daughter, she's seventeen years old, my daughter. I went on welfare with her. I went on welfare for a minute when I had Shantee. And I was on welfare with Alicia. And I'm gonna tell you right now, all the years I collected welfare, I worked. I did not sit and wait on the damn mailman. I did the damn fraud, whatever. Take me to jail now, I don't care. You can't live off that stuff. When I first moved out and I rented my

apartment, my apartment was $275 a month. My welfare check was
$273. I mean, there is not an apartment anywhere in the world for the
amount that welfare gives you. If you don't have Section 8, you can't
live. 'Cause then you have to have three jobs plus a husband and a boy-
friend on the side [laughter]. That's the only way you can live. You
can't do it. It's not physically working.

The rub comes, of course, when these same women confront welfare
and educational bureaucracies hostile to their notions of what it takes
to secure their children's survival:

NESTAR: *And I walked in and said, "Ms. Hogan, how you doing?"*
"I have one more minute for my coffee. Could you excuse me again?"
I wanted to kill her. I wanted to kill her. I said, "Ms. Hogan, I really
hate to tell you this, but you know, you sit around here and you don't
do nothing. You read the newspaper and gab on the damn phone. And
if it wasn't for bitches like me, you wouldn't have this job. So you really
shouldn't treat me like that." "Sit down right there!" I hate that.
BEATRICE: *No, they treat you so down. They treat you so low. So low.*
It's like they're too good to be bothered with people like . . .
MERCEDES: *You want to know what they did to me once? I was at wel-*
fare, with my little baby now. And I went to this. . . . lady and I was
like, "Listen, right now I don't have a place to stay. My father won't
take me back. I need a place to stay. I need furniture. I need every-
thing." "Well, honey, all I can tell you is to beg, borrow, and steal."
What? Now if I woulda went and did that . . .
BEATRICE: *The thing is, it's hard. It's hard. One thing I was telling you . . .*
I was talking to Katie. When I first moved here, we had to go to wel-
fare, and that was when we first started here. I hated going there
because they made me feel so low. The looks. I'm the kind of person
that looks intimidate me. You look at me wrong, I feel bad! I'm
already intimidated. We went and those were the looks that my case-
worker at the time . . . you just walked in and you got all these nasty
looks. When you come from an abusive situation, and you gotta go to
welfare. That negative feelings, plus that negative feeling that you get
in there. Because you expect that you're gonna go into the office and

you swear that you're gonna be treated nicely, decently. Show some type of courtesy that you are somebody. No, they treat you like garbage there too.

Refusing the Betrayal

Write with your tongues of fire. And, if you are going to spit in the eye of the world, make sure your back is to the wind.

— GLORIA ANZÁLDUA, *Borderlands—La Frontera*

With strong desire and passionate commitment, Latinas bring what Gloria Anzáldua calls "tongues of fire" – a particular blend of whispered critique and deep optimism – to securing their own and their children's survival within the family, the church, and schools. *Refusing the betrayal* of these institutions, these women author, quietly and usually with a smile, a growing critique, often much more muted than their African American sisters, but far more caustic than their white working-class and poor sisters. To each institution, they import an almost incomprehensible, compelling, and contagious belief that change is possible; that good things can flourish; that justice is right around the corner. *They are going to make good on the promise, on their own terms, alone if necessary.* So, for instance, despite much abuse, they (heterosexual Latinas) still look for a good man. Despite much evidence of church-based hypocrisy, many pray in their own corners, living rooms, over candles and incense in keeping with the traditions of their ancestors, with a vengeance. Despite much evidence of school-based inadequacies and inequities, they are deeply involved in their children's schools, searching for parochial schools, volunteering in public schools, and, to the extent that they feel capable, working with children on homework.

The depth of these women's culturally bound beliefs reflects profound ambivalence. These women carry, and give to their children, a shining sense of possibility. Things will get better. Trying to create change, they will not surrender self or their children to social injustice. Unwilling to accept the betrayal, they will fight to restore what is their due and their children's.

And yet, this sense of possibility bumps into culturally bound beliefs about being women. Their search for the "peaceful family" and their protectiveness of Latinos may blunt their sight of, and therefore hamper their exit from, violent domestic relations. Their insistence on blaming themselves for the ruination of their communities and their home lives may keep them from seeking options. To this end, we share the ambivalence expressed by Benmayor et al. (1987): "On the one hand, the assertion of family values and gender roles was a source of strength; on the other hand, these roles could also hold women back. At the same time that the women were struggling for change, they were struggling to recreate the cultural structures that supported them. Consequently, working from within the parameters of the culture could be both empowering and restrictive" (49).

With all the effort, and all the belief, there are still times when the burden of the betrayal, and attempts to keep children from feeling the assault, weighs too heavy:

> YOLANDA: *Sometimes I think it's like too late for me. I really think that. I do, but I'm trying. I'm trying. But I think I'm too old, man. Those questions like the guy asked me, "What do you think of five years from now?" It's like, give me a break. I don't know. I don't know what I want to do in . . . I want to be doing something, but exactly what, it's hard, you know. How much money would I want to be making? If it was up to me, $100,000 a year, but . . .*
> MUN: *Welfare was asking you?*
> YOLANDA: *No, this was from the school, yeah. I had told him $30,000. He said, "Thirty thousand dollars? Wow." [Laugh.] He said, "You don't have much of a dream, do you?" I was like [laugh] yeah, this is embarrassing. I was like, I don't know [laugh] . . . Oh, God.*

And far too much to do alone –

> MUN: *What does community mean to you?*
> CARMEN: *Community means to me people helping one another. But that's a joke, you know that . . . [laugh]. It is, that's what community is supposed to mean, but it's not.*
> MUN: *Why is it a joke?*

CARMEN: *Because nobody helps one another. You knock on people's doors, you know, "Fire, fire, fire," and they're scared to open the door because they think you gonna kill them or something. I swear to God.*[2]

Today's poor and working-class Latinas seek further education, work, and care for children. Those connected to men want men to do their share. Demanding that culture *not* be defined through gender subordination, these women are walking away from scenes of violence and uncertainty, and in the process boldly redefining gender and sexuality in quiet but collective moves toward redefining culture.

"You Can Never Get Too Much"
Reflections on Urban Schooling . . . for Grown-Ups and Kids

RECENT STUDIES SHOW, IN THE WORDS OF GITTEL ET AL. (1996), THAT "FOR welfare recipients, the additional earning capacity gained by a college degree can make the difference between independence and continued poverty. The most disadvantaged benefit most from education" (14). The men and women whom we interviewed, poor and working class, African American, white and Latino, couldn't agree more with these findings. They know that education matters. They chastise themselves for failures in the past and seek opportunities for advancing their own and their children's educational credentials. And yet they're not sure advanced schooling will pay off in terms sufficient to raise a family.

In this chapter, we tour the schooling biographies of our interviewees, taking note of the deep respect this generation carries for schooling despite often humiliating and typically disastrous educational histories, lingering doubts about the utility of the diploma, and the fearful hopes they pin on education for their children. The men and women whom we interviewed constitute a group trying to do it right, for themselves and their kids. For career advancement, knowledge, "maturity," or even just to "prove that I ain't stupid," across racial and ethnic groups, they believe fervently in education. While they may have serious reservations about particular institutions, proprietary schools, and some public schools in Jersey City, for instance, they desperately want to believe that more skills, more credentials, and more networks will produce better job opportunities and improved economic standing.

The Importance of Schooling

When asked about the importance of schooling, these women and men all confirm the significance of schooling, especially in today's labor market. At the same time they are also growing more agnostic about the trade value of advanced degrees. Storming ahead in their attempts to accumulate credits and credentials, they worry it may not pay off, or not enough. In a classic gendered splitting, women across racial and ethnic groups tend to voice strong belief in schools, while men across these same groups tend to voice concerns. Women are most engaged with their own and their children's schooling, and they *need* to believe in the power of education. Census data confirm what our narratives reveal. Women are scrambling for degrees; men are a bit more suspect.

When asked about schooling, Latinas reflect on how important education was to their mothers. Ana relates the stress her mother always put on education: "And that's when she [her mother] basically gave me an ultimatum: you either go to school or get out. So I went to school . . . [laughs]. It was like, you go to school, you get out, you know, and you give up your car, . . . so you kind of weigh, and you decide, well, going to school might not be that bad, which I'm glad she did."

African American women assert forcefully how essential schooling is for their children, that "you'd be cheatin' yourself" to leave school prior to graduation.

> MICHELLE: *What do you want Destiny to learn in school when she grows up?*
> ALLISON: Everything. *Whatever's out there that she can possibly learn, everything. I want her to learn everything because I'm still learning, so everything. Whatever the schools give her out of the books, that's what she'll learn.*

> NICOLE: *Education is very important, very important. She [her daughter] knows you can't get nowhere . . . and being black, you know, that's another thing. And bein' a woman . . . you know, so if you want any kinda life out here, . . . education is very important.*

Men, in contrast, across racial and ethnic groups, voice a more strident challenge about whether or not education really delivers to the poor and working class what we have all been led to believe it delivers. This parallels the generally more critical stance exhibited by men, especially black men, as noted in chapters 2 and 4. Julius explains, "I see myself as a very successful young black entrepreneur, and not only that, I see . . . that I can reach out and touch kids in a positive and physical way and I don't have a whole lot of money to do it. [But] it's not about the degrees no more. It's all about who you know. It's not what you know, it's who you know now if you want a serious job in a corporation or in the business world. The kids come out of school with a degree, and they can't find a job with a degree."

While almost everyone – across groups – agrees that schooling is (or should be) important to future success, groups part ways on those opportunities they have seen as available, and those opportunities they have accessed. Whites, followed closely by Latinos, are most likely to have enrolled themselves and their children in parochial schools, voicing concerns about a lack of "discipline, respect, and order" in the public schools: Viola, a white woman, sees a connection between home and school environment as being a lack of discipline. "I guess, I don't feel that there's a lot of order in the high school, the public schools. Because a lot, I mean, you get some kids who aren't really disciplined at home. I guess, stability, you know, you need discipline and stuff like that. 'Cause if there's no discipline at home, and they go to school, I mean there's a lot of violence directed toward teachers and just other students, and, you know. They just become rowdy, and there's just no order, you know."

African Americans are, in contrast, more likely to have enrolled themselves and their children in public schools. As Oliver and Shapiro (1995) so eloquently argue, there is simply more wealth available over generations in white families than in black families, even in poor and working-class white families, because of the ways in which class and race formations in America have disabled African Americans from amassing capital over time. In our data, African American interviews, therefore, carry far fewer references to parochial schools, although African Americans, too, worry that the public schools have "gone down," that too many teachers "don't care," that the schools are "falling apart" and suffer from being "overcrowded."

> ZEKEDA: *(African American woman) School is so laid back now, you know what I'm sayin', it's like, the teachers, I'm not going to say all the teachers, but some of the them just don't care. A lot of them just don't care about the kids nowadays, and it's like, so the kids, they end up not going to school, you know what I'm sayin'? So I think that they should more so get back into, the teachers and everything, should get back into the school, so that the kids can actually learn something.*

> ------

> BETTY: *(African American woman) The only good thing about public schools, the people . . . they can't afford to send their children to private schools [but they] are able to send their kids to public school, and they can still get a education, okay. But most—well, not all—but some teachers at these public schools don't give a damn if the students learn or not. And if you have a particular student in your class that's a troublemaker, okay, you have to realize that child is in trouble. He's crying out for help. He just doin' it in a different way. You know . . . really, financially is the only good thing about public schools.*

A few African Americans whom we interviewed, who are working for/in schools, express more sympathy with the difficulties of the task of schooling in a public sector under siege: "I think the schools do have an impact," says Bernard, "but I don't think their impact is as powerful as it has the potential to be, because it is up against so much. The teachers are up against so much. It's almost like fighting a losing battle. It's scary."

But it is African American men, in particular, who pose a sharp critique of the public school system, raising up questions of class, race, and social inequity:

> EDDIE: *I see a lot of anger that adults have, and young adults, but with the system that seems to have failed a generation of people. A school*

system that has failed. A church that has failed. A civil rights organiza-
tion like the NAACP that has failed. Politicians that have failed to
keep promises.

———————

LAURENCE: *Because we got mediocre teachers and they are teaching out*
of age shit that don't mean nothing to nobody, they're in a different
unrealistic world, and the teachers need more help than the children,
and the children sit up there wasting time trying to get in each other's
pants because the only thing it is, is a breeding ground for more drug
addicts and more criminals and more sex offenders than anything else
because those institutions ain't doing what they're supposed to be
doing. Our concept of schools are antiquated and outdated. They need
to be transformed. . . . My wife just started teaching last week, well,
this week as a matter of fact, on Monday, and she was amazed at how
the kids were as undisciplined and disrespectful of authority as they
were. She just couldn't believe it. We who have grown up in a different
generation have a different mind set about how kids should behave. So
when kids come through, it's almost like they're like little foreigners
from outer space and we just, we can't fathom, it just doesn't work. It
just doesn't fit, so, as a result, we treat the kids like little foreigners. We
treat them like little derelicts, little juvenile delinquents, and we don't
foster the sense of love and concern, but we do things as a means to an
end. I think there are some teachers who have been in the system so
long, not that they're ineffective, but they're just kind of burned out.
And so, as a result, the public school doesn't necessarily, is not neces-
sarily as effective and doesn't have the impact.

Latinos, like Carlos, also worry:

The social problem I'm really concerned about is AIDS and the politi-
cal problem I'm really concerned about is education. Because it is
political in a way, because a lot of people, you have to schedule a way
of bringing those people up. There is too many people that just fall into
the cracks. I mean they're not cracks anymore. It's like the Grand Can-
yon. Everybody is falling right down through it. It's a pit, and it
amazes me that nothing is being done.

It is interesting that in this set of interviews, some white men, most of whom were graduates of parochial schools, also pose critical questions about the inequities built into what Elvis calls the "two tiers of schooling" in Jersey City:

> Oh, without a doubt. I think that's very important. And you know, I support public education. I think we need to strengthen it. We need to improve it. We need to support it and make it, you know, have more equality so that you don't have a two-tier system of poor schools with bad education and rich schools with good education. You know, I think that the way things are now, it's very unfair. It's just, we're reproducing a class system, you know, through the education system.

But white men, like Latinos and black men raise important questions about the "trade value" of a diploma vis-à-vis a labor force that is downgrading and downsizing positions and incomes. Here is Armendo's take on the declining value of an education:

> I'm just looking at the future as being really terrible. I don't see like a great future out there. My whole thought is, I just feel that a couple years from now, even now it's happening, a college degree is basically gonna be like high school degree [diploma]. You can't get anywhere, well now, without a college degree, you can't get anywhere without a degree. And I feel that will be my goal. My thing is at least get a college diploma.

Across racial, ethnic and gender groups, these men and women voice desire for but also question the utility of advanced degrees. Their concerns, their ambivalence, is well placed for this generation of young Americans. As Sum, Fogg, and Taggart (1996) observe:

> [A] troubling – and broader – problem has received comparatively less notice: the steep and sustained decline since 1973 in the real (inflation-adjusted) earnings of *young* men and women generally. Even adjusting for demographic and socioeconomic characteristics, the labor market problems of *young workers* are disproportionately severe – they include

TABLE 11.1

MEDIAN WEEKLY EARNINGS (IN 1993 DOLLARS)

OF 16- TO 24-YEAR-OLDS, 1967–1994

Year	Men	Women
1967	$386	$294
1973	$417	$315
1979	$388	$299
1982	$349	$293
1989	$316	$286
1994	$286	$271

Source: U.S. Bureau of Labor Statistics, 1995.

higher than average unemployment and relatively low earnings when employed. This sustained drop in earnings has been especially dramatic for young adults with *no postsecondary school education.* . . . A young man under 25 years of age employed full time in 1994 earned 31 percent less per week than what his same-aged counterpart earned in 1973. . . . Whereas in 1973 the average young woman working full time earned only 75 percent of what her male counterpart earned, a young woman in 1994 typically earns 95 percent of what her male equivalent does. Near-equality of the sexes, sadly, has been attained only as a part of a broader decline in the earnings of all young adults. (83)

This worrisome trend is nowhere more apparent than in the median weekly earnings data presented in table 11.1. In 1967, median earnings for men was $386 as compared with $294 for women. By 1994, the gender gap among young adults narrowed substantially, but at the expense of a $100 drop in earnings for men.

Thus, to be clear, more education does bear economic fruit, even for the poor and working class, for both men and women. And yet two qualifiers need to be stipulated. First, a comment on race/gender parity in earnings. While each year of additional schooling does produce increased income *within* racial/ethnic and gender groups, additional schooling will *not* equalize income *across* racial/ethnic and gender groups. That is, black women with four years of college who work full time, on average, earn the equivalent of white male high school drop-outs who work full time (see table 11.4). "Equal" education does not translate across racial/ethnic and gender lines into "equal" income.

Our second qualifier addresses history and contemporary economic troubles for young workers. For the current generation of *young workers*, as Sum, Fogg, and Taggart (1996) have documented, unemployment rates are relatively high and earnings relatively low. This is particularly so for those with no college. This generation of young men and women, most profoundly those without college, are witnessing a shrinkage in the buying power of their educational credentials even as they accumulate more education than their parents did, and encourage their children to do the same.

Thus, what may sound like a contradiction – "I believe in education for myself and my children, and still I'm worried that my diploma has no value" – must be read as an accurate portrayal of the economic prospects of poor and working-class young adults in America in the 1990s. These men and women are giving voice to America's central contradiction at the close of the century.

Acquiring Credentials and Years of Schooling
Among the residents of Jersey City and Buffalo, we see enormous gains in educational attainment from 1980 to 1990 – with rises in percent of those with some college education and those who are college graduates. As table 11.2 suggests, Jersey City and Buffalo reflect national trends, with a rise in higher education due largely to increased enrollment by women – white, black, and Latina. Hard work and belief in education by women across colors and men of color could not be more visibly demonstrated than by the data shown in this table.

And yet the ambivalence about payoff is aptly reflected in Nestar's sarcasm: "[College] opens opportunities all right . . . [laughs]. . . . I see so many people that have college and you see them. . . . They don't have a job and they have all this degree and you see them working in McDonald's as managers, and, oh God, please. I don't know."

As Sum, Fogg, and Taggart (1996) and Gittell et al. (1996) have demonstrated, each additional year of schooling acquired post high school converts linearly into enhanced economic standing, within racial/eth-

TABLE 11.2

PERCENT OF U.S. HIGH SCHOOL GRADUATES ENROLLED IN OR HAVING COMPLETED
ONE OR MORE YEARS OF COLLEGE, 1970–1986

Year	High School Graduates Enrolled in or Having Completed 1+ Years of College (% of Total)			
	Male		Female	
	Black	White	Black	White
1970	41.2	60.8	39.0	47.1
1975	50.3	56.6	46.4	49.1
1980	44.4	51.8	47.5	51.0
1985	43.5	55.5	43.9	55.2
1986	43.7	55.0	50.2	55.6

Source: United States Bureau of the Census, *Statistical Abstract of the United States: 1988* (108th ed.; Washington, D.C.: Government Printing Office, 1988), table 233.

nic and gender groups. Our data, like the census data, indicate that poor and working-class-young adults are doing whatever they can to enhance their credentials. Across our interviews, men, and women even more so, are pursuing their G.E.D.s, enrolling in proprietary schools, and taking college courses, while rearing children, caring for parents, working one or two jobs, and paying off loans.[1]

Upon closer examination, it is clear that women's increased enrollment in college explains most of the rise in higher education from 1970 to 1990. But even prior to entering college, a number of the women whom we interviewed, particularly those on public assistance, were in the midst of studying for the G.E.D. exam, as a requirement of the "welfare reform" policy in New Jersey. Similar to the leap in college enrollment, the number of people taking the G.E.D. tests nationally increased by 247.3 percent from 1967 to 1987. The nation is rapidly approaching the point when one of every five persons completes high school via the G.E.D. Alice, a white woman in a G.E.D. program, tells what turns out to be a "typical story":

ALICE: *I quit school because I was pregnant, because I was embarrassed. The fact that I was not doing the right thing. I should not have been*

embarrassed. I could have come. I was in the eleventh grade. I had one
more year to go. I mean . . .
MUN: *Everything would have been different.*
ALICE: *Exactly, I mean . . . I went to business school, now I'm going*
back and taking my G.E.D. You know, it's just prolonging what I want
to do. And in fact, I could have finished, been done, been somewhere
else probably now.

Alice regrets that she didn't remain in school and save herself the delay
in career advancement she must now endure while she prepares to take
the G.E.D. Jennifer, a white woman who passed the G.E.D. while on
welfare, argues that passing the G.E.D. has not opened the doors she
had expected.

JENNIFER: *I used to work during the day, and I used to work at night.*
I stopped working during the day, and I went to school to get my
G.E.D., and I still work at night. Now I'm trying to get back into
school during the day. And it's like, there's no respect. I got my G.E.D.
and I'm fighting with my caseworker in the welfare, because she
always told me, "Get your G.E.D. and then we'll help you into
school." So I went and got my G.E.D., and I first wanted to go for nurs-
ing. "But we don't have any nursing courses" [said the welfare office].
So I said, "Okay, fine, then I want to be an accountant." And they're
giving me such a hard time to put me in school. And I told 'em, you
know, "You say, 'Oh, we're gonna help you get into school. We're
gonna send you help on this. You know, we want to reform you, we
want to take you off,' " but yet they prevent you from going. They actu-
ally give you a fight and a half to go. I feel that they feel that if they
reform all the people on welfare, they're not gonna have a job. They're
gonna start getting laid off, you know? They tell you, "Come back."
Every day of December I went, every day they were open, I went to
welfare and fought with my caseworker. "When you gonna send me
the papers to go to school? When are you gonna get me the papers for
this?" They made me take the same test three times. "Well, you have to
get recertified." Okay, fine. I went and took the test. Come back, "Oh

TABLE 11.3

GENERAL EDUCATIONAL DEVELOPMENT TESTS

Year	People Tested	% Who Pass	Avg. Years of Schooling	% Planning Further Study
1960	61,093	77.0	10.0	31.0
1970	331,534	70.8	9.7	40.1
1980	816,176	70.8	10.0	36.6
1987	758,367	74.1	9.9	51.8

Source: U.S. Department of Education National Center for Educational Statistics, 1990.

no, you have to get recertified again. They made a mistake on your papers." Then, it's "Oh they lost the papers." So, and it's a scandal, you know? I wrote that, I wrote in a letter, you know, "Dear Mr. Clinton, you have said you want to reform the welfare people. And I'm writing to inform you that the ones that wanna be reformed can't get no help."

These women's doubts and frustrations are voiced amid a national growing trend toward G.E.D. preparation, passage, *and* plans for advanced study, as table 11.3 illustrates, and alert us to the likelihood that with increasing numbers of people passing the G.E.D. will also come increasing frustration with "the system."

African American women, in proportions well beyond other groups, are busily engaged in educational enterprises, trying to acquire as much schooling as possible, to secure better employment, and to provide more for their children. As a group, they are most likely to be enrolled in the proprietary schools that line "the Boulevard" in Jersey City and exist throughout Buffalo. National exposés criticizing these schools have done little to halt their strong congressional lobby and continued "success." The national default rate hit an all time high of 22.4 percent in the 1990 fiscal year, while the default rate for proprietary schools that year was 41.2 percent. Our interviews revealed that while African American women continue to enroll in these schools and training programs, they are losing confidence in their value. Here, for example, is Tania: "I took up data entry trade at the School of Business

Equipment [altered name]. They said they would help you. You know, after you're finished, get a job, but they never help you. They didn't do anything. After that, they closed down and that was it. A couple of months after I got out. So I went searching for myself." Her story is echoed by Sylvia: "Then I went to International. That's when they tricked me into that student loan and shit. Yeah, so I didn't finish there. So now I gotta still pay for the student loan, even though I didn't finish. They talk you into applying for a student loan. Then you go right downstairs to the bank, around the corner, and you sign for the student loan." Trina volunteers another, now familiar sounding story: "Before I came here and after I took the G.E.D. test, I wanted to take up beauty courses. So I went to Beauty Academy. I wanted to do something, you know, but that wasn't a good experience either. I was goin' there and I had to sign a contract to go there, but I thought it was like a student loan. Okay. I had, I think it was $4,000. Okay, and I was learning, but as I was learning, they was rippin' me off left and right. It was a big rip off. So what I did was, I went to a public defender, explained the situation, you know. They told me it's a rip off. It's a game that the government allows. You know, and there's nothin' people can do."

Sara was one of the few women we interviewed who attended a federally funded job-training program. She completed the program, only to find that there were no jobs at the end, and has lost confidence in the idea that education and training will help improve one's life. She explains: "They tell you to go to a program working; they give you working skills, and there is no job. I mean, the programs they have I think sometimes doesn't even help you. I think they just want to see you doing something, you know? I have to go to school on the fourteenth for a training program. Am I gonna get a job from that? I'm gonna bust my butt doing this working program, and then what am I gonna get back in return? I'm still gonna be on welfare."

And here is Alfonso who has also earned credentials in a job-training program: "I mean, *here on my knees*, I really want to get educated and learn and to see that I have to get it in debt to do it. It's bugging me. It's still bugging me, so that whole aspect is still bugging me. But I always, always continue to go school and I want to. I don't want to . . . that's

TABLE 11.4

MEDIAN 1985 INCOME OF FULL-TIME WORKERS BY SEX AND RACE/ETHNICITY

	Men		Women	
Education Level	Black	White	Black	White
5+ years of college	$31,151	$39,834	$24,741	$26,014
4 years of college	$26,516	$33,487	$19,879	$21,694
1–3 years of college	$19,689	$27,737	$16,033	$18,415
4 years of high school	$18,452	$24,822	$13,806	$15,715
1–3 years high school	$15,633	$19,728	$11,282	$12,037
8 or less elementary	$13,722	$17,027	$10,280	$10,735

Source: Social and Educational Conditions, National Council of Educational Statistics, 1990.

something I realized, that knowledge, it's kind of, now it's playing a double role, but while I was growing up, I knew that it was always something interesting to learn something new."

Alfonso's story, too, speaks to a national growing problem – the yawning gap between the growth in tuition increases and much less accelerated growth in median household incomes.

All of our interviewees, and especially *women of color*, have good reason to be ambivalent about the market value of a degree. As table 11.4 demonstrates, education enhances economic standing *within* racial-gender groups, but the credential does not deliver equitably across race and gender. In other words, if you are a black woman working full time, a college degree does not yield the earning potential of a white man. In terms of 1985 income, *white male high school dropouts* employed full time still earned approximately the same median income as *black women college graduates* employed full time.

In fact, black-white wage differential *grew* from the early 1970s to the late 1980s, most dramatically for *college graduates* (Mishel and Bernstein 1994):

Among the workforce as a whole, the increase in blacks' wage disadvantage arises from the fact that the occupations and cities in which blacks are concentrated had lower wage growth, that blacks became relatively more concentrated in low-wage industries and nonunion settings, and that blacks were particularly disadvantaged by the failure of the minimum-wage threshold to keep up with inflation. . . . What we do know is that the racial wage gap widened despite a substantial closing of the racial gaps in educational attainment and education achievement. (189)

Improved educational standing will not insure economic parity cross race or cross gender, even if more education is better than less education for any one individual.

If, as our data indicate, poor and working-class mothers have been scrambling over the past twenty years for additional academic degrees and added years of education, and if they see some but diminishing payoff for their efforts, or, if welfare "reform" presses women to "work for welfare" rather than pursue education, then the implications for these women may stretch across two generations, curbing the opportunities for and aspirations of their children as well.

The deep desire for more education for this generation of poor and working-class young adults blends with serious reservations and concerns about the productivity of advanced education. If these men and women are actively but ambivalently engaged in their own educational pursuits, we need to inquire as to how they think about their children's schooling. And in answers to this question, we find a doubling of hope and fear.

Homework Picks Your Brains: Parents' Dreams and Fears About Children and Schooling

Dolores, an African American mother, tells us: "Even though he [my son is] seven, I tell him, 'Somebody's going to pick your brains. They'll ask you a question.' He'll say, 'Mommy, how am I going to answer?' I say, 'That's what I'm telling you. You have to listen in school. If the teacher gives you homework, when you get home, do it. If you need help, I'll help you. Homework picks your brain.'" In Dolores's insistence that her son do his homework we hear her faith that good will come of working hard for an education. The young men and women of today's poor and working class are devoted to acquiring education for themselves and their children not only as a means of advancement but also as a way to achieve more fulfilling lives. Education is seen as the way for a poor child to realize his or her dreams. Listen, for example, to Barbara's answer when asked what she'd like her children to learn in school:

> Okay, in school, I'd like to have them to first learn to develop a good attitude about learning. I'd like them to love to learn. I'd like them to be inquisitive. I think it's very important that they have a very good grasp of the English language, they be able to speak well, be able to write well, be good mathematically, sciences, art, music, culture. I'd like them to have a very good grasp of knowledge, of general knowledge, before going into a specific area, so before they even reach the college level, I'd like them to just be very well rounded in terms of travel and education and experiences.

And when Paco is asked the same question, he responds:

> Everything possible. I think that when they come here [to his college program], they'll see how in love I am with education. How I constantly push myself to go beyond what it is that's offered to me to learn. And I think that they're actually starting to acquire a very strong hunger or thirst for education.

How parents think about children's schooling is informed by their involvement in their own education and by the extent to which schools invite parents in, creating spaces in which parents can talk with other parents and educators about child rearing, schooling, and the strains of parenting in insecure times.

The evidence of parental involvement tends to be quite promising with respect to student outcomes (see Brooks and Sussman 1990, Comer 1986, Delgado-Gaitan 1991, Epstein 1991, Fine 1992, Fine and Cook 1991, Moore 1991). Byrk, Lee, and Smith (1990) report that volunteering by parents in schools tends to be associated with positive outcomes for students (particularly in elementary schools), and that when parents are regularly on site at schools, schools tend to develop more efficient and responsive organizations. The work of Comer (1985) also documents that increased parental involvement inside public schools (primarily elementary schools) dramatically alters the culture and the responsiveness of these schools to the needs of children.

Yet, the downward economic shift, and the corresponding ambivalence of the poor and working classes which we documented, must, we would argue, bear consequences for parental conceptions of/aspirations for their children's schooling (Lareau 1989). Our interviews allow us to capture how working-class and poor parents today conceptualize their children's schooling and their own involvement in public schools, that is, their tenuous capacity to advocate for their children, and their nervous desire to organize with other parents for reforms.

In "Free" Spaces for Parent Talk

Discussions about schooling generally concern what individuals and/or groups get when they obtain more years of education. But we now understand that other extremely important changes are afoot within educational institutions. At their best, public schools offer sites wherein parents meet together, compare notes, and work hand in hand to raise the next generation. Schools can, therefore, act as "free spaces" in which people negotiate day-to-day problems and begin to imagine and organize for "what could be," despite tough pasts and foreboding presents. Hope survives, even thrives, in some of the schools and educational sites which we visited. Poor and working-class parents got together in Head Start and EPIC (Every Person Influences Children), in particular, to wonder aloud how they would pay the bills, how to help with homework, how to live through adolescence. Our data in this regard are absolutely striking: *parents use programs like EPIC and Head Start to imagine "what could be" in the face of devastating poverty and diminished social resources*. These contexts allow them to raise their children within spaces of hope, sites of imagined opportunity.

Enter a conversation among six parents, all African American parents of adolescents, working within the EPIC project in Jersey City:

MARTHA: *Spare the rod and spoil the child.*
JOSEPH: *That was my father's philosophy [nodding in agreement].*
DIANE: *It is confusing to me now. I was raised with those same values.*

That was the way it was. And this is my child's society and it's not acceptable. You have to live with yourself, but here they'll call it abuse.

DOLORES: [instructor] If we are talking about spanking, beating, and whipping, we know these are issues for black parents in the United States. We were taught one set of rules for dealing with our children, and society says no.

MARTHA: Yes, it is upsetting. I won't hurt him, but that is how I was brought up to help, to teach him. There is a difference between discipline and abuse.

DOLORES: Do you know why black slaves used to beat their children? They would beat them before the master would. So they would save them from a beating. We are continuing that now, not realizing it is passed down from masters' treatment of slaves.

JOSEPH: I don't know what my child values.

TONY: There seems to be a reluctance to communicate on a level that I would like to see. He just goes to his room. I don't know what to do.

MARTHA: My son wants to stay home—no college, no army, no job. He hears Farrakhan and then he challenges the teachers, and they can't give him the answer he wants. "Raymond," I say, "you can't ask questions like that in class." The schools, really, don't offer enough for the kids. He's bored. He needs to be challenged.

MARTHA: We try to have family talks two times per month.

JANET: My teenager doesn't talk.

JOSEPH: When I grew up, children and adults were separated.

MARTHA: Not now. We need to communicate, not just allow them to get their way and not just say "no" to them. Need to talk more. Sometimes, I'm glad my mother's around. They talk to their grandmothers. That helps my children form values.

The focus group then shifts to a discussion of EPIC.

MARTHA: I like talking with other parents of teenagers, sometimes you just don't know what to do. You thinkin' it's you alone, and then you talk to these other mothers and even fathers, and well, you know, lots of people going through what you going through.

JANET: *I'm glad my children have Pre-CAP [a pre-college program attached to EPIC, for teens]. They get support when they can't go to us. This is something they want to do right.*

JOSEPH: *When we [parents] talk, I feel like I have choices. Somebody's going with me to make the next step.*

DIANE: *I need other parents to talk to, trying to raise up children in Jersey City is no easy task these days, and doin' it alone, Lord have mercy.*

Mothers and fathers meet weekly, coming together simply to talk the talk of child rearing amidst urban life in Jersey City with the delicate and inviting leadership of Dolores Perry. With all the anxieties and hair pulling that characterizes the parents of teens, these men and women joined in a small safe space, on the campus of St. Peter's College. In the group, listening was Michelle, who later was embarrassed to realize that she had expected to hear more about violence, pregnancy, AIDS, and sexuality, but the parents at EPIC were just like other parents with teenagers who don't listen, who go to their rooms, and who want more from school. Parents struggling with, working through, exasperated by, and loving their teenagers.

The EPIC program in Buffalo, this one designed for parents of younger children, plays a similar, that is essential, role in the lives of mothers and fathers. Gloria, an African American mother, describes in vivid language what EPIC did for her:

And all of a sudden I came to EPIC. I just sit in the room, with my head down, with my coat on, and wouldn't say anything to nobody and just walk out. And thank God for Bernice [community liaison], she did not give up on me. She told me, she says, she wasn't, she wasn't gonna pressure me. She didn't pressure me. I came at my own pace, my own time. And someone said, "There's another meeting going on." And I said, "Okay, I think I'm gonna go." I came, and all of a sudden [I] came every Wednesday, it seems like every strip of clothes came off, and I'm like, okay. But now I thank God for that. Because I wish that they had it then [earlier in life]. I think that's my vitamin. That's my . . . that's my food.

Diane, another African American mother, told us:

> Yes, I'm involved in EPIC. That helps me because when I first brought my son to school, I had a very low self-esteem due to the fact that the way I was being treated downtown, social services and the things that were going on in my personal life, with my landlord and me going back and forth to court. And also I enjoy it because it gives me peace of mind, and it helps me to look positive on things, and it gives me something to do instead of sittin' around all the time, watchin' TV . . . and so it helps.

Ayisha offers:

> [Things were going badly in my life] – the group sense something was wrong and after I came out of my little shyness, little shell, then I got to talking, and the principal, the head coordinator of the EPIC group, they contributed. They gave me numbers to call, the name of the county legislator or city council person to contact and they were helpful. They helped me, yes. Everyone was very helpful. I thank them a lot because, like I said, that's like a second family . . . I know I can always ask one of them because, for one thing, they're more educated. They're much older and they've gone through what I'm going through now.

Gloria reflects:

> EPIC was my salvation. . . . EPIC was where I thought I was alone and I thought nobody would go through the things I went through. I went every Wednesday. I came in shame and fear and I was with my coat and my hat, covered up over my head and sit in the cover corner. I just came every Wednesday like that . . . then I came out, you know, the flower was just . . . ready to bloom. . . . It gave me back my self-esteem. Without it . . . I wouldn't know what to do, where to go. How would I? It helped me in so many ways.

All parents need support, and all parents deserve a space within their children's schools and communities to learn and to engage. For poor and working-class parents, the latter is rarely available outside of Head Start, or, in this case, EPIC.

From both Jersey City and Buffalo, mothers involved in Head Start were extraordinarily practiced at school volunteerism. Across racial and ethnic groups, ages and living situations, across educational levels and housing circumstances, and across both cities, these women discussed how Head Start had offered them a chance to "learn to be a good mother," "talk to other parents," "ask questions I'm embarrassed to ask in other places."

> AMIRA: *Are there any people whom you would point to as significantly influencing your future decisions after high school?*
> KATHY: *No. Not that I can think of. Head Start has helped me now. At this point, since I started volunteering because I was in, I guess, a blue funk. I was sitting around not doing nothing, and I had been on social services since my six-year-old was born. So it's been six years, and social service tends to leave you numb. It gives you a view of yourself. Your self-esteem goes down and people always treat you badly.*

> RACHELLE: *[I was] so thankful for Head Start because I was a basket case. Because the only thing I had going for me then, so I thought, was motherhood, and they had challenged me. Told me I was a bad mother because I was spanking my children with a belt. And I didn't understand why were they picking on me? I was the mother that they called every time, every time they needed somebody to come in. I was the mother that's child they told me smelled so good, they couldn't believe that I kept him so clean. Everybody knew me around the school. And then these people pretended that they didn't know me, had called child protection and then did not want to help me deal with the fact that they had brought this into my life. And I was a problem.*
> AMIRA: *So Head Start helped you?*
> RACHELLE: *Yes. And from that point, for me, Head Start is something that I need to help too.*

Indeed, as noted in chapter 9, the Head Start and EPIC programs were among the few sites in which mothers could actively seek and provide help on questions of parenting without fear of judgement or being reported.

Nilda, a Latina mother, describes her parent participation at Head Start:

> NILDA: *I volunteered all the time. I was there three days out of the week.*
> MUN: *Did you like the Head Start there?*
> NILDA: *Yes, I like it. It was fine . . . I like it. I think it's good for kids.*
> MUN: *How much would you like to volunteer though?*
> NILDA: *If they would have let me work every day, I would have.*
> MUN: *Why didn't you?*
> NILDA: *Because you had to give other mothers a chance. I always stayed until the last, you know, and sometimes I would work in the kitchen. I would go with them in the church. Whenever I could, I participated in whatever they needed, you know, fixing up classrooms and all kinds of stuff.*

With comparable enthusiasm, Donna, an African American mother, describes her contribution to Head Start: "How much? I want to do everything. Whatever goes on in school, I want to be there, plays, parents' meetings at night, anything; I want to be involved. I think I will do it for my daughter because I think my daughter will want me involved because then she'll start asking questions, "Why don't you do this with me at school?" and stuff like that, so that's why . . . " Mary Jane, a white mother, describes her work at Head Start: "I stayed at the classroom for two hours each morning. Working with my kids, drawing, things made for holidays. I have a little . . . certificate. . . . That was good. Especially because I got my daughter . . . I just got my daughter and son back in my custody. So it was important to me to spend more time with them." Allison, who participates both in Head Start and EPIC in Buffalo, brimmed with delight at our questions, and in her response, describes her "dual expertise":

> ALLISON: *I'm learning so much about me, and I couldn't believe it. From Head Start opening my mind to different things because they have different workshops that they let you attend. Some are about self-esteem,*

some are about relationships, some are about disciplining your chil-
dren. I've been through the EPIC workshops and they kind of help
you realize things about yourself. And I find that all it takes is a little
thought. And then if somebody kind of opens your mind up, and you
say, "Wow, I could have thought about that myself."
LOIS: *So you're teaching yourself things now?*
ALLISON: *Yes, things that I have never even thought were there. The*
more mature you get, the more you realize things that you didn't real-
ize before, and I think that's what it is. So I'm learning that those three
things in my life have been a hindrance, but it's also enhanced me to be
the person that I am now. Because I can be very loving, very wonder-
ful, very giving. And most people that I'm involved with on whatever
level, will tell you that she always comes with a smile. She's always
willing to do. She's a good person. I pride myself on that. And a good
mom.

In contrast to the stereotypic, "they don't care about education," we
met many mothers and some fathers who were so deeply involved in the
Head Start parental participation effort that they, and some staff from
Head Start, complained that "welfare reform" in New Jersey had inter-
fered with, that is cut back, their available parental involvement hours.
Women receiving welfare, under "welfare reform" had to demonstrate
pursuit of schooling and/or job training and couldn't, therefore, commit as much time to volunteering at Head Start. As a consequence,
many contend, some women lost out on valuable time with their children, many sacrificed time with other mothers and with educators
"learning to be good mothers." And the centers lost revenues dedicated
to parental participation.

The story of parental involvement here reflects what is true in many
urban communities: when schools structure engaging opportunities for
parental participation, especially with younger children, the call is
heeded with enthusiasm. Head Start is a successful example. As children age, parents are less sure of their contribution (Lareau 1989) and
schools grow more ambivalent about, if not hostile to, parental involvement. The levels of participation drop off. If meetings are held during
the day, working mothers can't attend. Unless child care is provided,

single parents are unlikely. If no one really wants to hear what parents think, few will ultimately show (Fine 1994; Fruchter, Galletta, and White 1992).

On the other hand, rich, structured, and engaging parent participation projects – as those sponsored by Head Start – produce the possibilities for enhanced parenting, a space for sanity and reflection, and potentially two generations of activist citizens. Rachelle puts it this way:

> *Because I found out through Head Start, and it's going to be an extra link with the community. And there's going to be things that I may need to know about. Either for my children's sake or my sake, or something that's getting ready to happen that I might be a part of. Or protest about. This is the way I find out about it. I want the community to be the best thing it can be because my children have to play there. My children have to grow up there. And what they see is going to influence how they act when they get older.*

The arm wrestle between *desire for* and *doubts about* public education is fast approaching a stalemate. National, state, and local investments in education are diminishing, while personal investments are increasing, And yet the payoff for this generation – white, black, and Latino – is neither what economists promised nor what young adults trying to do it right expected. With each year of additional schooling, rewards do follow. But not enough to produce either race or gender equity in the economy and not enough for most families to survive well (Edin and Lein 1997).

Poor and working-class women, and to a lesser extent men, have dedicated themselves over the past two decades to acquiring skills and credentials presumably toward improved economic standing. They encourage their children to do the same. But the swell of suspicion looms. If there persists a relative decay in educational consequence, if educational opportunities are stolen in the form of tuition hikes, financial aid drops, and "welfare reform" that demands work not school, we may witness a generation who retreats from education. Yet for the moment, most still miraculously believe, "You can never get too much."

Work, the State, and the Body

Re-viewing the Loss and Re-imagining the Future

MUN: *When you talk about your stories and memories of your life, how has that influenced your visions and hopes for yourself? And for your kids? And for your community?*

KIM: *There are times I say that, wow. You know, the future is going to be really good. But then . . . I mean . . . I guess just like turning on the news, all you see is war, you know . . . or disease and, so, you're afraid to bring a life into this for the future. So it's like, you know, one day you're real hopeful and the next day you want to die.*

THIS BOOK WILL CLOSE AS WE FEEL THE TWENTIETH CENTURY WILL CLOSE, WITH pain, despair, and no easy resolution to the problems that confront all of us who live in, around, and even far from urban sites in the United States. As writers, we choose not to tie up the narrative neatly, not to offer up a soothing final chapter, leaving readers comforted by the fantasy of "if only," or eased by simple policy recommendations. Instead, we choose to offer a set of nagging questions, troubling observations, and policy recommendations that would be costly and politically difficult to enact given the state's retreat from both the economy and public programs. We leave you as this work has left us and the women and men we interviewed. Disturbed, moved, respectful, discomforted.

We will tell you in this chapter that despite the economy sailing overseas, and the state closing up shop, despite all this, many poor and working-class people are holding their own. There is even a belief in some quarters that "we don't need the government in this community, we need to empower ourselves." As private and public sector abandonment hijacks poor and working-class communities, in the ashes are left some very proud people trying to make ends meet. But many, like Kim above, at crucial moments, can't hold it together any longer, and so must admit, "one day you're real hopeful and the next day you want to die."

In our interviews with over 150 poor and working-class young adults, we hear whispers of hope amidst narratives of despair. In both Jersey City and Buffalo, our interviewers visited communities that have been ravaged by deindustrialization, a withering of the public sphere, and traumatic assaults of violence on the bodies of women and some men and children. Over the past two decades, Buffalo, in particular, has lost a substantial portion of its blue-collar labor market while Jersey City has watched its public sector safety net tatter. Both cities have suffered a withdrawal of private and public dollars and each epitomizes this loss dramatically. Both are marked by unbelievably high levels of reported (to us) violence. State, community, and domestic violence is witnessed, experienced, threatened, feared, sometimes resisted. Within this pattern of diminished economic and public resources sit young women and men coming of age. Men and women of a generation. Making families, shaping identities, raising babies, going to school, praying, searching for better, longing for a world of safety, prosperity, and comfort, they offer up analyses to explain their economic and social positions to themselves and their children.

Despite the evidence of diminishing jobs and declining returns for educational credentials, it would be profoundly irresponsible to argue that these working-class and poor women and men are simply depressed, despairing, or isolated, bereft of all hope. As much as our individual interviews did, at times, tell us this, our focus groups alerted us that much else is happening. These young women and men are "homesteading" – finding unsuspected places within their geographic communities, their public institutions, and their spiritual lives, to sculpt real and imagined spaces for peace, communion, personal, and collective work. We have explored some of these spaces, as in the black church, EPIC, and Head Start, in previous chapters.

These spaces offer recuperation, resistance, and "home." They are

not just a set of geographical/spatial arrangements, but theoretical, analytical, and spatial displacements – a crack, a fissure, a place to come
together and restore sanity, and to imagine possibilities. Individual
dreams, collective work, and critical thoughts are smuggled in and then
re-thought. Not rigidly bounded by walls/fences, the spaces often are
corralled by a series of (imaginary) borders where community intrusion
and state surveillance are *not* permitted. These are spaces where offen-
sive social stereotypes can be contested; where troubling questions of
parenting, schooling, and faith can be posed without recrimination.
Young women and men, in constant confrontation with harsh public
representations of *their* race, ethnicity, class, gender, and sexuality use
these spaces to break down public images for scrutiny, and invent new
ones. It is into these newly constructed "free spaces," as Boyte and Evans (1992) would argue, that young women and men are able to exit
from sites of historic pain and struggle, and enter into new identities,
create new alliances. While we know no space is "free," these are
spaces designed by and for community,[1] to reconstitute traditional cultural, racial, gender, or sexual identities. They provide contexts in
which individuals cross borders of race, ethnicity, gender, and sexuality
to find a small corner in which to breathe in peace.

Engaged, daily, in the sweat and the labor of living in poverty, these
young women and men are finding spaces in which they can make life
meaningful, pray, maintain a spiritual soul, try to sustain a proud sense
of self despite state policies that strip them of dignity, tutor their children because some schools don't, or "drag it up" one more time to attend an evening parents' meeting because, "I'm afraid I'm losing my
son to the streets." While we don't want to romanticize these spaces, or
mistake them for social movements, we do want to respect, recognize,
and speculate on their place in the larger project of social change and
consciousness.

Political scientist Nancy Fraser (1991) argues that it is advantageous
for "marginals" to create what she calls "counterpublics" where
groups may oppose stereotypes and assert novel interpretations of their
own shifting identities, interests, and needs. She theorizes that these
spaces are formed out of the very exclusionary practices of the public
sphere. While the once rich tapestry of community life of Buffalo and

Jersey City has been de-threaded as private, and public dollars have been removed from these communities, we nevertheless witness in our interviews, and, even more so in our focus groups, men and women trying to make sense of their lives, and trying to pass on a sense of hope to the next generation.

As we heard in chapter 4, for example, young men in both Jersey City and Buffalo have decided to "take the church back" from their elders, bringing the next generation of youth into a community spirit, service, and belief. They are eager to restore the church's relation to the community, to resurrect trust and resuscitate hope. In a lesbian and gay group in Jersey City, young men and women from a blend of races and ethnicities have a chance to reconstruct their cultural lives and reclaim their sexualities in the comfort of good company. In the "bathroom conversations" of a Jersey City workfare program, women on AFDC both critique the state's Welfare Act and pass on secrets to new young mothers, helping them to "survive in the system." In centers of art and creative works in both Jersey City and Buffalo, the cultural aesthetics of community life are invented and collected as an archive of class, racial, and ethnic struggles, and reimagined as public art. As we heard in chapter 11, mothers and fathers are finding essential support in EPIC parenting programs in both cities. In a shelter run by an activist nun in which homeless Latinas come together, maybe for the first time in their lives, as "cultural citizens" recognized for their strengths and valued for their contributions, men and women are reconstituting identities out of the cloth of history, the wisdom of tradition, and the power of resistance.

Having relished in these spaces, privileged to be invited and honored to be allowed to stay, we delight in the passions and solidarity expressed here. Nevertheless, we find ourselves worrying. We worry that these very spaces – the churches, the quiet havens for spirituality, the creative spaces for art and theater, the sessions in which parenting challenges and concerns are shared, the cloistered sites in which women share secrets and undress their lies – we worry that these spaces are so *fundamentally isolated, so severed from social movements and a broader critique*, so safe and disciplined (Foucault 1985) as to *secure*, that is to reinforce, the very systems of oppression which have organized the work, streets, schools, and homes of these women and men. We worry because so many warned us, that within poor communities there are too few leaders, too little trust, too much fear of neighbor and kin, too bankrupt a sense of social imagination. We worry, also, that too many of the few leaders who have run for office and have been elected to run City Council, to lead the church, the school board, the community have been bought and sold. Walking away from community needs and interests, the flames of social protest left behind, dampened. Sacrificed in the negotiations.

We find ourselves conflicted as to what we want to offer readers, as we draw toward the end of this volume and this century. Poor and working-class young people are surviving lives as complicated as yours, and worse; with more social scrutiny than you will probably ever have to face; with less security and fewer guarantees that a job, public assistance, a good school, a child care center will still be there next year; with more public humiliation and private violence than (maybe) you can imagine. And we want to say that these women and men are, nevertheless, sometimes carving out small spaces to celebrate, breathe, come together, share, and try to imagine what could be. Yet we need to remind you that talk, solidarity, and support are not the same as social justice. "Food in our stomachs" and a "roof overhead" are not the same as a decent life. And even these minor threads in the once expected safety net are fraying.

While intriguing and ultimately sustaining, little is known about the relation of these spaces to economic decay and state retreat. Are these spaces launching pads for social activism or are they distracting diversions from economic and political collapse? As Skocpol (1996) has written:

How ironic it would be if, after pulling out of locally rooted associations, the very business and professional elites who blazed the path toward local civic disengagement were now to turn around and successfully argue that *the less privileged Americans they left behind are the ones who must repair the nation's social connectedness*, by pulling themselves together from below without much help from government or their privileged fellow citizens. This, I fear, is what is happening as the discussion about "returning to Tocqueville" rages across elite America . . . Organized civil society in the United States has never flourished apart from active government and inclusive democratic politics. Civil vitality has also depended on vibrant ties across classes and localities. If we want to repair civil society, we must first and foremost revitalize political democracy. The sway of money in politics will have to be curtailed, and privileged Americans will have to join their fellow citizens in broad civic endeavors. Re-establishing local voluntary groups alone will not suffice. (p. 25)

As we continue to work with these spaces as sites of political engagement and personal resuscitation, as we continue to hear calls for community engagement, "1,000 points of light," "self-empowerment," and invitations for the clergy to heal our communities, we must ask: If "free spaces" are disconnected from a prospering economy, a government committed to democratic participation, and progressive social movements, do they have the capacity to interrupt social injustice and transform social arrangements? Or will they function instead as intermittently as steam valves on old radiators?

The Economy: On Work
We are heartened, if sobered, to see working-class and poor people struggling to create a life amidst a dismantling economy and a public sector collapsing around them. The broader apocalypse within which they construct their lives cannot, however, be forgotten. Specific decisions taken by elites in both the economic and political realm have created circumstances within which poor people live and more often than we wish, live in danger. The globalizing economy has meant that corporate interests, in order to remain competitive, indeed prosper, and keep their stockholders happy (Reich 1991), chose to relocate industries to places in which labor costs were not as high, unions were non-existent, and/or state regulations not so costly (worker's compensation in the state of New York, for example, is extremely costly to business). This set of moves, taken self-consciousnessly, presumably without government "interference" and yet with enormous state sanction, has meant that jobs are less and less available to poor and working-class

folks. This decline in jobs, coupled with racism, has assured that the mean income for African Americans and Latinos is substantially less than that of most urban whites, in spite of growing white poverty. The swelling service sector economy, while providing jobs to some people, has not provided reliable or adequate jobs or benefits to the people whom we interviewed, as chapter 1 suggests. Such jobs are either located in the suburbs, without adequate mass transit systems which cross city-suburban lines, or are so unstable, without benefits or security, that poor residents are reluctant to take them, given the problem of regaining access to welfare once these jobs evaporate. While all of the men and women with whom we spoke are vulnerable, white working-class men and women have, in the past, often had small nest eggs to sustain their extended families. But this minor edge of the white working class is crumbling. Substantially less real income is being generated within even these families. And yet, as Bell (1994) has written, racism keeps these men and women from seeing their class allies across race and ethnicity: "Racism is a critically important stabilizing factor that enables whites to bond across a wide socio-economic chasm. Without the deflecting power of racism, masses of whites would likely wake up and revolt against the severe disadvantage they suffer in income and opportunity when compared with those whites at the top of our system . . . " (p. 711).

The diminution of manufacturing-based employment, twinned with the shredding of the public safety net and the reduction in student financial aid, produce conditions guaranteed to exacerbate the growing inequality of rich and poor in the United States. As former Labor Secretary Robert B. Reich mused in his "parting benediction" to the Clinton Administration, contemporary social policy has abandoned "the implicit social contract it has maintained with workers for a half a century" (*New York Times*, Jan. 1, 1997, B8). Reich notes that the loss of jobs reverberates in what he calls a "growing 'benefits gap' in which top executives and their families receive ever more generous health benefits and their pension benefits are soaring in the form of compensation deferred until retirement." In contrast, only 14 percent of workers with incomes ranging from $10,000 to $20,000 are covered by retirement savings plans, with 34 percent involved in a pension plan.

Demanding major attention to both jobs creation and systematic retraining, Reich left the Clinton administration as he came in, with a significant critique of the economy. We join Reich in his concerns, echoed and elaborated by William Julius Wilson, Michael Katz, and others, and add that this economic devastation is exacerbated substantially by the curtailment of public assistance – limiting who is eligible, for how long, under what conditions and with what consequences – combined with the shrinkage of funds for federal and state higher education.

The consequences of the private and public sphere betraying the poor are already in clear evidence. Families are barely scraping by; reports of neglect rise, abuse sweeps through homes and pours onto the streets. Drug use and sales are reviled and yet often relied upon in these neighborhoods to sustain an economy of subsistence. The media and policy makers surveil and ridicule "those people" for living as they do.

Our data suggest one more outcome of this set of conditions, noted most recently by Hochschild (1995). That is the loss of the belief in the American Dream. A perhaps naive fantasy historically accessible to only a fraction of Americans, the belief has, nevertheless, kept young adults in the United States pursuing education, obeying the law, imagining a future better than the present, struggling through low-paying jobs because they anticipated better, socializing children to imagine what could be. As the economy floats overseas, the public sector packs its bags, and poor communities implode, along with all the praying, all the desire to believe in education, all the "free spaces," all the loving of children and mommas, there is also a sprawling continually reinforced suspicion that there is "no exit." African American men have advanced this critique, laced with substantial self-blame. Few listen. White men are beginning to suspect it to be true, although many (not all) still cling to the sad belief that, "if only blacks didn't take away my job," all would be well. Women are living the critique, as it affects home life, with African American women among the most articulate. And yet these very same women and men are still going to school, trying to get better jobs for themselves, and trying to secure better futures for their children. What a terrifying legacy of this millennium: the cynical defeat by capital and the state of social equality and the belief in the American Dream. If things are bad now, imagine what they will be like once the dream is officially dead.

This economic devastation is particularly hard-hitting in inner-city black communities. The National Urban League notes in their recently released *The State of Black America* (1996) that "jobless rates three to four times the national average and with labor force participation rates even worse, inner cities are well into the third decade of economic and social despair that matches the depths of the depression of the 1930s. . . . With all of America's economic future hanging in the balance, it's imperative to end the Great Depression in America's ghettos" (8–9). We join with the National Urban League in calling for an urban policy on jobs, one in which *all* Americans have access to paid work. What is required is a policy that also has a "laser-like focus on jobs for the inner city poor" (9).

> Make no mistake, inner city folk want to work. We've got to spread the job action around if inner city folk are to work – and if cities are to work. There is no macroeconomic policy, no economic growth scenario, no model cities approach, no black capitalism strategy and no enterprise zone experiment imaginable that can match the Depression-era Works Progress Administration in jumpstarting hope by driving unemployment down in a hurry. [There is] nothing un-American about spending public money to fill gaping holes in the labor market. (9)

The Public Safety Net/The State

William Julius Wilson (1996) has said better than we that it is imperative to create more jobs for city residents – jobs that enable *men and women* to earn a decent wage, enjoy the benefits of insurance and protection from unfair labor practices, to live meaningful productive lives and raise their children. Yet our analyses assure us that national policy for jobs must be linked to a full restoration of a public sphere that serves and supports poor and working-class young adults and families. Even within a job-rich society there must be a public sphere rich in support for those who can't work, who don't work, or haven't worked, and those eager to be educated and in need of health care. Within the past several years, the once public, always inadequate, safety net has been shorn from poor and working-class adults and children. Under Republican-driven federal and state legislatures, there has been less and less money available for schooling, housing allotments for the poor, college loans, and the multiple supports needed by poor children. With President Clinton's endorsement of various forms of "Welfare Reform," the sixty-one-year-old federal guarantee of cash aid to poor children, now administered under the Aid to Families with Dependent Children program, has come to an end. States have already adopted new rules replacing AFDC with programs designed to crack down on "illegitimacy," reduce aid to disabled children, limit family size and length of time on public assistance, curtail benefits to immigrants, and establish "workfare" programs.

Our interviews alert us, and even New Jersey State Assemblyman Joe Doria drove home the point, that at present there is not enough work to go around. And even if there were, some adults can't or won't work and/or are in shifting life circumstances where they need help, and children pay an unfair price. The state posture on "dependency" masquerades as being in both society's and the individual's best interest; when, in fact, the working class and poor are increasingly expendable in economic terms. Yet the "dependency" of elites, via corporate welfare and tax cuts for the rich, flourishes unacknowledged.

Our chapter on schooling vividly demonstrates the shortsightedness of federal, state, and local withdrawal from public education, early education through higher education. These are perhaps our wisest national investments. And yet today the federal government appears to be going out of the education business; states are slashing financial aid and student loans and demanding higher education cutbacks, while fighting for minuscule tax refunds to citizens. At the same time, local school boards are hijacking public education budgets to allay the concerns of those 80 percent who do not have children in the public schools. While all evidence confirms that education is a necessary (if not sufficient) vehicle through which economic and social gains are reaped (assuming there are jobs), the state flees its social responsibility.

Retreating, ironically or not, on the promise of public education just when poor and working-class men, and especially women, are acquiring the credentials *we* say *"they"* need to succeed. As African American men told us repeatedly, once "they" acquire the "tools," "we" change the rules for social mobility (Hochschild 1995).

On Violence and Bodies

Amidst inspiring "free spaces," a brutal economy, and a bankrupt public sphere, we find we must contend with one more axis of social life – one more sphere of needed public policy – the *violence* that rips through our interviews. As we discussed in chapter six, this violence comes in many forms: at least three categories, state, community, and domestic, to be sure. As Rodney King will forever remind us, confirmed by the many subsequent videotapes of police brutalizing the bodies of young men of color, concerns of harassment and abuse "in blue" have understandably defined a particular stance toward the state in communities of color. Distrust and desperate need of police feverishly twin through these communities like a tornado, and this is reflected in our interviews. Not a day goes by without some city spiking up another story of a man of color being beaten, pulled over, searched, handled too harshly by a cop. And, as our middle-class and elite friends of color will testify, this kind of treatment is not limited to poor and working-class men. Police departments and Human Relations Commissions should not wait for another "case" to come forward, dependent on the fortuitous presence of a videographer who chooses to tape and report. The data are in. Communities await and deserve response.

A perhaps more subtle form of state abuse is narrated most markedly by women, African American, Latina, and white, working with the welfare system. Here the abuse is that of surveillance, suspicion, humiliation. As many have written far more eloquently that we (see Abramowitz 1996; Piven 1972, 1996; Sidel 1990, 1996), welfare has been constructed, and delivered, in this country, as punishment and humiliation for the poor. Polakow (1993) ups the ante when she argues that women who stray from the traditional heterosexual family or patriarchal mold of family are the ones most likely to be punished. While a number of women told us they cherished their caseworkers and recognize the support they embody, many didn't. Many report disrespect, late checks, chronic distrust, frequent public humiliation, mandates to attend courses not needed, and being banned from pursuing academic work that would enhance their economic prospects. Most feel forced to lie about income, men, and life's complexities, and those who don't, learn fast the price of truth. Few feel free to ask for real help. If welfare was tough then, when we conducted our interviews, we worry about its current and future incarnations. Particularly with respect to violence against women.

The beating of American women's bodies, across racial and ethnic groups, is a problem both connected to and disconnected from the economy and the state. Probably there would be less violence in our homes if there were more work to be had – if men were less frustrated at their lack of ability to "be men" across racial and ethic groups, given that masculinity is so intimately tied up with economic maintenance. But terror in the home runs across classes and is also linked to patriarchy. That is, policies, structures, and beliefs that men should control women, and that women are male property to be done with as men wish. As women assert their economic and educational selves, in the midst of eroding bases of exclusively male power, male violence may *increase*, as men struggle to remain dominant in the face of women who question this right. This is no better displayed than in the documented *rise* in domestic violence and stalking *after* women leave abusive men (Castellino 1996). Again the tattering of the public safety net does not bode well here. Many of the women we interviewed were able to leave abusive relationships only because they could receive tuition assistance and/or welfare benefits. Without such benefits, they would have been unable to leave and set out on their own. Support for battered women's shelters has been slashed along with a host of programs necessary for women and children to survive without men. Surely there has to be much more education about this subject, both among boys and girls, men and women, but the drain on resources in this area is devastating and will only exacerbate the violence we uncover here. As important as jobs and restoration of a public safety net are, a full federal policy initiative dedicated to the curtailment of state violence, community violence, and domestic violence must be considered simultaneously.

―――――――

What we have here is a story of two northeastern cities, Buffalo and Jersey City. We chose them because we assumed they were different. Carved through distinct histories, hit by deindustrialization and the shriveling of the public safety net at different moments in time, what has been most surprising to us has been the comparability of stories emanating from the two cities. We didn't expect it, any more than we expected the extent of domestic violence which we stumbled upon. This makes us think that there is a broader urban American story being told here, about a generation mostly trying to do it right. A generation which is relatively unsuccessful, perversely misrepresented, and fundamentally unknown. Surely in Texas and California the ethnic groups and the issues differ, given a shared border with Mexico, raw anti-immigrant sentiment, the anti-Affirmative Action flare-ups on university campuses. The stories brewing in Atlanta, Miami, and Detroit also carry distinct histories and contemporary circumstance. Yet we suspect that the stories we are hearing and those we are telling run through urban sites in the United States at the end of this millennium. These are stories of pain, passion, violence, fear, and enormous strength.

We have no easy answers to the problems unraveled here, through the words of those with whom we worked. At once, the economy, the public sector, and the body are under siege. All must be attended to. While it must be admitted that there are no easy solutions, it also must be asserted that, at the moment, our country is headed in the diametrically wrong direction. We urge social political movements toward justice, in which the politics of race, ethnicity, class, gender, disability, and sexuality are engaged in all their complexity. We invite others to mobilize to open the twenty-first century, with liberty and justice, this time, for all.

Epilogue

Writing the "Wrongs" of Fieldwork
Confronting Our Own Research/
Writing Dilemmas in Urban Ethnographies

WITH THIS EPILOGUE, WE HOPE TO PRY OPEN A CONVERSATION ABOUT METHODS in need of public shaping. When we have discussed some of these research/ethical dilemmas with friends and colleagues, many say they are relieved that someone is "saying aloud" this next generation of methodological and conceptual troubles. And yet answers evade us. With this writing we wedge open this presumably needed conversation in the hope that colleagues working ethnographically "in our own backyards" will engage with us in excavating the next generation of always tentative resolutions. As we write, we straddle the semifictions of empiricism and the intellectual spheres of critical theory, feminism, and post-structuralism. As we read and hear our friends (and ourselves) pleading for researchers to be critical and self-reflexive, we note that many of these same friends have long stopped collecting data. As we consume the critical literatures on "race" and "gender," we ask our informants to talk about both, and they keep responding, "Really I'm black, why do you keep asking?" or, "A woman – what do you think?" We write in the space which exists between despair and hope because while we hear much despair from our informants, we hear from them whispers of hope as well, and because that is the space within which we ourselves can live. Yes, structures oppress, but we *must* have hope that things can be better.

We speak now because we worry that many of us, ourselves included, in order to "cope" with the apocalypse, are simply studying it, as one more piece of the sky falls. This epilogue represents a concrete analysis "in the midst" of what Michelle (Fine 1994) has called "working the hyphen."

Much of qualitative research has reproduced, if contradiction-filled a colonizing discourse of the "Other." This essay is an attempt to review how qualitative research projects have *Othered* and to examine an emergent set of activist and/or postmodern texts that interrupt *Othering*. First, I examine the hyphen at which Self-Other join in the politics of everyday life, that is, the hyphen that both separates and merges personal identities with our inventions of Others. I then take up how qualitative researchers work this hyphen. . . . Through a messy series of questions about methods, ethics, and epistemologies as we rethink how researchers have spoken "of" and "for" Others while occluding ourselves and our own investments, burying the contradictions that percolate at the Self-Other hyphen.

This epilogue, then, offers up our concerns as we grapple with what it means to be in the midst of a study which attempts to work across many borders, always searching for ways to "work the hyphen." We take our cue from Richardson (1995) who invites what she calls "writing-stories":

With the poststructural understanding that the social context affects what we write, we have an opportunity – perhaps even an ethical duty – to extend our reflexivity to the study of our writing practices. We can reflect on and share with other researchers what I think of as writing-stories, or stories about how we came to construct the particular texts we did. These might be of the verification kind, or they might be more subjective – accounts of how contexts, social interactions, critiques, review processes, friendships, academic settings, departmental politics, embodiedness, and so on have affected the construction of the text. Rather than hiding the struggle, concealing the very human labor that creates the text, writing-stories would reveal emotional, social, physical, and political bases of the labor. (191)

Echoes (and Aches) in Our Head

On Community

Perhaps our most vexing dilemma at the moment concerns the question, "What constitutes community?" How do we write about communities in which we find little sense of shared biography or vision? When we write, currently, we write "as if" the contours of geography or SMSA (Standard Metropolitan Statistical Area) adequately define the boundaries of these two "communities." Coherence organizes life within, while difference defines life between.

And yet we recognize from our theoretical interests, confirmed by the narratives we've collected, that piercing fractures define life within communities and some pronounced similarities emerge across the two cities. Internal geographic coherence seems a naive fiction, while blunt cross-community contrasts seem deceptively polarized.

Simple demographic fractures, by race/ethnicity, gender, class, generation, and sexuality marble each city. Within local neighborhoods or racial/ethnic groups, gender, sexuality, and generational divisions boldly sever what may appear to be, at first glance, internal continuities (see West 1992).

For instance, within the presumably "same" community, African Americans will refer to local police with stories of harassment and fear while whites are far more likely to complain about a rise in crime and brag about a brother-in-law who's a cop.

Jersey City whites describe "good old days" of economic security and pine for the day when they'll be moving to Bayonne, while African Americans harbor few wistful memories of "good old days" and try to avoid "getting stopped at red lights" in Bayonne, lest their stay be extended beyond what they expected.

At historic moments of job security and economic hard times, the presumed harmony of working class/poor communities grows ravaged by interior splits, finger-pointing, blame, and suspicion. Coalitions are few, even if moments of interdependence-for-survival are frequent. Within homes, differences and conflicts explode cross-gender and cross-generation. A full sense of community is fictional and fragile, ever vulnerable to external threats and internal fissures. A sense of coherence prevails only if our methods fail to interrogate difference. And, at the same time, commonalities *across* cities – by demography and biography – are all the more striking.

So, for the moment in our writing, we script a story in which we float a semifictional portrait of each community, layered over with an analytic matrix of differences "within." For our analysis – within and between cities – we delicately move between coherence and difference, fixed boundaries and porous borders, neighborhoods of shared values and homes of contentious interpretations.

On "Race"

As with "community," "race" emerges in our data as both an unstable and an enduring aspect of biography. Henry Louis Gates, Jr. (1986) has written beautifully about "race" always using quotes; Michael Dyson (1996) argues against narrow nationalistic or essentialist definitions for either skin color or language; Stuart Hall (1981) narrates the contextual instability of racial identities. Like these theorists, our informants are sometimes quite *muddy* – other times quite clear – about race. Indeed, some of our informants, like Luisa below, suggest that "race" constitutes inherently undefinable territory. This is not a narrative of denial as much as is one of complexity.

> LUISA: *Yes, my dad was the craziest Puerto Rican you had ever seen in the '70s. Oh my Lord. Mom was raised Catholic, but in my mother's days, when an Irish and German woman went with a Chinese guy, in those days that was like, oh no, no that cannot happen. My grandfather had to drop his whole family for my grandmother, so they could be together. Everybody disowned him in his family [because] he married my grandmother.*
> MUN: *So you looked very different?*
> LUISA: *Yeah, I'm a mixture.*
> MUN: *You have Chinese blood?*
> LUISA: *Right. I got Irish and German, I got Puerto Rican and Italian, I have a lot. I'm a mixed breed.*
> MUN: *I was wondering. The first time I saw you I thought you were from the Middle East.*
> LUISA: *From the Middle East?*

MUN: *Yeah.*

LUISA: *Oh, golly gee, no. I'm, like, really mixed. I'm like everything. I got all these different personalities that just come out all the time. I swear to God. No lie. No lie.*

Jorge, a gay Latino man, does a wonderful job of scrambling—that is, "deconstructing" race/ethnicity.

JORGE: *Like to me the black race is, to me, one of the more beautiful things that I've ever seen in my life. Because of just the way that they practice certain things. Like the way they go to church and stuff. To me, those things are like so wonderful. Their spirituality in those terms, I mean, are amazing. And yet, in the Spanish race, I just love the whole, the dance, the loudness of it. I just love all that kind of stuff. So, to me there are certain things in different races. And yet in the Oriental, I just love the way that they can, everything to them is so calm and no yelling and all that kind of stuff. So it's like so opposite. I mean, so, you know, I can never like, want to categorize myself as just being this. Because I just like so much of so many different things. But yet when you're asked to fill out questionnaires and stuff, you have to like fill in the box and . . .*

ANDY: *How does it feel to fill in a box?*

JORGE: *Sometimes I want to fill them all in.*

ANDY: *Why?*

JORGE: *Because I think they're, I personally am not just, what I am right now, is just not Puerto Rican.*

ANDY: *What is it?*

JORGE: *[Laughs] . . . I'm black. I'm Puerto Rican. And I'm white. I'm so many different things that I've taken from different people that I've met through life. Different ways of thinking. Different philosophies that have made me what I am right now, that I cannot just see myself as relating to just Puerto Rican.*

When we began our interviews in Jersey City and Buffalo, we were well influenced by post-structural thinking on questions of "race." With Hall (1981) particularly in mind, willing to acknowledge the artificiality, the performances, and indeed, the racist "roots" of the notion of race (1/32nd drop of blood, for example), we constructed an interview protocol that generously invited our informants to "play" with "race" as we had. We asked for them to describe time/context specific racial identifications—for instance, when they fill out census forms, walk through supermarkets, when alone or among friends. Informants of color, trying to be polite, by hour three grew exasperated with these questions. White folks were sure we were calling them racist, or they went on about being Irish, Italian, human—never white. Needless to say, the "playfulness" of the questions didn't work.

Many argue that race *shouldn't* make much of a difference. *Yet the life stories as narrated are so thoroughly raced that readers can't not know even an "anonymous" informant's racial group* once they read the transcript. Personal stories of violence and family structure, narrative style, one's history with money, willingness to trash (and leave) men and marriages, access to material resources, relations with kin and the state, descriptions of interactions with the police are all profoundly narrated through "race," fluid though it is.

"Race" is a place in which post-structuralism and lived realities need to talk. "Race" is a social construction, indeed. But "race" in a racist society bears profound consequence for daily life, identity, social movements, and for the ways in which most groups "other." Du Bois noted that race was the dividing line for the twentieth century. He may have been a two-century prophet.

But how we write about "race" in our work worries us. Do we take for granted, as if unproblematic, the category? Do we problematize it theoretically knowing well its full-bodied impact on daily life? Reflecting on our writings thus far, we seem to tip toward theorizing "for" and about whites who deny they have one (a race) (Weis, Proweller, and Centrié 1977; Weis and Fine 1996); while we offer much more open latitude around the "voices" of people of color who articulate their thoroughly embodied experiences within "race." We try to construct theoretical structures of racial formations, borrowing from Omi and Winant (1986), recognizing that whiteness requires, indeed creates, blackness in order to see the self as moral, hard-working, family-oriented, good citizens. Yes, "race" *is* a social construction, but it's so deeply confounded with racism that it bears enormous power in the lives of people. To the informants with whom we spoke, "race" does exist – it saturates every pore of their lives. How can we destabilize the notion theoretically and at the same time recognize the lived presence of "race"?

To give some trivial, but telling, examples: Here's a problem that may appear, at face value, to be a "sampling problem" related to "race." We struggled in both cities to find "equally poor" and "equally working-class" African American, Latino, and white young adults so that comparisons by race/ethnicity would not be compounded by class. Guess what? The world is lousy with confounds. While we found poor and working-class whites, the depth of their poverty, their cross-generational poverty, their spread and depth of their poverty was nowhere near as severe as in the African American sample (see chapter 1).

White informants were sometimes as well off, but more often slightly worse off than their parents. But – and here's the *unacknowledged* impact of U.S. federal government subsidies in the 1940s and 1950s for the white working class/middle class – these young adults often had access to a small house or apartment their parents were able to buy; a small "nest egg" of cash the family has squirreled away; or the union-based pension Dad saved up. In contrast, our African American and Latino informants are in very tough financial straights but they are not, for the most part, worse off than their parents. Their parents rarely had a home, a small stash of monies, pensions that they could pass on. Further, some of our African American and Latino informants who have, themselves, amassed small amounts of capital over time, at some point lost it, when someone in the extended family bumped into a health crisis, a housing crisis, a problem with the law.

Our ambitious search for sampling comparability, despite our meticulous combing of raced neighborhoods, lost hands down to the profound "lived realities" of multigenerational poverty disproportionately affecting poor and working-class families of color. What may appear to be a methodological problem has been revealed as constitutive of the very fabric of society. Problematizing race alone does not help us confront the very real costs and privileges of racial categorization.

On "Bad Data"

Moving from worries of epistemology to worries about data, we excavate more headaches:

> MUN: *Do you feel that your word is not trusted, that you need someone else—you need a lawyer or psychiatrist to say everything is okay now?*
> TARA: *Because of DYFS [Division for Youth and Family Services], yes. They won't just take you for your word, no. You need to have—*
> MUN: *You need to have somebody else say that for you?*
> TARA: *Yes. DYFS, yes.*
> MUN: *How would DYFS treat your kids, though?*
> TARA: *Because when you get child, they say I put their life in danger, because I did, but I was . . . I was in jail, I was in the psychiatric ward. They had to do the best interest for the children; I couldn't take care of them at the time.*
> MUN: *Oh, so DYFS took your kids?*
> TARA: *Yeah, so DYFS gave them to their father. I'm in court now.*
> MUN: *At least it's not foster care, though.*
> TARA: *That's what I said. They're with family. They might hate it there, they can't stand it. My kids say that they're treated worse.*
> MUN: *They hate their father?*
> TARA: *No, they don't hate their father, they hate their grandmother, [my] mother-in-law. [And] they don't like their aunts, their uncles.*
> MUN: *They are a lot of Puerto Ricans?*
> TARA: *They're all Puerto Ricans, but my kids were always like the outcasts because they didn't like me, so my kids . . . you know, my kids got dumped into a family that they know nothing about.*

What does it mean to uncover some of what we have uncovered? How do we handle "hot" information, especially in times when poor and working-class women and men are being demonized by the Right and by Congress? How do we connect troubling social/familial patterns with macrostructural shifts when our informants *expressly don't* make the connections? The hegemony of autonomous individualism forces a self-conscious, imposed theorizing of data—especially "bad data" – well beyond the consciousness expressed by most of our informants. So, for instance, what do we do with information about the ways in which women on welfare virtually have to become welfare cheats – "Sure he comes once a month and gives me some money. I may have to take a beating, but the kids need the money" – in order to survive. A few use more drugs than we wish to know; most are wonderful parents but some underattend to their children well beyond neglect. These are the dramatic consequences, and perhaps also the "facilitators," of hard economic times. To ignore the data is to deny the effects. To report the data is to risk their likely misinterpretation.

In a moment in history when there are few audiences willing to reflect on the complex social roots of community and domestic violence, the impossibilities of sole reliance on welfare, and few even with a willingness to appreciate the complexity, love, hope, and pain that fills the poor and working class – how do we put out for display the voyeuristic dirty laundry that litters our data base? At the same time, how can we risk romanticizing or denying the devastating impact of the current assault on poor and working-class families launched through the state, the economy, neighbors, and sometimes kin?

Because of our early questions about both perspectives and representations, the interview schedule was originally created utilizing input from a group of activists and policy makers of varying racial and ethnic backgrounds from Jersey City and Buffalo, working with the research teams. Many questions were inserted to satisfy local concerns, for example, questions about police harassment, welfare reform and its effects on children born to women on welfare, state takeover of schools. Nevertheless, with data collection and analysis virtually completed, we continue to struggle with how to best represent treacherous data; data that may do more damage than good, depending on who consumes/exploits them; data about the adult consequences of child physical and sexual abuse; data suggesting that it is almost impossible to live exclusively on welfare payments encouraging many to "lie" about their incomes so that they feel they are "welfare cheats"; data in which white respondents, in particular, portray people of color in gross and dehumanizing ways; data on the depth of violence in women's lives, across race/ethnicity.

We spend much time reading through the *Handbook of Qualitative Research* (Denzin and Lincoln 1994), Gregory's (1993, forthcoming) ethnographies of Queens, Scheper-Hughes's (1992) analysis of mothering in poverty-stricken communities of Brazil, Connell's (1995) representations of white male identity formation in Australia, Dyson's *Reflecting Black* (1993), re-reading Gwaltney's *Drylongso* (1980) and Ladner's *Tomorrow's Tomorrow* (1971) to reflect on how to best write authentically and critically about the narratives offered, in ways that serve communities, theory, and public policy. We present these as dilemmas with which all field-workers must currently struggle. There is nothing straightforward or objective about reporting *or* withholding these data. Each strategic decision of scholarship bears theoretical, ethical, and political consequences.

On the Mundane
Sticking with dilemmas of data, we turn now to questions about mundane details of daily life.

> *Well, I take . . . I get $424 a month, okay? And I get $270 in food stamps, so I take . . . there's four weeks to a month, so I take . . . I take the $270 and I divide it by four. And that's what I spend on food. It's just me and my daughters. And my oldest don't eat that much and I don't eat . . . I only eat once a day. I only eat dinner. I'm not hungry in the morning and I don't have breakfast. I have a cup of coffee or hot chocolate. My little one is the one that eats a lot. And whatever I don't . . . like I spend $65 a week in food. I go and I buy meat every day and I buy their breakfast, their lunch, her snacks for school. And whenever I can . . . I work at night . . . I work . . . if I get a call I go and clean somebody's house. I do that. Their father gives me money, you know. So I do whatever I . . . you know, whatever it takes, you know? Shovel your snow . . . [laughs] I don't care. You know, to me money's money, as long as your kids got what they need. But basically their father helps me the most. You know, he'll come in . . . oh, my dad does this, too, and I get really pissed off at him. He'll come in and he'll start looking through my cabinets and in my refrigerator, and my closet. "Well, what do you have here?" And it's like, "I'm fine. Johnny's coming over*

later." "No! Blah, blah, blah." And he'll go out and he'll come back
with food, and their father's always coming in looking through the
refrigerator, and things like that, you know? I always . . . my kids have
food, so that's good, you know? They never go hungry. You know, I . . .
I hate to say this, but if I had . . . I mean, if it came to where my kids
were gonna go hungry, I'd sell my body. To hell with that! My kids ain't
gonna starve, you know? I'd do what it takes. I would give two shits.
People could . . . my friends could tell me whatever they wanted. I
have a . . . I have two friends that sell their bodies for money for their
kids. And thank God, I have to knock on wood, I never had to do that.
But I mean, if I had to, I would. If that's what it took to feed my kids
. . . I mean, if their father . . . a lot of people that are on welfare have
husbands worth shit. They don't care. If they had a father, but I guess
that's, if that's what it took . . . I would try every aspect before doing
that. But if that's what it really took to feed my kids, that's what I
would do. I would do whatever it takes to feed and clothe my kids,
you know, and put a roof over their head. I wouldn't care what the hell
it was. I guess that's what I would do, you know?

These are the dull and spicy details of negotiating daily life in poverty. When we listen to and read narratives we (researchers) tend, with embarrassment, to be drawn to, in fact, to *code for* the exotic, the bizarre, the violent. As we reflect, though, we nevertheless feel obligated to explore meticulously the very tedious sections of the transcripts: those sections not very sexy, exciting, or eroticizing. The mundane spots, when "they"–the informants–do what "we"–the researchers–admit that "we" do. Walk their kids to school, read the newspaper in horror, turn on the television for a break, look for a doctor they can trust, hope their children are safe on the way home from school. These mundane rituals of daily living–obviously made much more difficult in the presence of poverty and discrimination, but mundane nonetheless–are typically left out of ethnographic descriptions of life in poverty. They don't make very good reading, and yet these are the stuff of daily life. We recognize how carefully we need to be to *not* construct life narratives spiked only with the hot spots . . . like surfing our data for sex and violence.

On "Safe Spaces"

In our first Spencer study, we heard from young women and men who survived in the working-class and poor segments of our society, how they viewed economic opportunities, how they would spin images of their personal and collective futures, especially as related to the power of schooling, how they conceptualized the shrinking public sector, economy, labor, and the military, and how they reflected upon progressive social movements which have historically and dramatically affected their ancestors' and their own life chances. With respect to policies written allegedly *for* the poor and working class, our data enable us for the first time to hear from them. What we have tripped upon, however, and desperately need to explore further, are those pockets of possibility excavated by these young men and women. For amidst their despair lies hope, and hope is cultivated in these "safe" spaces.

These spaces offer recuperation, resistance, and the makings of "home." They are not just a set of geographical/spacial arrangements, but theoretical, analytical, and spacial displacements—a crack, a fissure in an organization or a community. Individual dreams, collective work, and critical thoughts are smuggled in and then reimagined. Not rigidly bounded by walls/fences, the spaces often are corralled by a series of (imaginary) borders where community intrusion and state surveillance are *not* permitted. These are spaces where trite social stereotypes are fiercely contested. That is, these young women and men, in their constant confrontation with harsh public representations of *their* race, ethnic, class, gender, and sexuality, use these spaces to break down these public images for scrutiny, and invent new ones.

These spaces include the corners of the African American church where young men huddle over how to "take back the streets" to "save the young boys;" the lesbian and gay center carved out quietly by working-class late adolescents and young adults, seeking identities and networks when their geographic and cultural contexts deny them sexual expression; the Head Start and EPIC programs in which poor mothers, and sometimes fathers, come together to talk the delights and the minefields of raising children in a culture showered in racism, decimated by poverty; the cultural arts programs where men and women join self-consciously cross racial and ethnic borders to create what is "not yet," a space, a set of images, a series of aesthetic products that speak of a world that could be.

Spaces such as these spring from the passions and concerns of community members; they are rarely structured from "above." They may be a one-time fiction, transitory, or quite stable. They can be designed to restore identities devastated by the larger culture or they may be opportunities to "flirt with" identities and community rejected by both mainstream culture and local ethnic groups. These spaces hold rich and revealing data about the resilience of young adults, without denying the oppression which threatens the borders and interiors of community life amidst urban poverty.

These "free spaces" (Boyte and Evans 1992) are rarely studied by social scientists. Typically we enter people's lives and communities and ask them the questions that titillate "us," creating "unfree spaces." As Keith and Pile (1993) argue, by asking questions of "arbitrary closure," social scientists fail to see the world as it unfolds and is reshaped by community members across "spacialities" and time. Typically, social sciences fix (our) gaze on public (or private) programs that are offered to low-income adults. Then we collect evidence of "their" noninvolvement—laziness, resistance, helplessness. But we now know that there is a rich underground to community life that is vibrant, alive, and fundamentally self-created. These are spaces designed by and for community, into which we, after three years of interviewing in Buffalo and Jersey City, have been invited. They may be transitory, healing, and mobilizing. They may be "official" or absolutely ad hoc. They may be a way to reconstitute traditional culture, racial, gender, or sexual identities, or they may be contexts in which individuals cross borders of race, ethnicity, gender, and sexuality to find a small corner in which to breathe in peace. These "free spaces," of which we have only glimmers, have raised a set of questions which need attention. When should these data about "private/free spaces" float into public view? Does the public/private distinction need to be problematized as Gubrium and Holstein (1995) have argued?

Legitimately one may ask (and some have) whether we have any business floating through, writing about these sequestered quarters. Do the conditions of our whiteness, femaleness, class status, and staccato appearances adversely affect or interrupt the music of life within "free spaces"? Does our social scientific voyeurism shatter the sanctity of that which is presumably (although recognizably *not*) "free"?

We come down on this question, for the moment at least, by presenting two different incidents. One occurred in a basement office in which New Jersey community activists meet to discuss local politics. We were welcomed for the initial interview, but the notion of our sustained presence clearly provoked a discomfort. Not asked to return, we left. In contrast, for instance, we have been invited into some spaces (for example, an EPIC parenting group, a black church, a lesbian and gay club) in which members, directors, and others indicate they are eager for documentation, anxious for others to know who they "really" are, what functions their programs serve, how deeply spiritual and religious "those teenage mothers" can be, how organized and supportive "those gays and lesbians" are. In these latter cases, informants have welcomed us into their spaces to "exploit" our capacity and willingness to write and to testify to those aspects of community life that the straight media ignore, that trenchant stereotypes deny, that mainstream culture rarely gets to see. Our rights, responsibilities, and relationships influence how (and if) we have access to these spaces.

There are lots of academics writing about these things, but few are really grappling with trying to meld *writing about* and *working with* activists within these communities (for wonderful such work, see Lykes 1989; Austin 1992). We try to work with communities and with activists to figure out how to say what needs to be said without jeopardizing individuals or presenting a problem that is universal as though it were "particular" to this class. And yet cracking *their silence* — especially among white working-class women who are exceedingly reluctant to discuss or reveal what goes on in their lives for fear that the ideology of domestic family life will crumble and their role as savior of the family will be exposed — is a feminist and intellectual responsibility fraught with dilemmas.

On Self-Reflexivity

We have certainly read much, and even written a fair amount, about researchers' subjectivities (Fine 1994). Our obligation is to come clean "at the hyphen," meaning that we interrogate in our writings who *we* are as we coproduce the narratives we presume to "collect." It is now acknowledged that critical ethnographers have a responsibility to talk about our own identities, why we interrogate what we do, what we choose not to report, on whom we shed our scholarly gaze, who is protected and *not* protected as we do our work. As part of this discussion, we want, here, to try to explain how we, *as researchers*, work *with* communities to capture and build upon community and social movements. In other words, we will put forward parts of our ever-evolving political agenda, sharing the kinds of scholarship/action that we are focusing upon. We draw from our past work to illuminate what's possible "at the hyphens" of researcher and researched (Fine 1994), and what feels impossible.

Thus far, in Jersey City and Buffalo, we have been able to document how state policies and local economic/social shifts have affected young women and men's belief systems, worldviews, social consciousness. Through individual interviews we have gathered much of these data. Through the focus groups, for example, in the lesbian and gay club, in the African American and white churches, in the EPIC parenting group, in the Latina homeless shelter, in the Pre-Cap program for young adolescents, we have been able to encourage settings in which our interviewees have begun to weave together analyses that weren't entirely formed, have begun to piece together their commitments, for instance, to the "next generation of African American boys," or to "practicing the ways of my grandmother" around Latina spiritual rituals. Sister Kristin, from the York Street Project, and Dolores Perry, from Head Start, have both invited us to work more closely with groups of women and men in their programs, running focus groups that would raise questions, press issues, and help the participants reshape programs. In the EPIC group, we were told that the involvement of several members was raised due to the kind of individual and group work we were engaged in. For these women, the group interviews offered a way of piecing together the strengths of their lives, involvement forward movement as they were raising their families in the midst of poverty.

Further, throughout the course of our three years of research, we have moved across the researcher-researched hyphen to apply our work to support local policy and community efforts. Michelle Fine testified at state hearings on the state takeover of local schools, advocating with community groups that the state remain in control until local participation can be encouraged and sustained. Research assistant Mun Wong coordinated a project among women on welfare who were eager to document the differential supermarket prices of similar items, at different points in the month and in different markets in the community; and we have provided census and qualitative data to city council members from the Latino community. Lois Weis supplied testimony in support of continual funding for EPIC. Across communities, numerous conversations have taken place with key policy makers on a number of issues arising from our data.

We take for granted that the purpose of social inquiry in the 90s is not only to generate new knowledge but to inform critical public policies, existent social movements and daily community life. A commitment to such "application," however, should not be taken for granted. This is a(nother) critical moment in the life of the social sciences, one in which individual scholars are today making moral decisions about the extent to which our work should aim to be "useful." Distinct camps are lining up with arrows nastily poised.

We have colleagues who embrace the commitment to "application," as we do, even if some think it is naive to imagine being able to infiltrate current policy talk on life within poor and working-class communities; other colleagues have long seen their own scholarship as explicitly aimed toward political and social change (see, for example, the work of Piven 1972; Lykes 1994; Mullings 1984; Powell 1994); and we hear a growing chorus of colleagues who presume that if you are interested in policy and/or social practice, your data are thereby less trustworthy. This latter position was perhaps in retreat for a moment in time, but it seems to be returning to the academy in well-orchestrated volume. We do, of course, reject this latter position, but would ask again that academics who see their work as deeply nested in community life (recognizing the notion of "community" is up for grabs) come together to argue cogently, responses to the litany of questions – "Is this science?" "Is *only* progressive work biased?" "Is this politics or policy?" We must probe fundamentally to discover where are the sites of intellectual leverage by which our work can begin to fissure public and political discourse. That said, we take our responsibilities to these communities seriously, and both of us are educating our graduate students to work with – not on or despite – local community efforts.

Throughout the design, the "doing," and the interpretation of our fieldwork, we talk and write about the anxiety (much of which is represented in this paper), the struggles, passions, and pains. But we ask now *how much* do we insert of our relatively privileged lives into essays when we are chronicling lives under assault from the economy, the state, within communities, and even homes? Yes, *we* write the stories, we determine the questions, we hide some of the data, and we cry over interviews. But self-conscious insertion of self remains an exhilarating, problematic, sometimes narcissistic task. What more do we say than we are two white Jewish women, deeply committed to a better world? The post-structuralist question of "who are we" is, indeed, an important one, but what does that mean as we weave together lives of passion, pain, and assault? A narcissistic look at self seems misplaced here. Whiting ourselves out seems equally wrong-headed.

So, in Whose Voice?

Tom, a white working-class informant, tells us:

> *It goes into another subject where blacks, I have nothing against blacks. Whether you're black, white, you know, yellow, whatever color, whatever race. But I don't like the black movement where, I have black friends. I talk to them and they agree. You know, they consider themselves, you know, there's white trash and there's white, and there's black trash and there's blacks. And the same in any, you know, race. But as soon as they don't get a job, they right away call, you know, they yell discrimination.*

In whose voice do we write? Well, of course, our own. But we also present long colorful narratives from informants in our scholarly and more popular presentations, essays, and articles. Some of these narratives, particularly from "angry white men," contain hostile or grotesque references to "others" – people of color, police, men on the corner. As theorists we refrain from the naive belief that these voices should stand on their own; or that voices should survive without theorizing. However, we also find ourselves *differentially theorizing and contextualizing* voices. That is, those voices which have been historically smothered – voices of white women, and men and women of color – we typically present "on their own terms," perhaps reluctant as white academic women to surround them with much of "our" theory. And yet, when we present the voices of white men who seem eminently expert at fingering African American men for all their pain and plight, we theorize generously, contextualize wildly, rudely interrupting "them" to reframe "them" (Weis and Fine 1996; Weis, Proweller, and Centrié 1997).

Is this an epistemological double standard in need of reform, or is it a form of narrative affirmative action, creating discursive spaces where few have been in the past? Hurtado and Stewart (1997) in a new and fascinating essay on "whiteness and feminist methods", argue that feminist scholars should self-consciously *underplay* (for example, not quote extensively) hegemonic voices in our essays and as relentlessly create textual room (quote) for counterhegemonic narratives. While we agree, we also think it is vitally important for us to analyze, critically, what it is that white men are saying about us, about "them," about economic and social relations. To do this, we interpret their words, their stories, their assertions about "others."

All of this raises what we have come to think of as the "triple representational problem." In our texts we ponder how we present (1) *ourselves* as researchers choreographing the narratives we have "collected"; (2) the *narrators*, many of whom are wonderful social critics, while some, from our perspective, are talented ventriloquists for a hateful status quo; and (3) the "*others*" who are graphically bad-mouthed by these narrators, for example, caseworkers blamed for stinginess by women on welfare; African American men who are held responsible for all social evils by white men; the police who are held in contempt by communities of color which have survived much abuse at the hands of police. Do we have a responsibility to theorize the agency/innocence/collusion of these folks, too? When white men say awful things about women of color do we need to represent women of color, denounce and replace these representations? If not, are we not merely contributing to the archival representations of disdain that the social science literature has so horrifically chronicled?

Since all these groups deserve to be placed within historical and social contexts, and yet power differences and abuses proliferate, how do theorists respect the integrity of informants' consciousness and narratives, place them within social and historical context, and yet not collude in or dignify this perverse denigration of people of color? In what seems like a too shallow resolution, we have diversified our research teams; hired local activists and community members, when appropriate, to consult with us on design and interpretation; and read, endlessly, in an effort to get out of these boxes. However, these issues are *not* being raised by those in the field. Perhaps defensively we notice that many of our friends and colleagues who now write on critical ethnography are writing about theory and methods, but not through *data*. Critical work on representations, post-structuralism, and ethnography has taken many of our once-in-the-field colleagues up and out, looking down now (as we have been wont to do) on a set of dilemmas that have nasty colonial pasts, and precarious futures. Those of us still in the field, "on the ground," so to speak, worry through this set of issues in highly concrete ways. We worry with no immediate resolution and only rare conversations. We know, though, that these points must be considered.

There are no easy answers to these dilemmas. In each of the chapters in this book, we have tried to contextualize the narratives as spoken within economic, social, and racial contexts so that no one narrator is left holding the bag for his/her demographic group, but indeed there are moments when, within the narratives, "others" – people of color, caseworkers, men, women, the neighbor next door – are portrayed in very disparaging ways. Then we are waged in the battle of *representation*. We work hard to figure out how to represent and contextualize our narrators, ourselves, and the people about whom they are ranting. We try, with the tutelage of historians Joan Scott (1992), Michael Katz (1995), and psychologist William Cross (1991) to understand how and why these categories of analysis, these "others," and these accusations are being cast at this moment in history, and who is being protected by this "scope of blame" (Opotow 1990). At times, however, audiences have nevertheless been alarmed at the language in our texts, at the vivid descriptions and the portraits. We are working on these issues, and welcome help from others who are also struggling with both theory and empirical data.

On a Disappearing Public Sphere

Tamara explains:

> I didn't want to be with the father of my children anymore. And at that time he really gave me a lot of headaches. "If you don't stay with me, then I'm not gonna help you with the kids." Which he really didn't do, which I'm thankful. But I just figured, "Well, the hell with it. Then I'll work . . . get the welfare." Because I pay $640 for this apartment. That's a lot of money for a two-bedroom apartment, you know? And the welfare only gives me $424, so I have to make up the difference. And plus I have a telephone, you know. I have cable for my daughters, you know. And it's just a lot of money. And I figure, you know, I figured, well, I couldn't make it on my own. I wasn't making enough to make it on my own back then, so I had to go on welfare. So I did it, and it was . . . I didn't like it. I didn't like sitting there. I didn't like the waiting. I didn't like the questions they asked me, you know?
> MUN: What kind of questions did —
> TAMARA: Well, they asked me if I was sexually active, how many times I went to bed with him, you know? And I told the guy, "I'm sorry, but that is none of your business" and I refuse to answer the questions. Because to me, well, what they ask you if you, he asked me if I slept with black men or white men, Puerto Rican men. What was my preference. And to me that was the questions —
> MUN: Was this on a form, or he —
> TAMARA: No, he was just asking questions, you know? And I refused to answer them, you know. And he kind of like got upset. "We have to ask you this." I was like, "Bullshit." You know, they just wanted to, they asked, he asked me how many times I had sex in a day, and just really, you know, if I douched, if I was clean, if I took a shower. I don't think these are any of your business, you know? I take a shower every night and every day, you know? I think those are stupid ques-

tions he asked. I was, he asked me how many men I had in my life that I had, you know, if I have more than one man. And I turned around and told him, "I'm not your mother." I never heard of questions like [laughs] . . .

MUN: *Neither have I [laughs].*

TAMARA: *They asked the weird questions.*

MUN: *So, how, what was the procedure like?*

TAMARA: *It was embarrassing. Like, with Medicaid, for kids it's good. For kids, you know, you can go anywhere you want with the Medicaid. You can go to the doctors for kids. You know, they pay for braces. When it comes to an adult, I was going to, I was hemorrhaging. I was going to a doctor. I'd been bleeding since December, okay, and they're telling me, I've been going to a gynecologist through the welfare. "It's normal, it's normal. Don't worry about it. It's normal." So last week I was getting ready, for the past week I was feeling really dizzy and really weak, and I said the hell with it. Let me go see a gynecologist. And I paid her. Thank God, you know, the Medicaid took care of the hospital. But I had to pay her $700 for the procedure that I had to have done [laughs]. I had to do it. It was either that or bleed to death, you know [laughs]. But a lot of doctors, I asked her, because she used to take Medicaid. And I asked her, "Why don't you, you know, take Medicaid anymore?" And a lot of doctors that don't, doctors tell you because they don't pay them. She said she's been waiting for people that were on Medicaid to get paid for two years, three years, bills, that's how old the bills are, and she's still waiting to get paid.*

We have collected data for the past five years on communities, economic and racial relationships and individual lives, deeply affected by public policies and institutions that had been rotten for many years before that. And yet these very same public policies and institutions, the ones about which we have deeply incriminating data, are today disappearing, yanked away from communities as we speak. Defunded. Public schools, welfare, social services, public housing. Positioning a critique of the public sphere as it evaporates, or more aptly, as it is decimated, seems an academic waste of time; worse, it anticipates collusion with the Right.

Our responsibility in this work, as we see it (and if it is doable) is *not* to feed the dismantling of the state by posing a critique of the public sector as it has been, but instead to *insist* on a state that serves well and equitably its citizenry. That is, social researchers must create vision and imagination for "what could be" and demand the resurrection of a public sphere that has a full and participatory citizenship at its heart. Then we can layer on the critiques of "what has been." That said — it's not so easy when Newt and others are just waiting to use our narrative words to do away with welfare; when Brett Schundler, Mayor of Jersey City, is pushing hard to get voucher legislation passed in a city in which public schools enjoy little to no positive reputation; when George Gilder and Charles Murray, conservative scholars, will gleefully abduct our phrases as they paint poor women as lazy and irresponsible. Creating a *safe space* for intellectual, critical, and complicated discussion when the Right has been so acutely talented at extracting arguments that sustain the assault may be a naive, but worthwhile, wish.

Responsibilities for Our Writing

We watch the apocalypse and write about it. What is the relation between what we see, the outrage we gather and feel, the relatively tamed texts we produce, and our audiences, many of whom are alternately too depressed or too cynical to be mobilized? We feel the weight of academics, that is, as public intellectuals who need to tell the stories from the side of policy that is never asked to speak; to interrupt the hegemony of elite voices dictating what is "good for them," and yet we feel the need to document, at once, the pain and suffering in these communities and the incredible resilience and energy that percolates. It is important to note, therefore, another "underground debate" within community studies which concerns the tension between representing historically oppressed groups as "victimized" and "damaged" *or* as "resilient" and "strong." This may seem an artificial and dangerous dichotomy — we think it is. But we have encountered colleagues within feminism, "critical race theory," poverty work, disability studies, and most recently queer theory, arguing across these intellectual stances, with these two "choices" carved out as the (presumably only) appropriate alternatives.

We share the worries, but worry more about the fixed "choices" that are being offered. Simple stories of discrimination and victimization, with no evidence of resistance, resilience, or agency, are seriously flawed, deceptively partial, and they deny the rich subjectivities of persons surviving amidst horrific social circumstances. Equally dreary, however, are the increasingly popular stories of individual heroes who thrive despite, denying the burdens of surviving amidst such circumstances.

We stretch toward writing that spirals around social injustice and resilience; that recognizes the endurance of structures of injustice and the powerful acts of agency; that appreciates the courage and the limits of individual acts of resistance, but refuses to perpetuate the fantasy that "victims" are simply powerless and collusive. That these women and men are strong *is not evidence that they have suffered no oppression.* Individual and collective strength cannot be used against poor and working-class people as evidence that "Aha! See, it's not been so bad!" We need to invent an intellectual stance in which structural oppression, passion, social movements, evidence of strength, health, and "damage" can all be recognized without erasing essential features of the complex story that constitutes urban life in poverty.

We take solace in the words of many of our African American male informants – drawn from churches and spiritual communities – who testify: "Only belief and hope will save our communities. We have come a long, long way . . . and we have much further to go. Only belief will get us through." Amidst the pain, the despair, survives hope. This, too, is a big part of community life, rarely seen in the light of day. It is time to recognize the full nature of community life.

Full Circle

Coming full circle, we are still a couple of white women, well-paid Thelma and Louise, if better protected with laptops, out to see the world through poor and working-class eyes, words, and stories that we collect across and within communities. We work with activists, policy makers, church leaders, women's groups, and educators in these communities trying to figure out how best to collect data that will serve local struggles, rather than merely document them. We are surrounded by wonderful students of all races/ethnicities, languages, and sexualities, and come to few conclusions with any illusion of consensus. We draw upon community activists and policy makers to help us invent interview questions and interpret the data; we use our data to write up "evaluations" for community programs surviving on shoestring budgets. We write through our own race and class blinders, and we try to deconstruct them in our multiracial and multiethnic coalitions. Decisions about design, sampling sets, interview schedule, interpretation, representation, and dissemination of findings have been developed, clumsily but broadly, through an open process among the research team, with consultation from community members. Questions have been added – and omitted – by research assistants and community members. Phrasing of questions concerning social class, language, neighborhood violence, and childhood abuse have been best articulated by people who know community life, needs for privacy and acceptable places for inquiry. Researchers can no longer afford to collect information on communities without the information benefiting those communities in their struggles for equity, participation, and representation. While such collaborations are by no means easy (see Fine and Vanderslice 1992, on participatory activist research), they are essential if social research is to serve the public good.

At base we are trying to work the hyphens of theory and research, policy and practice, whiteness and multiracial coalitions, and at this moment in history we find few friends who don't demand that we choose one side (or the other) of each dichotomy and stake it out! Our commitments to "floating across" satisfy few. Policy makers want clear, usually victim-blaming descriptions of social problems. Communities would prefer that we keep dirty laundry to ourselves. Some academics think we should stay out of policy talk and remain "uncontaminated" by local struggles. More than a few whites see us as race traitors, while a good number people of color don't trust two white women academics to do them or their communities much good.

In somewhat weak response, to colleagues and graduate students, we are trying to build theory, contextualize policy, pour much back into community work, and help to raise the next generation of progressive, multiracial/ethnic scholars. We try to position ourselves self-consciously and hope that our colleagues who are engaged in critical work and still plowing the fields for data will enter with us in this conversation about writing the wrongs (and rights) in the field. When ethnography came "home," informants moved next door and *read* our books. Academics were reluctant, remiss, too arrogant to clear up some of these questions of ethics, methods, and theory. Many of our colleagues, on the Right and Left, have retreated to arrogant theory or silly romance about heroic life on the ground. Others meticulously, and persuasively, deconstruct the very categories we find ourselves holding onto, in order to write a simple sentence about community life. We toil on . . . looking for friends, writing for outrage, searching for a "free" space in which social research has a shot at producing both social theory and social change as the world turns – rapidly to the Right.

TABLE A1

OCCUPATIONS BY YEAR FOR BUFFALO, SMSA, ALL PERSONS*

Year	Occupations					
	Managerial, and Professional Specialty	Technical, Sales, and Adm. Support	Service	Farming, Forestry, and Fishing	Precision, Production, and Craft and Repair	Operators, Fabricators, and Laborers
1960	19.2%	22.8%	10.1%	1.0%	16.8%	25.3%
1970	21.9%	25.4%	12.9%	0.6%	15.4%	23.6%
1980	21.7%	30.7%	13.9%	0.9%	12.5%	20.2%
1990	25.8%	32.7%	14.7%	0.9%	11.0%	14.8%
Absolute Change	6.6%	9.9%	4.6%	−0.1%	−5.8%	−10.5%
Net % Change 1960–90**	34.4%	43.4%	45.5%	−10.0%	−34.5%	−41.5%

*Occupations not reported 5.1%.
**(Absolute Change/1960 figure) × 100 = Net % Change 1960–90.

TABLE A2

OCCUPATIONS BY RACE AND GENDER FOR BUFFALO, SMSA, 1960–90

	1960				1990			
	Black		White		Black		White	
Occupations	Male	Female	Male	Female	Male	Female	Male	Female
Managerial, and Professional Specialty	0.6%	0.7%	70.6%	28.1%	2.0%	3.5%	48.0%	46.5%
Technical, Sales, and Adm.	0.7%	0.8%	43.2%	55.3%	2.0%	5.1%	28.7%	64.3%
Service	3.1%	8.9%	35.8%	52.2%	5.9%	16.5%	33.2%	44.4%
Farming, Forestry, and Fishing	1.2%	0.3%	87.3%	11.3%	4.2%	.0.4%	91.5%	3.8%

| Occupations | 1960 | | | | 1990 | | | |
| | Black | | White | | Black | | White | |
	Male	Female	Male	Female	Male	Female	Male	Female
Precision, Production, and Craft and Repair	2.4%	0.1%	95.3%	2.3%	4.6%	0.6%	87.9%	6.9%
Operators, Fabricators, and Laborers	7.9%	1.2%	75.3%	15.6%	14.2%	3.5%	64.8%	17.5%
Occupations not reported	7.9%	3.6%	56.5%	32.0%	...	...	...	...

TABLE A3

OCCUPATIONS FOR PEOPLE 16 YEARS AND OLDER

IN JERSEY CITY: 1960–1990

| Year | Occupations | | | | | | | |
	Total Employed	Managerial, and Professional Specialty	Technical, Clerical, and Admin. Support	Operators, Fabricators, and Laborers	Precision, Production, Craft, and Repair	Service	Farming, Forestry, and Fishing	Sales
1960*	112,172	13.9%	21.5%	31.6%	12.0%	10.6%	N/A	5.1%
1970	105,172	15.1%	26.1%	29.6%	11.0%	13.0%	0.2%	4.9%
1980	88,239	17.1%	27.7%	25.4%	9.6%	13.7%	0.3%	6.2%
1990	104,595	24.1%	26.3%	17.7%	7.7%	14.0%	0.4%	9.8%
Absolute Change 1970–90	577	9.0%	0.2%	−11.9%	−3.3%	1.0%	0.2%	4.9%
Net % Change 1970–90**	0.5%	59.6%	0.77%	−40.2%	−30%	7.7%	100%	100%

*5.4% of the people did not report an occupation and 1960 data were compiled for
people fourteen years and older.
**(Absolute Change/1970 figure) × 100 = Net % Change 1970–1990.

PERCENT OF PEOPLE 16 YEARS OR OLDER

UNEMPLOYED IN JERSEY CITY BY RACE: 1960–1990

Year	Population				
	General	White	Black	Asian or Pacific Islander	Hispanic
1960†	5.8	...	...	...	...
1970	4.2	...	5.7%	...	6.1%*
1980	9.8	8.5	12.9%	4.9%	12.4%**
1990	10.8	9.1‡	14.8%	5.8%	14.1%

†The unemployment rate is calculated for people 14 years or older.
‡The unemployment rate for whites drops to 7.8% when Hispanics are excluded from
this category.
*Only people from Puerto Rico.
**People of Spanish origin.

Sources for tables A1–A4: U.S. Department of Commerce, Bureau of Census (1962). *1960 census of the population and housing. Census tracts Jersey City, N.J., standard metropolitan statistical area.* Washington, D.C.: U.S. Government Printing Office. U.S. Department of Commerce, Bureau of Census (1972). *1970 census of population and housing. Census tracts Jersey City, N.J., Standard Metropolitan Statistical Area (PHC(1)-96).* Washington, D.C.: U.S. Government Printing Office. U.S. Department of Commerce, Bureau of Census (1983). *1980 census of population and housing. Census tracts Jersey City, N.J., standard metropolitan statistical area (PHC80-2-194).* Washington, D.C.: U.S. Government Printing Office. U.S. Department of Commerce, Bureau of Census (1993). *1990 census of population and housing. Population and housing characteristics for census tracts and block numbering areas. New York–Northern New Jersey–Long Island. Jersey City, NJ PMSA (1990-CPH-3-245D).* Washington, D.C.: U.S. Government Printing Office.

Data for this volume were collected primarily by means of in-depth interviews and focus group interviews. Desiring to find out how regular people, who constitute the poor and working classes, view contemporary social policies, prospects for work and education, satisfying family and spiritual life, engaging community involvement and social activism, we constructed an open-ended interview schedule which tapped a number of substantive areas. In consultation with graduate students and social activists, we developed a set of interview questions, which were then pretested in the field and revised as necessary. Questions targeted issues relating to neighborhood, schooling, experience with jobs, family, gender relations, violence, social activism, religion, racial and ethnic identification, children, and desires for the future, both one's own future and that of the children (see Appendix 3). The questions were open-ended, designed to encourage interviewees to talk about their experiences in these areas. All interviewers were extensively trained in qualitative techniques of investigation, with ongoing meeting and consultation as we moved through the interviews.

We adopted a quasi-life history approach in which a series of in-depth, two to five hour interviews were conducted with young people, twenty-three to thirty-five of varying racial and ethnic backgrounds in order to ascertain how these groups conceptualize and experience education, employment, and family in Jersey City and Buffalo. This research was designed to hear from young men and women who survive in the working class and poor segments of our society, how they spin images of their personal and collective futures, how they conceptualize the shrinking public and private sectors, and how they reflect upon progressive social movements which have historically and dramatically affected their ancestors' own life chances and those of their children. As policies are written today *for* the poor and working class, we have yet to hear from them. Our goal, then, was to unearth the "voices" of people usually not heard, and to excavate these voices across a range of life's activities.

We drew from a sample of young adults who have basically "followed the social rules" (attended school, often beyond high school), focusing on people who were connected to "meaningful urban communities." We selected "communities," defined not by geographic location alone (given what Wilson 1987, and Fine and Cook 1991, have found about the lack of connection and trust in low-income urban communities), but by meaningful social connections. Our goal was to generate a broad analysis of the "coming of age in urban America" during the 1980s and 1990s. We focused, in both cities, on four sets of urban institutions: (1) schools and post-secondary institutions, (2) churches and spiritual sites, (3) social agencies and self-help groups, and (4) community centers and activist organizations. All individuals whom we interviewed were involved in at least one of these institutions. So, for example, white, African American, and Latino men and women were drawn as equally as possible from across the four sectors in each city. Schools refer to either their childrens' school, or, in some cases, their own. Churches which serve the poor and working class tend to be Catholic in urban northeastern white communities, and Baptist and/or Holiness churches in the black communities. Latinos/Latinas were drawn from both Catholic churches and Pentecostal churches. Social agencies refer to those agencies which actively seek (and receive funding) to train and place those who attend their programs in literacy, job training, public assistance, or domestic violence. Community centers can at times double as social agencies, but also serve as spaces in which communities are drawn together; for example, a well-known community arts center located in the fruit belt in Buffalo, parental groups, a lesbian/gay center, and theater projects. In spite of our desires, it was not possible to come up with exactly equivalent numbers in each category. White men, for example, are less well represented in social agencies (because they tend to attend in fewer numbers) than the other groups, and Latinos are disproportionately represented in community centers, due to the prominence of particular community centers in the communities in which we worked. All in all, 154 black, white, and Latino/Latina men and women were interviewed across the two cities. (See table B1.) Over half of the Latino/Latinas were interviewed in Spanish, that being their language of choice for the interview.

Lists of potential institutions within each of the four target categories were drawn up and particular institutions were selected within each category, by racial and ethnic group and gender. Lois and Michelle went and met virtually all of the gatekeepers at each institution, explaining the purpose of the project and enlisting their help. Gatekeepers provided us with the actual names of inter-

INTERVIEWEES BY CITY, GENDER, AND RACE/ETHNICITY

	African American		White		Latino	
	Male	Female	Male	Female	Male	Female
Buffalo	18	15	13	15	11	10
Jersey City	12	16	14	12	7	11

viewees and, whenever possible, their phone numbers or ways to locate them (not all the people had phones). Once we had a list of names, we used the "snowball effect" in order to obtain additional names. We (Michelle, Lois, or our graduate students) contacted all individuals directly and set up interview times. Interviews were generally held at the institution from which names were obtained. Thus, interviews were conducted in churches, city schools, Head Start centers, social agencies, and various community centers.

We fanned out through Buffalo and Jersey City, working intensely with select institutions and the individuals we contacted. Interviews were generally conducted in two segments, spanning two to five hours total. Individual interviews took place over an eighteen-month period. Each interviewee was paid forty dollars for the interview. All interviews were tape recorded, with explicit conversations about confidentiality, anonymity, privacy, and informed consent. The tape recorder was fully visible on the table and all interviewees were invited to turn off the tape at any time, if they wanted information to be "off the record." Few availed themselves of this opportunity, however. Protocol was followed with respect to Human Subjects Review and all individuals were apprised of the purpose of the study and informed that their real names would not be used. Almost without exception, interviewees wanted to tell their stories—they felt that they had something to say and that nobody was listening. They ached to share their frustration at the lack of work; wanting to let the world know their disgust at the ways in which they were treated by the welfare office ("downtown"); desiring to let us know, and all the world know, their fears for their children in the midst of a drug economy that seemed to spare no one, and to some, an equally relentless police force. And we were there, promising to tell their story—assuring them we would write this book so that you would hear the analyses of the poor and working class at the close of the century.

Upon completing the individual interviews, all data were transcribed (put into hard copy) and input into either Hyperqual (Buffalo) or Ethnograph (Jersey City), computer-based analytic programs for qualitative data. Using traditional qualitative analysis techniques (Bogdan and Taylor 1975; Bogdan and Biklen 1982; and Goetz and LeCompte 1984), we read through over a quarter of the transcripts (across all racial, ethnic, and gender groupings) and established "coding categories" – labels through which the data could be chunked up and analyzed. These empirically developed coding categories added to our preestablished theoretically driven codes, ultimately numbering 184, and ranging from "Physical abuse," to "Where from," "Family when growing up," "Childhood fears," "Children," "What community means," and so forth. It is important to note here that in qualitative research most categories stem from the data themselves, as filtered, of course, through the investigators' eyes. In other words, few coding categories are predetermined by the investigator; the data have to "speak" to this category in order for it to be set up as one. Inter-rater reliability scores of at least 0.80 were established between raters for each code. Each category was assigned a shorter code ("Viol" for "Violence," for example), so that the coding itself was less cumbersome. We then took the code sheet and coded each interview, marking codes on the hard copy. Coding is done such that interview segments can be double coded or even triple coded; that is, one interview segment can be coded as "Church" and "Hard times," and "Father" at one and the same time. After coding on hard copy, the transcripts, which were input into the respective programs, were coded on the screen. We found the qualitative analysis packages useful in this regard, although any word processing program can be set up to do the same, at far less cost. The packages were terrific as a filing system, but the actual analysis was done by us, using the sorted interview segments as the basis for our analysis. Once all data were coded on screen, print files were established and data were printed out by our gender and racial categories. A manila file folder was set up entitled "Current Employment, White Male," into which all utterances by white men related to current work were placed. A similar file on work was set up across all demographic groups, so that ultimately statements about work by white females could be compared with those by white males, for example. In this regard, it is noteworthy that no white male talked about domestic violence, whereas 92 percent of white females did. Since these men and women come from exactly the same communities (churches, schools, and so forth), this led to some of our theorizing as to the silence about this subject in this particular community.

Once data were all printed out and placed in appropriately labeled manila file folders (for example, "Neighborhood, Latino"), our analysis could begin. Michelle and Lois read and re-read all the full narratives as well as all somewhat decontextualized folders of data snippets, ultimately coming to conclusions about the broader themes which swirled through these stories. As noted throughout the book, the themes which circulated in each community were very different, thus leading to the chapters that we constructed. We must also point out that in qualitative research, the coding categories are constituted of, but not necessarily identical to the themes which constitute later writing. Coding categories are numerous, (in our case, 184), and they serve as a way of chunking up data so that they can be looked at. Once all data are examined in this way (it is impossible to analyze systematically thousands of pages of field notes or interview transcripts without coding), the categories are recombined by the investigators in order to produce the written research product. The process of setting up coding categories and the actual coding are extremely tedious and must be done exceedingly carefully. We and our graduate students engaged painstakingly in this process, over many months time. Coding categories and later on, themes, are not established at the whim of an investigator.

After conducting individual interviews, we conducted focus group interviews, interviews in which two to seven people met with us at one time in order to probe further issues that came out earlier (Morgan 1988). In Buffalo, focus groups were conducted in an early childhood center with five African American women; in a Catholic church with four white women; in an African American church with four black men; and in a Catholic church with three white men. (The overwhelming number of poor and working-class whites in Buffalo are Catholic.) With only two exceptions, all individuals who participated with us in the focus groups had participated in individual interviews as well. In Jersey City focus groups were conducted with a group of young Latina mothers; white men civil servants; African American, Latina, and white women on public assistance; an African American parenting group; a group of church-based African American men.

Data from the focus groups were coded similarly to those gathered in individual interviews, although different coding schemes were set up. Questions in focus groups were designed to extend topics which came out as important within gendered and raced communities. Thus the questions posed in each of the focus groups were very different. Groups met over a range of times, from one long substantive meeting to those which sustained themselves over a two-month period, and one, the African American men's group in Buffalo, which met again a year later.

We found that group interviews tended to be far more hopeful than individual interviews as we sat with interviewees through many a tearful individual session. While certainly tears flowed in the groups, other members of the group supported and jumped in to tell the tearful person how they had handled particular situations (either with men, children, welfare, or a job). The individual is not left so emotionally spent in a group interview as participants share their experiences, faith, and hope. While we try to do this in the individual setting, the ambiance of the group is much different and more hopeful things emerge. In both sets of interviews, we had available information on activist organizations, support groups, and/or therapists who would be available and willing to talk with our interviewees. We provided agency names to the interviewees if we felt that it would be useful. Ultimately, however, the decision to call these agencies had to be their own.

The process of analyzing the data took over a year. And then we began to write. Writing was truly collaborative in that Michelle, Lois, and a number of graduate students circulated working papers back and forth, (between five and ten drafts per chapter) before producing the final essays you see here. Although one of us always took the lead on a chapter, the final chapter reflects collaborative work at its best, drawing upon our strengths as we construct a volume which sets the voices of the poor and working class of a generation potentially at the center of the policy debates rather than at the margins, where they are now. As we close the century, it is important that those historically disenfranchised be heard. It is our hope that policy makers will take their stories seriously; our future as a nation depends on it.

Background Questions

1. Let's start with growing up. Can you describe your family?
2a. What did you love to do when you were growing up?
2b. What were the kinds of things that frightened you? Or things that you worried about?
3. Can you tell me about the neighborhood you live in now? How is it the same/different from the neighborhood you grew up in?
4. Would you consider moving? If so, why and where? If not, why not?
5. Do you have family nearby? Tell me about the family nearby.
6. How old are you?

Education

Questions 10–14 in this section were asked only in Jersey City. In Buffalo, comparable data were picked up in other questions.

1. Where did you go to elementary school? High school? Did you complete high school?
2. When you think back on your high school, what kind of student were you?
3. Can you tell me a story about your education, something that stands out, that you remember about any point in your education? How did you feel in that situation? In what ways have you changed since then? If a child or niece or nephew of yours were in the same situation today, what would you advise them to do?
4. Who were your best friends in high school? What did they do with their time? How would you describe them as students? What are they doing now? Are you surprised at what they are doing?
5. Did you like high school? Why or why not? What were the positive things about your high school experience? The negative things?
6. Think back to high school. What were your hopes and dreams for the future? Do you have or are you doing the things you dreamed about? Why?

7. Did you have responsibilities at home while in high school? Can you discuss them? Was it difficult to do these things and go to school at the same time? [Push on child care, taking care of the elderly, and so forth.] Think about your teenage years – outside of school.

8a. Did a particular person or persons influence your future decisions after graduation/leaving high school? If so, how? [Push on influence of counselors, parents, teachers, peers.]

8b. Did something in particular, once or over time, make you change your life? Was there an important event/person and/or experience that became a turning point for you? Did anyone or group provide important role models, messages, information, warnings, or experiences that you found particularly meaningful?

9. Did you think about continuing your education after high school? Did you? Why or why not?

10. When you left high school, did you think about attending college?

10a. [If the response is Yes] If so, what did you study? What kind of college were you interested in? Did you actually apply to a college? What happened? Did you attend? If not, why not? What was college like? Was it difficult? If so, why? [Probe whether studies were hard, hard to work, didn't you have enough money?] Did you accomplish what you went to college for? Did you complete your degree? Did college studies help you? In what way?

10b. [If the response is No] Why didn't you consider college? What was the biggest reason why you didn't consider college? What kind of work were you thinking of doing? Did you get a job in that area? If not, why not? Did you have the training needed for the job? Do you ever think you might like to go to college someday? What would convince you it was worth attending a college? Do you know what kinds of programs colleges offer? Do you know what it would cost to attend college?

11. If you didn't, do you intend to go on to school? Why or why not?

12. If you have a child in Head Start or preschool – how much parent participation can you do? How much would you like to? What gets in the way?

13. If you could change five things about Head Start or preschool, what would you change or improve?

14. What else needs to be offered to meet your needs?

Race

1. How do you define yourself in racial/ethnic terms? [self-defined]
2. Why do you respond the way you do? [In other words, why do you call yourself black as opposed to African American?]
3. Whenever we fill out forms, we are asked to put ourselves in a category. I'm going to give you a list. Where do you usually put yourself and why? What does it mean to you to be an(a):
    (1) African American man
    (2) African American woman
    (3) Latino/Hispanic man
    (4) Latino/Hispanic woman
    (5) White (non-Hispanic) man
    (6) White (non-Hispanic) woman
4. How would you describe relationships among the various races/ethnic groups in this community? Are there issues that divide you? Enable you to come together?

Work Experience

1. When you were in high school, what kind of work did you hope to do in the future? Do you do this work now? If no, what happened between then and now that you don't do what you had wanted to do? [Skip if information is picked up in the above section.]
2. What was your first work experience after high school? Did you stay there? Why or why not? How many hours did you work a week? Did you want to work more/less hours per week? Why didn't you? [Go on to get information on second, third job, etc. Discuss why they left each job.]
3. Where are you working now? Do you hope to stay there? What is good about the job? What would you like to see changed? Have you ever been in a union? What do you think of unions?
4. In five years, what will you be doing? What could get in the way of that? What could make it happen?
5. [If work experience] Can you tell me about a time at work, when you felt that you were treated unfairly? What did you do about it? If the same thing happened to someone you care about, what would you tell them to do?
6. Did you ever go through any job training? How did you get into this pro-

gram? What was your experience with this (these) program(s)? Did you get a job as a result of this program? Why or why not?

Alternative Income

1. Given that it is hard to get by these days, people sometimes use money or other things that they add to their regular income (for example: play the numbers, buy hot goods, sell hot goods). Do you sometimes use any of these things to get by? If so, what? (Remember your answer is confidential.)
2. Have you ever applied for welfare?
3. Did you receive benefits?
4. How would you describe that experience?
5. If you got welfare, would you be willing to go through the same procedures again? Why or why not?

Family

1. Do you have a partner (husband, wife, lover)? How would you describe your relationship?
2. When you were in high school, how did you think your personal life would look now? Does it? Why or why not?
3. How did you meet your current partner?
4. What do you see as the good parts of your relationship? What would you like to see changed? Do you think it will?
5. Do you think about leaving the relationship you are in? Who do you talk to about troubles in your personal life, if you have them? What do you worry about – children, violence, racism, daily hassles?
6. Describe a typical weekday in your home, beginning with the morning.
7. Describe a typical Friday night.
8. How do you and your partner spend your time when you are together? How do you spend most of your social time when you are apart?
9. Could you tell me about a situation in your relationship in which you feel that you were treated unfairly or not well? What did you do about it? If a friend were in the same situation, what would you suggest to her/him?
10. How would you like your life to look five years from how? Do you think it will look this way? Why or why not? [Stress personal life, but if you picked up in the earlier section, delete.]

11. Can you imagine a time when you got pregnant [women] or there was an unplanned pregnancy [men] and you didn't want a child, what would you do? What do you think your partner would say? If s/he did not agree with your decision, would that change your decision? Why or why not?

Violence

1. Have you ever had a negative experience in childhood or adolescence? People have a lot of different reactions to these experiences: silence, talking to a friend, confronting the person. What was your reaction? Did you do anything about it? What would you advise your own children to do about it if the same thing happened to them?
2. Have you ever experienced abuse in your family, on the streets, and at work? Verbal? Physical? Sexual? Under what circumstances. Did you do anything about it?

Gender

1. Think about the women and men in your neighborhood. Tell me about the images of women and men in this community. What are the kinds of things they do? What are the expectations for women/men? How do you feel about these expectations? Do you meet them?
2. How would you describe relations between women and men in your neighborhood? Are there issues that divide you? Enable you to come together?

Class

1. Think about your family when you were growing up. Was there ever a time when money was tight? Can you remember embarrassing situations when money was a problem? Can you remember a situation when you were proud of yourself or your family even though money was an issue?
2. What is your money situation like now? Did life get better, worse, stay the same over the last decade? What is the same and/or different?
3. Have these stories and memories of your life influenced your vision/ hopes for yourself, your children, family, and your community?

Social Movements, Political Organizations, and Activism

1. What does community mean to you? In light of what you've told me about your community and your neighborhood, let's talk about the

people you feel most comfortable with. What groups do you feel most attached to? What groups of people do you most care about? Feel responsible for?

2. What groups do you belong to? Do you belong to any organizations/ groups that try to change things in the community? If so, which ones? If not, why not?

3. Can you tell me how you got involved in your group work?

4. What social/political problems are you most concerned with today? If it were up to you, how would these problems be solved? What would make this happen?

5. Do you think your public school can have an impact on your community? How?

6. Do you have any sense of the several movements that are trying to help women and men gain social and political rights? For example, the women's/feminist or civil rights movement. Have these movements helped you or hurt you? In what ways? Do you identify with any of them? Why? Why not? Do you think these are important and relevant movements? Why? Why not?

Political Alienation and Institutions

1. There are lots of institutions in Jersey City/Buffalo that shape our lives: police, welfare, courts, schools, hospitals. Can you tell me about a time you had to struggle with one of these institutions for yourself or a relative? What happened?

2. Bill Clinton is now having town meetings across the country. If he came to Jersey City/Buffalo, what kinds of problems should be dealt with here? What specifically would you like him to do about it?

3. There are a lot of young men in jails. How do you explain this? Why do you think this is the case?

Coping

1. When you feel low, how do you cope with your problems? For example: sports, movies, sleeping, church, drinking, drugs, video games.

2. How do members of your family cope?

3. Has there been anything that has happened to your family recently that has added to your stress? What?

4. Do you belong to any self-help group? If so, how does the group help you cope? Would you consider joining such a group? Has anyone ever suggested you join? If so, why didn't you?

5. Do you go to church/temple/mosque? If so, why? If not, why not? What do you think about the church/temple/mosque?

Children

1. Do you have children? If so, how many?

2. Do they live with you? If not, who do they live with? Why don't they live with you?

3. Describe a time you spent with the child/children that will give me a good sense of your relationship.

4. If you take care of a preschool child, who takes care of the children when you are out? How do you pay for this child care? If you have school-age children, what do they do after school? Who takes care of them?

5. If you have a child in school, what kind of school does your child attend? Do you like the schools these children are in? Why or why not?

6. How involved are you with your children's schools? Would you like to be more involved? Why can't you? Who helps your child with schoolwork? Are you happy with the amount of time that you are able to help them? What do you like to do together?

7. What do you want your children to learn in school? Do you think they learn it? Why or why not?

8. What kind of student is your child? [Take each child separately.] Are you pleased with that?

9. How far do you want your children to go in school? Do you think they will go this far? Why or why not?

10. If you have problems/worries about your child, who do you talk to? Who can you rely upon? Who wouldn't you tell? Why?

11. What do you tell your children about schoolwork; about violence; about race relations; pride; how men and women get along; about being a man/woman? Can you tell me the kinds of things you think he/she should know?

12. What do you hope for your child's future?

Chapter 1

1. We complicate the term "Latino" in chapters 4 and 10; for the moment we rely on this term to reflect a group of men and women – almost all of whom, in this study, come from Puerto Rico.

2. There has been much debate regarding how it is that social identities are produced (or how individuals and collectivities produce themselves). Excellent work by Giroux (1991), Apple (1995), McClaren (1986), Lather (1991), Foley (1990), Willis (1977), McCarthy and Crichlow (1993), Levison, Foley and Holland (1996), Holland and Eisenhart (1990), MacCleod (1995), Wexler (1987), Hurtado (1996), bell hooks (1982, 1989), Michael Dyson (1996), Steven Gregory (1997), Patricia Hill Collins (1991), Leslie Roman and Linda Christian-Smith (1988), to name only some, pushes our thinking in this direction. We have participated in these debates (Weis 1990; Fine 1991; Weis and Fine 1993), and our work has been profoundly influenced by post-structuralist critiques of reproduction theorists (Bowles and Gintis 1976). We think it particularly important to acknowledge that one's perspective, or standpoint, influences strongly the ways in which one sees and ultimately experiences the world.

   Unfortunately, however, in all the theorizing about voices and standpoint, much of which we have contributed to, and still feel to be of enormous value, the fundamental importance of the economy in people's lives has been buried. Too much recent theorizing ignores the very real fact that people exist within a material realm and that this realm has impact on their lives through the economy, the state, and the body.

3. While we could have extended the sample to reflect the rapid growth of Asians and West Indians in Jersey City in particular, we decided to focus on the three racial and ethnic groups who form – at the moment – the "native" population base of both cities. An extension grant from Spencer Foundation is now helping us to collect data from recent immigrant groups.

4. African Americans have not shared equally in the nation's prosperity. They earn less than whites, and they possess far less wealth, whatever measure one may use. The table below presents data on income along with median wealth figures. The black-to-white median income ratio has hovered in the mid-50 to mid-60 percent-

age range for the past twenty years or so, Fluctuations have been relatively minor, and in many ways American society became accustomed to this standard of inequality. In 1988 results from SIPP (the Survey of Income and Program Participation, a Census Bureau instrument introduced in 1984 to track entry into and exit from participation in various government social programs) showed that for every dollar earned by white households, black households earned sixty-two cents.

The median wealth data expose even deeper inequalities. Whites possess nearly twelve times as much median net worth as blacks, or $43,800 versus $3,700. In an even starker contrast, perhaps, the median white household controls $6,999 in net financial assets (NFA) while the median black household retains no NFA nest egg whatsoever (Oliver and Shapiro 1995, 85–86).

WEALTH AND RACE

Race	Median Income	Median NW[a]	Mean NW	Median NFA[b]	Mean NFA
White	$25,384	$43,800	$95,667	$6,999	$47,347
Black	$15,630	$3,700	$23,818	0	$5,209
Ratio	0.62	0.08	0.25	0.0	0.11

Source: 1988 Survey of Income and Program Participation.
[a] Net Worth.
[b] Net Financial Assets.

5. The gap in the median household income between races has widened even in the ten-year period from 1980 to 1990. The median household income in 1990 for white households was $21,186 as compared with $13,042 among blacks. In 1980, however, the median income for whites was $12,617 as compared with $8,573 for blacks. This represents approximately a $4,000 difference in 1980 as compared with an over $8,000 difference in 1990 (census figures).

The mean income is also striking. In 1990, mean household income for whites was $27,367 as compared with $19,509 for blacks; in 1980, the mean income was $15,814 for whites as compared with $12,014 for blacks. This large increase between races from 1980 to 1990 is in spite of the somewhat higher proportion of blacks in the work force in the larger SMSA. Latinos in 1990 are in even worse shape than blacks relative to whites in Buffalo. Median income is $11,037 in 1990 and the mean income is $16,573. This latter figure represents mean household income; mean family income for Latinos in 1990 is $11,429. This contrasts with the mean family income of $27,645 for whites and $16,574 for blacks.

The proportion of people living in poverty in Buffalo is rising as well. In 1990, 18 percent of whites were living in poverty. This compares with 38 percent of blacks and 52 percent of Latinos. In 1980, only 14 percent of whites lived in poverty compared with 36 percent for blacks. Again, data for Latinos are not available prior to 1990. Poverty rates are climbing for all groups, but are climbing relatively more for whites than blacks.

Chapter 2

1. Some exceptions here include Kathy Borman's (1991) analysis of entering the labor force and Claire Wallace's (1987) qualitative study of school leavers in England. Recently William Julius Wilson (1996) provided qualitative data as well.
2. All respondents were asked the same set of initial probe questions, this being one of them. In this chapter we present data related to social critique. Critique tended to emerge by group in relation to different questions.
3. Phillippe Bourgois has explored this point recently in *In Search of Respect* (1995).
4. Derrick Bell makes a similar assertion in *Faces at the Bottom of the Well* (1992). Our thanks to Mwalimu Shujaa for pointing out that Malcolm X insisted as early as the 1960s that we must look beyond the poor to explain the health of the drug economy.

Chapter 3

1. A similar erosion of privilege existed for white working-class males in the southern United States after the Civil War. The obsolescence of white male overseers, sharecroppers, and others associated with the care and management of slaves following the Emancipation Proclamation found this group of white men "retaliating" for their felt loss of privilege through the organization of hate groups like the Ku Klux Klan.
2. There is some excellent recent theoretical work on the production of "whiteness." We have discussed this at length in the introductory chapter to Fine et al., *Off White* (1997), and essays in this volume are exemplary examples of such work. See also Frankenburg (1993), Morrison (1992), Roediger (1991), and Mohanty (1988).

Chapter 4

1. Our thanks to LaVonne Ansari for pointing out this pair of facts.

Chapter 5

* *Boricua* derives from *Boriquén*, the original name of the Island of Puerto Rico given by the Taino Indians.

** *El Barrio* means neighborhood and here refers to Spanish Harlem.

1. In this chapter and in chapter 10 we focus on Puerto Ricans. The focus on Puerto Ricans is not to deny the pan-ethnicization occurring in some Latino/Latina communities. In Buffalo, though, the community in which we did our work is virtually all Puerto Rican. Although the community is more varied in Jersey City, the interviewees were almost entirely Puerto Rican. For important discussion of pan-ethnicization, see Flores (1996).

2. Roberto is the only non–Puerto Rican in the group. He is from El Salvador.

3. An exception here is very light skinned blacks who have, over the years, "passed" as whites. This does not deny the racial order, however.

4. The fact that Puerto Ricans in the United States create a special "Puerto Rican" ethnic category, refusing, thus, to adopt the dichotomous black and white racial categories of the mainland, may suggest that Puerto Ricans consider themselves racially homogeneous, or that racism has escaped the island and the Puerto Rican population in the United States.

   The scholarly work on racism in Puerto Rico is quite limited. A doctoral dissertation from 1961 (Bouquet 1961) cites some pertinent studies. Although dated, these studies might still be useful for a clearer understanding of how racism is manifested in Puerto Rico. One study of two hundred prominent families from San Juan states that whiteness is associated with higher class while dark skin implies "certain restrictions to mobility into that class, mainly in social life" (Scheele 1956, cited in Bouquet 1961, 9) For lower-class Puerto Ricans, biracial social activities and intermarriage are more common and dark skin color "does not affect employment opportunities" (ibid., 10) The author concludes that "colored ancestry is a greater handicap among those of the upper than the lower class."

   Anecdotal evidence of racism in Puerto Rico exists. Consider, for example, the experience of Juan Valentin-Juarbe, co-author of the original manuscript from which this chapter draws, who grew up in Puerto Rico and has lived in the United States for twenty-two years. During that time Juan has returned to Puerto Rico regularly. There he is seen as a "Jabao," a light-skinned person with light eyes, African features, and light curly hair. He states, "I have experienced and continue to experience racist attitudes which are part of the Puerto Rican culture. A common teasing during elementary school included being called 'Negro.'" Ironically, the term "Negro" can also be used as a term of endearment without any color connotations.

   Further complicating the possible assumption that racism does not exist among Puerto Ricans is the opening in the summer of 1996 of a new play, *Un mime en la leche (A Bug in the Milk)* by a San Juan playwright. Its theme concerns the homecoming of a lost relative, whom, much to everyone's chagrin, turns out to be a black man.

5. Although Juan embraces the notion of "machismo," there has been critique of this idea as applying only to Latin cultures. See Andrade (1992).

Chapter 6

1. Data presented here are drawn from Jersey City. We do, though, speak to the two-city sample since data drawn from both cities are, by and large, remarkably similar by gender, race, and ethnicity.

2. The Latinos in Jersey City offer a critique of the police that is far more expansive than that offered by Latinos in Buffalo. We explain this discrepancy based on both the physical proximity of Jersey City to New York, where discourses of police harassment and abuse are rampant, and on the long, painful history of corruption in the Jersey City public sector. With respect to city hall, the schools, and the police and fire departments, Jersey City has had a long history of patronage and favoritism "cleaned up," in part, only recently. And yet on the ground, community-based suspicion of the schools, the mayor's office, the police and fire departments remains widespread, particularly in communities of color.

3. The following table is drawn from data provided by the U.S. Department of Justice (1995).

AFRICAN AMERICANS AND DRUG POSSESSION

Population Group Studied	African American Percentage
U.S. Population	12%
Monthly Drug Users	13%
Drug Arrests	35%
Drug Conviction	55%
Prison Sentence	74%

Note: Data are for 1992 or 1993 depending on the most recent available figures.

Chapter 7

1. The violence that these women do narrate is a violence of the past, not current. This raises important theoretical and methodological cautions about women's self-reports of current violence. As Fine and MacPherson (1995) describe in research with adolescent girls, a critique of hetero-relations is more likely to be nar-

rated *in retrospect* than about a current relationship. Stories take time to construct and stories of trauma take much time to utter, let alone construct. Thompson (1994), in a study of women's experiences with eating problems, writes, "Like many qualitative anthropologists and sociologists, I am not sure there is such a thing as a complete story: future experience keeps adding to and revising what the present offers. Partial truths and circuitous narratives of lived experience are often the closest approximation of the whole story available" (24). Lived stories take time and space to construct and these women tell stories of the past. A woman in a study conducted by Kidder, Lafleur, and Wells (1995), which examines women's recollections of "the sexual transformation of professional relationships," later recalled "sexual harassment," offers more clues to the lack of current violence narrations. She describes her feelings of guilt and shame after a professor sexually harassed her and adds, "I can say this now that it's history." She wonders if she could have avoided the incident. The women in Jersey City and Buffalo have a language for domestic violence as evidenced by their descriptions of past abuse, a language to which women of previous generations may not have had access. They are, therefore, not "preverbal" in Kidder, Lafleur, and Wells's sense. However, like the woman in this study, the women we interviewed may seek safety in history, a place where guilt and shame are not felt as immediate emotions.

2. At least in recent history – although current movement toward globalization has shifted many of these once secure white male jobs out of the country, out of the unions, out of the Northeast. See chaps. 1 and 2.

3. In fact, recent research suggests that separated women are the most vulnerable group for domestic violence, with divorced women next, and married women last. The National Crime Survey Data (cited in Stark and Flitcraft 1988), indicate that "whereas 15.6% of all assaults among married women are domestic, fully 55% of assaults among separated women are by a male intimate" (308). Kurz (1995) finds that 11 percent of women in their sample reported they are battered during separation as well as marriage. Four percent of the women stated that they were assaulted during separation even though they had not been assaulted during marriage. Our point here is that separating from an abusive partner is no guarantee that violence will end.

Chapter 8

1. This chapter has benefitted from discussion with Curlane Jones-Brown, Carolyn Thompson, and Virginia Batchelor.

Chapter 10

1. Latino culture is often seen to be machismo. According to Ramirez (1993), machismo is not only a Latin thing, and not only bad. Rarely highlighted aspects of machismo include strength, responsibility, and the preservation and protection of the family. For Latinos, masculinity embodies an ideology, a social construction which privileges attributes considered masculine and devalues attributes considered feminine. Those men who have to compete unsuccessfully for material goods, those men who are today trying to figure out what it means to be a man when there is no work, may become more likely to exhibit derogatory, stereotypic behaviors (Ramirez, 26–27). De La Cancela (1981) posits that in order to "expose the ideological underpinnings of the machismo construct, [one must undertake] an examination of the economic sphere in which Puerto Ricans find themselves" (11–12). He goes on to argue that generations of Puerto Ricans continue to represent an "acutely oppressed sector" of the North American population. Such a statement obviously supports a consideration of the material conditions of Puerto Rican men. De La Cancela would probably agree with Benmayor et al. (1987) that the experience of male socialization is neither homogenous nor categorical in nature. It is a dynamic process, full of contradictions and tensions.

2. One of our interviewers and colleagues, Rosemarie Roberts, a second-generation Latina of Cuban and Puerto Rican parents, reacts personally to the Latina narratives she helped collect and analyze: "I could hear our culturally bound 'promise' and the subsequent betrayal of that 'promise' as Latinas struggle through a reworking of gender, sexuality, and motherhood. With many walking a tightrope in the United States between violence and welfare, we find ourselves in the midst of a quiet revolution."

   She frames the voices we hear in this chapter in this way: "Latinas live under a cultural promise about gender and sexuality. Love and honor your man – cook his meals, clean his house, be available and ready when he wants to have sex, have and care for his children, and look the other way at marital infidelities, all the time working *una doble jornada* (working inside and outside the home). In return, he will agree to protect you and your children, work, pay the bills. Even if our mothers worked, which was often the case, our fathers were supposed to be treated as if they were the primary wage earners. Indeed, in the '40s and '50s and as early as the '30s, our fathers migrated here for better job opportunities. Jobs for both our mothers and fathers were easier to come by then. But times have changed. The loss of manufacturing jobs in the United States and the lack of social mobility between our mothers' generation and our own have created a radically different experience for us, Latinas coming of age in the '80s and '90s. The conditions necessary to be the perfect wife, work, cook, clean, and raise children have been stolen from us."

The Latinas we interviewed, all of whom presented themselves as heterosexual, started relationships with men intent on fulfilling the promises their mothers had made. Except soon they learned that the economic conditions for their men had slipped. It had become increasingly difficult for them to fulfill their end of the promise. They watched as these men were sucked into the dangerously seductive, momentarily lucrative, street life of drugs and violence. They saw how dead-end menial jobs with no opportunities for advancement dealt small and consistent blows to their sense of self. Hombre – be a man. Unlike their fathers, they could neither protect nor provide. These blows accumulated. Anger and seething rage turned inward toward self. And against the women and children they loved.

Rosemarie Robert's work has been supported under a National Science Foundation Graduate Research Fellowship. Any opinions, findings, conclusions or recommendations expressed in this publication are those of the author(s) and do not necessarily reflect the views of the National Science Foundation.

Chapter 11

1. The following table provides national data on college enrollment increases, identifying gender and enrollment status of students and the type of educational institution in which they are enrolled.

PERCENTAGE OF U.S. COLLEGE ENROLLMENT INCREASES, 1970 TO 1990

	Type of Institution		
	Four Year	Two Year	Graduate
Women			
Full-time	23.6%	11.1%	7.6%
Part-time	10.7%	17.1%	7.3%
Subtotal	34.0%	28.2%	14.9%
Women Subtotal	77.4%		
Men			
Full-time	4.8%	0.5%	2.5%
Part-time	5.7%	6.5%	2.6%
Subtotal	10.5%	7.0%	5.1%
Men Subtotal	22.6%		

Source: U.S. Bureau of the Census, Current Population Reports, Series P-60,
No. 178, U.S. Government Printing Office, Washington, D.C., 1992, p.6.

Chapter 12

1. The Spencer Foundation and Carnegie Foundation have generously funded our current work in these "free spaces." We are conducting a series of ethnographic investigations in three sites, in Jersey City, New York, and Buffalo.

Abramowitz, M. 1996. *Under attack, Fighting back: Women and welfare in the United States.* New York: Monthly Review Press.

Anderson, E. 1990. *Streetwise: Race, class, and change in an urban community.* Chicago: University of Chicago Press.

Andrade, A. R. 1992. Machismo: A universal malady. *Journal of American Culture* 15 (Winter): 33–41.

Anzáldua, G. *Borderlands—La Frontera: The New Mestiza.* San Francisco: Aunt Lute Books.

Apple, M. 1995. *Education and power.* 2d ed. New York: Routledge.

Aronowitz, S. 1992. *The politics of identity: Class, culture and social movements.* New York: Routledge.

Attar, B. K., N. G. Guerra, and P. H. Tolan, 1994. Neighborhood disadvantages, stressful life events, and adjustment in urban elementary-school children. *Journal of Clinical Child Psychology* 23(4): 391–400.

Austin, R. 1992. "The Black community," its lawbreakers, and a politics of identification. *Southern California Law Review* 65(4): 1769–1817.

Bambara, T. 1995. *The salt eaters.* Excerpted in *My Soul Is A Witness: African American Women's Spirituality,* edited by G. Wade-Gayles, 299–304. Boston: Beacon Press.

Bean, F., and M. Tienda. 1988. *The Hispanic population of the U.S.* New York: Russell Sage Foundation.

Bell, D. 1992. *Faces at the bottom of the well: The permanence of racism.* New York: Basic Books.

Bell, D. 1994. The freedom of employment act. *The Nation* 260: 708–14.

Belle, D. 1989. *Children's social networks and social supports.* New York: White.

Belton, D., ed. 1996. *Speak my name: Black men on masculinity and the American dream.* Boston: Beacon Press.

Benmayor, R., A. Juarbe, C. Alvarez, and B. Vazquez. 1987. *Stories to live by: Continuity and change in three generations of Puerto Rican women.* New York: Centro de Estudios Puertorriqueños.

Benmayor, R., R. Torruellas, and A. Juarbe. 1992. Responses to poverty among Puerto Rican women: Identity, community and cultural citizenship. Report to the Joint Committee for Public Policy Research on Contemporary Hispanic Issues of the Inter-University Program for Latino Research at the Social Science Research Council.

Blount, M., and G. Cunningham. 1996. *Representing Black men.* New York: Routledge.

Bluestone, B., and B. Harrison. 1982. *The deindustrialization of America: Plant closings, community abandonment and the dismantling of basic industry.* New York: Basic Books.

Bogdan, R., and S. K. Biklen. 1982. *Qualitative research for education.* Boston: Allyn and Bacon.

Bogdan, R., and S. Taylor. 1975. *Introduction to qualitative methods: A phenomenological approach to the social sciences.* New York. John Wiley and Sons.

Borman, K. 1991. *The first "real" job: A study of young workers.* Albany: SUNY Press.

Bouquet, S. 1961. Acculturation of Puerto Rican children in New York and their attitudes towards Negroes and Whites. Ph.D. dissertation, Columbia University.

Bourgois, P. 1995. *In search of respect: Selling crack in El Barrio.* Cambridge, England: Cambridge University Press.

Bowles, S., and H. Gintis. 1976. *Schooling in capitalist America: Educational reform and the contradictions of economic life.* New York: Basic Books.

Boyte, H. C., and S. M. Evans. 1992. *Free spaces: The sources of democratic change in America.* Chicago: University of Chicago Press.

Brickman, P., V. C. Rabinowitz, J. Karuza, D. Coates, E. Cohn, and L. Kidder. 1982. Models of helping and coping. *American Psychologist* 37(4): 368–84.

Brooks, M. G., and R. A. Sussman. 1990. *Involving parents in the schools: How can third party interventions make a difference?* Boston: Institute for Responsive Education.

Byrk, A., V. Lee, and J. Smith. 1990. High school organization and its effects on teachers and students: An interpretive summary of the research. In *Choice and Control in American Education*, edited by W. Clune and J. Witte. New York: Falmer Press.

Campbell, J., M. Poland, J. Waller, and J. Ager. 1992. Correlates of battering during pregnancy. *Research on Nursing Health* 15: 219–26.

Castelino, C. 1996. *Staying Put: Why, how, and to what effect do some battered women (re)-claim their home.* Unpublished dissertation proposal, Environmental Psychology Program, City University of New York Graduate Center.

Cole, J. 1995. Jesus Is a Sister. In *My soul is a witness: African American women's spirituality,* edited by G. Wade-Gayles, 299–304. Boston: Beacon Press.

Coley, S. M., and J. O. Beckett. 1988. Black battered women: A review of the empirical literature. *Journal of Counseling and Development* 66(6): 266–70.

Collins, P. H. 1991. *Black Feminist Thought: Knowledge, Consciousness, and the Politics of Empowerment.* New York: Routledge.

Collins, P. H., and M. Anderson. 1992. *Race, Class and Gender: An Anthology.* Belmont, Calif.: Wadsworth Publication Co.

Comer, J. 1986. Parent participation in the schools. *Phi Delta Kappan* 67(6).

Connell, R. W. 1995. *Masculinities.* Cambridge, England: Polity Press.

Crenshaw, K. 1989. *Demarginalizing the intersection of race and sex: A Black feminist critique of antidiscrimination doctrine, feminist theory and antiracist politics.* Chicago, University of Chicago Legal Forum: 139–67.

Crosby, F. 1976. A model of egoistical relative deprivation. *Psychological Review* 83(2): 85–113.

Cross, W. E., Jr. 1991. *Shades of Black: Diversity in African-American identity.* Philadelphia: Temple University Press.

Currie, E. 1993. Missing pieces: Notes on crime, poverty, and social policy. Paper prepared for the Social Science Research Council's Committee for Research on the Urban Underclass, Policy Conference on Persistent Urban Poverty, November, Washington, D.C.

Deaux, K., and K. A. Ethier. 1994. Negotiating social identity when contexts change: Maintaining identification and responding to threat. *Journal of Personality and Social Psychology* 67(2): 243–51.

De La Cancela, V. 1981. Towards a critical psychological analysis of machismo: Puerto Ricans and mental health. Unpublished doctoral dissertation, City University of New York, New York.

Delgado-Gaitan, C. 1991. Involving parents in the schools: A process of empowerment. *American Journal of Education* 102 (November): 20–46.

Denzin, N. K., and Y. S. Lincoln, eds. 1994. *Handbook of qualitative research*. Thousand Oaks, Calif.: Sage.

Downs, W. R., B. A. Miller, and D. D. Panek. 1993. Differential patterns of partner to woman violence: A comparison of samples of community, alcohol abusing, and battered women. *Journal of Family Violence* 8(2): 113–35.

Dyson, M. 1993. *Reflecting Black: African-American cultural criticism*. Minneapolis: University of Minnesota Press.

Dyson, M. 1996. *Race Rules: Navigating the color line*. Reading, Mass.: Addison-Wesley Publishing Co.

Edin, K., and L. Lein. 1997. *Making ends meet: How single mothers survive welfare and low-wage work*. New York: Russell Sage Foundation.

Edwards, R. 1979. *Contested terrain: The transformation of the workplace in the twentieth century*. New York: Basic Books.

Epstein, J. L. 1991. School and family connections: Theory, research, and implications for integrating societies of higher education and family. In *Families in Community Settings: Interdisciplinary Perspectives*, edited by D. G. Under and M. B. Sussman, 99–126. New York: Hayworth Press.

Fspin, O. 1995. "Race," racism, and sexuality in the narratives of immigrant women. *Feminism and Psychology* 5(2): 223–38.

Ethier, K., and K. Deaux. 1994. Negotiating social identity when contexts change: Maintaining identification and responding to threat. *Journal of Personality and Social Psychology* 67(2): 243–51.

Fagan, J., D. Conley, J. Debro, R. Curtis, A. Hamid, J. Moore, F. Padilla, J. Quicker, C. Taylor, and J. D. Vigil. 1993. Crime, drugs and neighborhood change: The effects of deindustrialization on social control in inner cities. Paper presented for the Social Science Research Council's Committee on the Urban Underclass, Policy Conference on Persistent Urban Poverty, November. Washington, D.C.

Fine, M. 1991. *Framing dropouts: Notes on the politics of an urban public high school*. Albany: State University of New York Press.

Fine, M. 1992. *Disruptive voices: The possibilities of feminist research*. Ann Arbor: University of Michigan Press.

Fine, M. 1994. Working the hyphens: Reinventing self and other in qualitative research. In *Handbook of Qualitative Research*, edited by N. R. Denizen and Y. S. Lincoln, 70–82. Thousand Oaks, Calif.: Sage.

Fine, M., and D. Cook. 1991. *Evaluation Reports "with and for parents."* Washington, D.C.: National Committee of Citizens for Education.

Fine, M., and P. MacPherson. 1995. Hungry for an us: Adolescent girls and adult women negotiating territories of race, class, and gender difference. *Feminism and Psychology* 5(2): 181–200.

Fine, M., L. Powell, L. Weis, M. Wong, eds. 1997. *Off white*. New York: Routledge.

Fine, M., and V. Vanderslice. 1992. Qualitative activist research: Reflections in methods and politics. In *Methodological Issues in Applied Social Psychology*, edited by F. B. Bryant, J. Edwards, R. S. Tindale, E. J. Posavac, L. Heath, E. Henderson, and Y. Suarez-Balcazar, Vol. 2. *Social Psychological Applications to Social Issues*, 199–218. New York: Plenum.

Fine, M., and L. Weis. 1996. Writing the "wrongs" of fieldwork: Confronting our own research/writing dilemmas in urban ethnographies. *Qualitative Inquiry* 2(3): 251–74.

Fine, M., L. Weis, J. Addelston, and J. Marusza. 1997. White loss. In *Beyond Black and White*, edited by Maxine Seller and Lois Weis, 283–301. Albany: State University of New York Press.

Flores, J. 1996. Pan-Latino/trans-Latino: Puerto Ricans in the "New Nueva York." *Centro* 8, 1(2): 171–86.

Foley, D. 1990. *Learning capitalistic culture: Deep in the heart of Tejas*. Philadelphia: University of Pennsylvania Press.

Foucault, M. 1980. *The history of sexuality.* Vol. 1. New York: Vintage Press.

Foucault, M. 1985. *Discipline and punish*. New York: Vintage Press.

Frankenberg, R. 1993. *White women, race matters: The social construction of whiteness*. Minneapolis: University of Minnesota Press.

Fraser, N. 1991. Rethinking the public sphere: A contribution to the critique of actually existing democracy. In *Habermas and the public sphere*, edited by C. Calhoun, 56–77. Cambridge: M.I.T. Press.

Fruchter, N., A. Galletta, and J. L. White. 1992, *New directions in parent involvement*. Washington, D.C.: Academy for Educational Development.

Furstenberg, F. F. 1996. Teen pregnancy and parenting: What is the problem? Paper presented at Wellesley College, Wellesley, Mass., April.

Gates, H. L., Jr., ed. 1986. *"Race," writing, and difference.* Chicago: University of Chicago Press.

Gelles, R. 1988. Violence and pregnancy: Are pregnant women at greater risk of abuse? *Journal of Marriage and Family* 50: 841–47.

Ginsburg, C. 1989. *Race and media: The enduring life of the Moynihan report.* New York: Institute for Media Analysis, Inc.

Giroux, H. 1991. *Postmodernism, feminism and cultural politics: Redrawing educational boundaries.* Albany: State University of New York Press.

Gittell, M., K. Vandersall, J. Holdaway, and K. Newman. 1996. *Creating social capital at CUNY: A comparison of higher education programs for AFDC recipients.* New York: Howard Samuels State Management and Policy Center.

Goetz, J., and M. LeCompte. 1984. *Ethnography and qualitative design in educational research.* Orlando, Fla.: Academic Press.

Gordon, L. 1993. Women's agency, social control and the construction of "rights" by battered women. In *Negotiating at the margins: The gendered discourses of power and resistance,* edited by S. Fisher and K. Davis, 122–44. New Brunswick, N.J.: Rutgers University Press.

Gregory, S. 1993. Race, rubbish, and resistance: Empowering difference in community politics. *Cultural Anthropology* 8(1): 24–48.

Gregory, S. Forthcoming. *Black corona: Race, class, and the politics of place.* New York: Ithaca University Press.

Gubrium, J. F., and J. A. Holstein. 1995. Qualitative inquiry and the deprivatization of experience. *Qualitative Inquiry* 1(2): 204–22.

Gwaltney, J. L., ed. 1980. *Drylongso: A self-portrait of Black America.* New York: Random House.

Hall, S. 1981. Moving right. *The Socialist Review* 55 (1): 113–37.

Hare, N. 1971. Will the real Black man please stand up? *Black Scholar* 2(10):35. Quoted in M. Blount and G. Cunningham, eds., *Representing Black men* (New York: Routledge, 1996).

Haug, F. 1987. *Female sexualization: A collective work of memory.* London: Verso.

Helton, A., J. McFarlane, and E. Anderson. 1987. Battered and pregnant: A prevalence study. *American Journal of Public Health* 77: 1337–39.

Hochschild, J. 1995. *Facing up to the American dream: Race, class and the soul of the nation.* Princeton: Princeton University Press.

Holland, D., and M. Eisenhart. 1990. *Educated in romance: Women, achievement, and college culture.* Chicago: University of Chicago Press.

hooks, b. 1982. *Ain't I a woman: Black women and feminism.* Boston: South End Press.

hooks, b. 1989. *Talking back: Thinking feminist, thinking black.* Boston: South End Press.

hooks, b. 1990. Yearning: Race, gender, and cultural politics. Boston: South End Press.

Howell, J. 1973. *Hard living on Clay Street: Portraits of blue collar families.* New York: Anchor Books.

Hsieh, C. C., and M. D. Pugh. 1993. Poverty, income, inequality, and violent crime: A meta-analysis of recent aggregate data studies. *Criminal Justice Review* 18(2): 182–202.

Hurtado, A. 1996. Strategic suspensions: Feminists of color theorize the production of knowledge. In *Women's Way of Knowing Revisited*, edited by N. Goldberg, M. Belenky, B. Clinchy, and J. Tarule. New York: Basic Books.

Hurtado, A., and A. J. Stewart. 1997. Through the looking glass: Implications of studying whiteness for feminist methods. In *Off white*, edited by M. Fine, L. Weis, L. Powell, and M. Wong, 297–311. New York: Routledge.

Ignatiev, N. 1995. *How the Irish became white.* New York: Routledge.

Institute for Puerto Rican Policy, Inc. 1992, March. *Puerto Ricans and other Latinos today in New York City.* Number 9/10. New York: Author.

Jaffe, P., D. Wolfe, and S. Wilson. 1990. *Children of battered women.* Newbury Park, Calif.: Sage.

Janoff-Bulman, R. 1979. Characterological versus behavioral self-blame: Inquiries into depression and rape. *Journal of Personality and Social Psychology* 37(10): 1798–1809.

Jencks, C., and P. Peterson, eds. 1991. *The urban underclass.* Washington, D.C.: The Brookings Institute.

Jones, A. 1992. *When love goes wrong: What to do when you can't do anything right.* New York: HarperCollins.

Katz, M. 1995. *Improving poor people: The welfare state, the "underclass" and urban schools as history.* Princeton: Princeton University Press.

Keith, M., and S. Pile, eds. 1993. *Place and the politics of identity.* London: Routledge.

Kidder, L., R. LaFleur, and C. Wells. 1995. Recalling Harassment, Reconstructing Experience. *Journal of Social Issues* 51(1): 53–67.

Kurz, D. 1995. *For richer for poorer: Mothers confront divorce.* New York: Routledge.

Ladner, J. A. 1971. *Tomorrow's tomorrow: The Black woman.* Garden City, New York: Doubleday.

Lareau, A. 1989. *Home advantage: Social class and parental intervention in elementary education.* New York: Falmer Press.

Lather, P. 1991. *Getting smart: Feminist research and pedagogy within the postmodern.* New York: Routledge.

Lemann, N. 1991. The other underclass. *Atlantic Monthly* 273(12): 96–110.

Levin, H. M., and R. W. Rumberger. 1987. Educational requirements for new technologies: Vision, possibilities, and current realities. *Educational Policy* 1(3): 333–54.

Levison, B., D. Foley, and D. Holland, eds. 1996. *The cultural production of the educated person: Critical ethnographies of schooling and local practice.* Albany: State University of New York Press.

Lorenzo, J. 1995. Nuyorican adolescents negotiating identities. Ph.D. diss. CUNY Graduate School and University Center.

Luker, K. 1996. *Dubious conceptions: The politics of teenage pregnancy.* Cambridge: Harvard University Press.

Lykes, M. B. 1985. Gender and individualistic vs. collectivist bases for notions about the self. *Journal of Personality* 53(2): 356–83.

Lykes, M. B. 1989. Dialogue with Guatemalan Indian women: Critical perspectives on constructing collaborative research. In *Representations: Social constructions of gender,* edited by R. K. Unger, 167–85. Amityville, New York: Baywood Publishing.

Lykes, M. B. 1994. Speaking against the silence: One Maya woman's exile and return. In *Women creating lives: Identities, resilience, and resistance,* edited by C. E. Franz and A. J. Stewart, 97–114. Boulder, Colo.: Westview Press.

Marsh, C. E. 1993. Sexual assault and domestic violence in the African-American Community. *Western Journal of Black Studies* 17(3): 149–55.

Marusza, J. 1997. Urban white working class males and the possibilities of collective anger: Patrolling Riley Road. *Urban Review* 29(2): 97–112.

May, M. 1987. The historical problem of the family wage: The Ford Motor Company and the five dollar day. In *Families and work*, edited by N. Gerstel and H. E. Gross, 45–62. Philadelphia: Temple University Press.

McCarthy, C., A. Rodriguez, S. Meecham, S. David, C. Wilson-Brown, H. Godina, K. Supryia, and E. Buendia. 1997. Race, suburban resentment, and the representation of the inner city in contemporary film and television. In *Off white*, edited by M. Fine, L. Powell, L. Weis, and M. Wong, 229–41. New York: Routledge.

McCarthy, M., and W. Crichlow, eds. 1993. *Race, identity and representation in education*. New York: Routledge.

McClaren, P. 1986. *Schooling as a ritual performance: Towards a political economy of educational symbols and gestures*. Boston: Routledge and Kegan Paul.

MacCleod, J. 1995. *Ain't no making it: Aspirations and attainment in a low-income Neighborhood*. 2d ed. Boulder: Westview Press.

Melendez, E., C. Rodriguez, and J. B. Figueroa, eds. 1991. *Hispanics in the labor force: Issues and policies*. New York: Plenum Press.

Mills, C. W. 1959. *The sociological imagination*. New York: Oxford University Press.

Mishel, L., and D. Frankel. 1990. *The state of working America*. Washington, D.C.: Economic Policy Institute.

Mishel, L., and J. Bernstein. 1994. *The state of working America 1994–95*. Washington, D.C.: Economic Policy Institute.

Mishel, L., J. Bernstein, and J. Schmitt. 1996. *The state of working America*. Washington, D.C.: Economic Policy Institute.

Mohanty, C. T. 1988. Under western eyes: Feminist scholarship and colonial discourses. *Feminist Review* 30: 61–88.

Moore, D. R. 1991. *The case for community and parent involvement*. Chicago: Designs for Change.

Moore, J., and R. Pinderhughes, eds. 1993. *In the barrios: Latinos and the under class debate*. New York: Russell Sage Foundation.

Morgan, D. 1988. *Focus groups as qualitative research*. Newburg, Calif.: Sage.

Morrison, T. 1992. *Playing in the dark: Whiteness and the literary imagination*. Cambridge: Harvard University Press.

Mullings, L. 1984. Minority women, work and health. In *Double exposure: Women's health hazards on the job and at home*, edited by W. Chavkin, 84–106. New York: Monthly Review Press.

Muñoz, V. 1995. *When something catches: Work, love and identity in youth*. Albany: State University of New York Press.

National Urban League. 1996. *The state of Black America*. New York: National Urban League, Inc.

Newman, K. 1993. *Declining fortunes: The withering of the American dream*. New York: Basic Books.

Oliver, M., and T. Shapiro. 1995. *Black wealth/white wealth: A new perspective on racial inequality*. New York: Routledge.

Omi, M., and H. Winant. 1986. *Racial formations in the United States: From the 1960s to the 1980s*. New York: Routledge and Kegan Paul.

Opotow, S. 1990. Moral exclusion and injustice: An introduction. *Journal of Social Issues* 46(1): 1–20.

Parker, B., and J. McFarlane. 1991. Identifying and helping battered pregnant women. *Maternal and child nursing* 16: 161–64.

Pastor, J. 1994. Possible selves and academic achievement among inner-city students of color. Master's thesis, CUNY Graduate School, New York, New York.

Perry, D. 1987. The politics of dependency in deindustrializing America: The case of Buffalo, New York. In *The capitalist city: Global restructuring and community politics*, edited by M. P. Smith and J. R. Feagin, 113–37. New York: Basil Blackwood.

Perry, D., and B. McClean. 1991. The aftermath of deindustrialization: The meaning of economic restructuring in Buffalo, New York. *Buffalo Law Review* 39: 345–84.

Piven, F. F. 1972. *Regulating the poor: The functions of public welfare*. New York: Vintage.

Piven, F. F. 1996. Was welfare reform worthwhile? *The American Prospect: A Journal for the Liberal Imagination* 27 (July–August): 14–15.

Polakow, V. 1993. *Lives on the edge: Single mothers and their children in the other America*. Chicago: University of Chicago Press.

Polikoff, A. 1978. Housing the poor: The case for *heroism*. Cambridge, Mass.: Ballinger Publishing Co.

Powell, L. 1994. Interpreting social defenses: Family group in an urban setting. In *Chartering urban school reform: Reflections on public high schools in the midst of change*, edited by M. Fine, 112–21. New York: Teacher's College Press.

Ramirez, R. L. 1993. *Dime capiitan: Reflexiones sobre la masculinidad*. Rio Pedras, Puerto Rico: Ediciones Huracan, Inc.

Reich, R. 1991. *The work of nations: Preparing ourselves for 21st century capitalism*. New York: A. A. Knopf.

Richardson, L. 1994. Writing: A method of inquiry. In *Handbook of Qualitative Research*, edited by N. K. Denzin and Y. S. Lincoln, 516–29. Thousand Oaks, Calif.: Sage.

Ritchie, B. 1996. *Compelled to crime: The gender entrapment of battered Black women*. New York: Routledge.

Rodriguez, C. 1989. *Puerto Ricans: Born in the USA*. Boston: Unwin Hyman.

Rodriguez, C. 1990. Racial identification among Puerto Ricans in New York. *Hispanic Journal of Behavioral Sciences* 12: 366–79.

Rodriguez, C. 1992. Race, culture and Latino "otherness" in the 1980 census. *Social Science Quarterly* 73(4): 930–37.

Rodriguez, C. 1994. *Challenging racial hegemony: Puerto Ricans in the United States*. In *Race*, edited by S. Gregory and R. Sanjek, 131–45. New Brunswick, N.J.: Rutgers University Press.

Roediger, D. 1991. *The wages of whiteness: Race and the making of the American working class*. New York: Verso.

Roman, L. G. 1993. White is a color! White defensiveness, postmodernism, and anti-racist pedagogy. In *Race, Identity, and Representation in Education*, edited by C. McCarthy and W. Crichlow, 71–88. New York: Routledge.

Roman, L., and L. Christian-Smith, eds. 1988. *Becoming feminine: The politics of popular culture*. Philadelphia, Penn.: Falmer Press.

Rubin, L. 1976. *Worlds of pain: Life in the working class family*. New York: Basic Books.

Ruddick, S. 1990. *Maternal thinking: Toward a politics of peace*. Boston: Beacon Press.

Sachs, K. B. 1989. Toward a unified theory of class, race and gender. *American Ethnologist* 16: 534–50.

Sachs, K. B. 1994. How Jews became white folks. In *Race*, edited by S. Gregory and S. Sanjek, 78–102. New Brunswick, N.J.: Rutgers University Press.

Sandefur, G., and M. Tienda, eds. 1988. *Divided opportunities: Minorities, poverty and social policy*. New York: Plenum Press.

Schechter, S., and A. Jones. 1992. *When love goes wrong: What to do when you can't do anything right*. New York: HarperCollins.

Scheper-Hughes, N. 1992. *Death without weeping: The violence of everyday life in Brazil*. Berkeley: University of California Press.

Schwab-Stone, M. E., T. S. Ayers, W. Kasprow, and C. Voyce. 1995. No safe haven: A study of violence exposure in urban communities. *Journal of the American Academy of Child and Adolescent Psychiatry* 34(10): 1343–52.

Scott, J. W. 1992. Experience. In *Feminists theorize the political*, edited by J. Butler and J. W. Scott, 22–40. New York: Routledge.

Sharff, J. W. 1987. The underground economy of a poor neighborhood. In *Cities of the United States: Studies in urban anthropology*, edited by L. Mullings, 19–50. New York: Columbia University Press.

Sidel, R. 1978. *Urban survival: The world of working-class women*. Boston: Beacon Press.

Sidel, R. 1990. *On her own: Growing up in the shadow of the American dream*. New York: Viking.

Sidel, R. 1996. *Keeping women and children last: America's war on the poor*. New York: Penguin.

Skocpal, T. 1996. Unraveling urban America. *American Prospect* 61: 20–25.

Smith, D. 1987a. *The everyday world as problematic: A feminist sociology*. Boston: Northeastern University Press.

Smith, D. 1987b. Women's inequality and the family. In *The women's movements of the United States and Europe: Consciousness, political opportunity, and public policy*, edited by M. F. Katzenstein and C. M. Mueller, Philadelphia. Temple University Press.

Smith, D. E. 1988. Femininity as Discourse. In *Becoming feminine: The politics of popular culture*, edited by L. G. Roman and L. K. Christian-Smith, 37–57. Philadelphia: Falmer Press.

Smith, T. 1982. *The powerticians*. Secaucus, N.J.: Lyle Stuart, Inc.

Spivak, G. C. 1990. Can the subaltern speak? In *The post colonial critic: Issues, strategies, dialogues*, edited by S. Harasym, 271–313. New York: Routledge.

Stack, C. 1974. *All our kin: Strategies for survival in a Black community*. New York: Harper and Row.

Stack, C. 1996. *Call to home: African Americans reclaim the rural south*. New York: Basic Books.

Stack, C., and L. M. Burton. 1994. Kinscripts: Reflections on family, generation, and culture. In *Mothering: Ideology, experience and agency*, edited by E. Nakano Glenn, G. Chang, and L. R. Forcey, 33–44. New York: Routledge.

Stark, E., and A. Flitcraft. 1988. Violence against intimates: An epidemiological review. In *Handbook of Family Violence*, edited by Dr. Von Haselt et al. New York: Plenum Press.

Steinmetz, S., and M. Strauss, eds. 1974. *Violence in the family*. New York: Dodd Mead.

Sullivan, M. L. 1989. *"Getting paid": Youth crime and work in the inner city*. Ithaca, N.Y.: Cornell University Press.

Sum, A. M., N. Fogg, and R. Taggart, 1996. The economics of despair. *American Prospect* 27 (July–August): 83–88.

Taylor, I. 1992. The international drug trade and money laundering: Power controls and other issues. *European Sociological Review* 8(2): 181–93.

Thompson, B. 1994. *A hunger so wide and so deep: American women speak out on eating problems*. Minneapolis: University of Minnesota Press.

Thorow, L. 1995. Companies merge, families break up. *New York Times*, September 3, p. 11.

Tienda, M. 1989. *Immigration and Hispanic educational attainment: Challenges for the 1990s*. University of Wisconsin-Madison, Institute for Research on Poverty.

Torres, A., and C. E. Rodriguez. 1991. Latino research and policy: The Puerto Rican case. In *Hispanics in the Labor Force, Issues and Policies*, edited by

E. Meléndez, C. E. Rodriguez, and J. B. Figueroa, 247–63. New York: Plenum Press.

Trinh, M. 1989. *Women, native, other: Writing postcoloniality and feminism.* Bloomington: Indiana University Press.

Wade-Gayles, G., ed. 1995. *My soul is a witness: African-American women's spirituality.* Boston: Beacon Press.

Wallace, C. 1987. *For richer, for poorer: Growing up in and out of work.* New York: Tavistock.

Ward, J. V. 1996. Raising resisters: The role of truth telling in the psychological development of African American girls. In *Urban girls: Resisting stereotypes, creating identities*, edited by B. J. Ross Leadbetter and N. Way, 85–99. New York: New York University Press.

Weis, L. 1985. *Between two worlds: Black students in an urban community college.* New York: Routledge.

Weis, L. 1990. *Working class without work: High school students in a deindustrializing economy.* New York: Routledge.

Weis, L. 1995. Identity formation and the process of "othering": Unraveling sexual threads. *Educational Foundations* 9(1): 17–33.

Weis, L., and M. Fine. 1993. *Beyond silenced voices: Class, race, and gender in United States schools.* Albany: State University of New York Press.

Weis, L., and Fine, M. 1996. Narrating the 1980s and 1990s: Voices of poor and working-class white and African American men. *Anthropology and Education Quarterly* 27:493–516.

Weis, L., A. Proweller, and C. Centrié. 1997. Re-examining "a moment in history": Loss of privilege inside white working-class masculinity in the 1990s. In *Off white*, edited by M. Fine, L. Weis, L. Powell, and M. Wong, 210–26. New York: Routledge.

Weiss, H. B., and J. C. Greene. 1992. An empowerment partnership for family support and education programs and evaluations. *Family Science Review* 5(1,2): 18–35 (Cambridge: Harvard Family Research Project).

West, C. 1992. Black leadership and the pitfalls of racial reasoning. In *Raceing justice en-gendering power*, edited by Toni Morrison, 390–401. New York: Pantheon.

Wexler, P. 1987. *Social analysis of education: After the new sociology.* New York: Routledge and Kegan Paul.

Whatley, M. 1991. Racing hormones and powerful cars: The construction of men's sexuality in school sex education and popular adolescent films. In *Postmodernism, feminism, and cultural politics: Redrawing educational boundaries*, edited by H. Giroux, 119–43. Albany: State University of New York Press.

White, E. 1985. *Chain change: For Black women dealing with physical and emotional abuse*. Seattle: South End Press.

Willis, P. 1977. *Learning to labour: How working class kids get working class jobs*. Farnborough, England: Saxon House.

Wilson, A. 1995. Foreword. In *Speak my name: Black men on masculinity and the American dream*, edited by Don Belton, xi–xiii. Boston: Beacon Press.

Wilson, W. J. 1980. *The declining significance of race: Blacks and changing American institutions*. 2d ed., Chicago: University of Chicago Press.

Wilson, W. J. 1987. *The truly disadvantaged: The inner city, the underclass and public policy.* Chicago: University of Chicago Press.

Wilson, W. J. 1996. *When work disappears: The world of the new urban poor*. New York: Knopf Books.

Wong, M. 1994. Di(s)-secting and di(s)-closing whiteness, "Two Tales from Psychology." *Feminism and Psychology* 4: 133–53.

Woodcock Tentler, L. W. 1979. *Wage earning women: Industrial work and family life in the U.S. 1900–1930*. New York: Oxford University Press.

Benmayor, R., 87, 89, 95, 208, 223, 226
betrayal, 207, 215, 216, 226; refusing the,
    225
biracial continuum, 97
black males, 23, 59–83; as discursive subject
    or object, 59; and school expulsion, 69.
    See also African American males
black men, 78, 155; and church, 61, 71–76;
    as fathers, 76; fathering children, 60; mar-
    ried, 60; "need to come together," 61;
    poor, 60, 70; and religion, 71; representa-
    tion of, 65; working-class, 60, 61; and vio-
    lence, 63
Black Panthers, 82
black women, 64, 76, 155, 186; college grad-
    uates and median income, 240; and do-
    mestic violence, 170; and religion, 71. *See
    also* church, prayer, religion
blacks, 20–25, 40–41, 44, 86; African Amer-
    ican, 97; and government programs, 26;
    have America's attention, 86; as lazy, 22,
    24–25, 41; and media, 58; and median
    family income, 85; in mixed neighbor-
    hoods, 47
blame, 19, 22, 122, 129–30; for own abuse,
    150–51; outside black community, 81;
    scope of, 282; self, 68, 194, 216
block: associations, 107; clubs, 45–47
Bluestone, B., 18
borderguards, 161–62
borderlands, 48
border-patrolling, 48, 76, 79, 155, 161
borders, 61, 253, 265; between home and
    streets, 162–69; of community, 48, 61, 76,
    79, 161; crossing of, 44; family, 169–74;
    patrolling, 76, 79, 155, 161–62; of public
    and private sectors, 174–81; of threat-
    ened violence, 169; of white working-
    class males, 39
boundedness, 100
Bourgois, Phillipe, 90, 165
Boyte, H. C., 253, 276
Brooks, M. G., 242
Buffalo (NY), 28–30, 35, 37, 42, 60–61, 67,
    76, 89, 90, 95, 103, 174, 207, 252, 263;
    changes in, 110; and crime, 109; Crimi-
    nal Index, 121; and deindustrialization,
    20, 37; drug dealers, 165; early childhood

program, 169; education in, 235; and
    EPIC, 201, 245; job loss in, 29, mean
    black income in, 24; mothers in, 188;
    North, 93; proprietary schools in, 238;
    poverty rate in, 40; and Puerto Rican
    fruit pickers, 88; and view of police, 123
Byrk, A., 242

Campbell, J., 151
capital, 230, 259, 270; flight of, 110; move-
    ment of, across borders, 28
capitalism, 107
caseworkers, 25, 27, 181, 200, 224, 237, 262,
    282; as gatekeepers, 179; white, 180
Catholic, 183; schools, 85
census data, 98–99, 190, 229, 236
child: advocacy, 190; birth of, and height-
    ened stress, 151; care, 162, 177, 193, 196;
    rearing, 186, 193, 200–201, 242, 245; sup-
    port, 115, 121–22, 152
childbearing (early), 192
childhood, 188, 197; programs, 201
children, 23–24, 45, 48, 54, 61, 76, 100; beat-
    ing of, 244; being protected, 113; to care
    for, 104; cared for by community, 119; co-
    ercive loss of, 198; communicating with,
    244; diminished resources for, 159; dis-
    abled, 260; effects of crime on, 108; and
    family interconnections, 174; and fa-
    thers, 162; futures envisioned for, 207;
    "giving up," 193–94; losing, 199, 200;
    losing custody of, 155; and mothers'
    working, 176; parents advocating for,
    243; poor, 203, 260; pride in, 203; pro-
    tected from rage, 153; protected from vio-
    lence, 154; Puerto Rican, 88–89; raised
    by kin "down South," 162; raising, 18,
    73; rearing, 186; removing, 190; as safe
    through God, 182; and schooling, 69;
    subjected to violence, 100; and urban vio-
    lence, 109, 111; and violence, 64; in
    working-class family, 137
church, 53, 61, 72, 75, 80, 82–83, 101, 182,
    184, 216, 248; African American, 275;
    and African American men, 74; black,
    71, 73, 252; for community, 76; as com-
    munity of worship and commitment, 76;
    that has failed, 232; leaders, 75; and man-

within, 215; dominant, 60, 81; oppositional, 67; popular, 49; Puerto Rican, 98–
99, 102, 208; in Puerto Rico, 90; revisionist definitions of, 206; shop-floor, 48;
street, 165; working-class, 39, 53
curricula (sexuality), 55
Currie, E., 108–9
custody, 194, 199, 200, 202, 248; battles, 195

data, 279, 280, 282–84; base, 272; treacherous, 272
day care, 50; home, 197
Deaux, K., 95–96
degrees, 230, 241; additional, 241; advanced, 229; college, 233, 235; market
value of, 240
deindustrialization, 39, 252, 263; and Buffalo, 20, 37
Delgado-Gaitan, C., 242
demography, 128–29
differential sentencing policies, 131
discipline, 50, 77, 99, 230; and abuse, 244; of
children, 249
diploma, 228, 235; high school, 61, 233;
trade value of, 233
discrimination, 24–25, 95
disinvestment, 19
Division for Youth and Family Services
(DYFS), 195, 198, 202, 271
divorce, 102–3
domestic violence, 81, 111, 115, 120, 123,
133, 147, 154, 185, 202, 207, 263, 272;
abuse, 198; across generations, 135; in
America's inner-city neighborhoods,
169; family knowing about, 172; in lives
of poor and working-class women, 170;
in relationship, 170; as permeating society, 134; public nature of, among poor African American women, 171; as theme in
women's lives, 134
dominance: male, 155; of men as waning,
137; waning, in all spheres, 58; waning,
in material sector, 52; in working-class
family, 47–48
domination, 221; masculine, 53
Downs, W. R., 136
downtown, 32, 181, 246. See also welfare
drinking, 32–33, 101, 103, 141; mothers,
144; and violence, 143

drug: addict, 114, 152, 232; addiction, 194;
arrests, 129; dealers, 32–35, 109, 165;
dealers, and deals gone bad, 166; economy, 36, 111, 163, 165, 169; markets, 109;
use, 129
drugs, 30–33, 62, 73, 79, 81, 108, 116, 154,
184, 194, 196, 198–99; dealing, 43; doing,
195; domestic cycle of, 122, 151; harder,
and gang behavior, 167; in neighborhoods, 215; selling, in neighborhood, 64,
163–64; at street level, 35; and urban terror, 110; used by informants, 272; war
on, 33, 36. See also cocaine, crack
Dyson, M. E., 179, 267

early childhood program (Buffalo), 169
earnings, 234–35
East Harlem, 165
Economic Policy Institute, 16; studies, 18
economic restructuring, 27
economics, 19, 213
economy, 28, 37, 81, 95, 179, 206, 280; American, 21; changing, 37; crack, 28; crushing the middle-class and poor, 159; dismantling of the, 217; drug, 31, 65, 71;
expansion of, 17; failing, 19; globalizing,
256; household, 162, 169; inhospitable,
134, 185; insular, in Puerto Rico, 87; and
men in jail, 117; new, 18–19, 21; place in
the, 107; restructured, 18–19, 60; sailing
overseas, 251; service, 37, 61; tight, 177–
78
Edin, K., 250
education, 30, 68, 97–98, 174, 192, 211; advanced, 241; bad, 233; benefits to disadvantaged, 228; cuts in public funds for,
87; good, 233; and hard living women,
134; higher, 191, 217, 235; as important,
229; investments in, 250; as political
problem, 232; public, 81, 233, 260–61;
sex, 55–56; system, 233; thirst for, 242
educators, 242; parent, 201
Effective Parenting Information for Children (EPIC), 201. See also Every Person
Influences Children
elites, 19, 37, 46, 206, 260; bureaucratic, 75;
business and professional, 255; white,
21–22, 28, 36, 86
employment, 17, 177; city, 138; and educa-

ments, 217; being rewritten, 206; and black men, 116; borders of, 100, 206; expectations, 100, 139; and fear, 109; police prejudiced by, 127; positions, 57; positions, in U.S., 128; redefining, 227; regimes, 100, 105–6; relationships, 52, 147, 213, 223; roles, 48, 52, 100, 104, 215; as socially constructed, 128; traditional conceptions of, 106; worlds of, 207

generation (story of), 206

generations, 109, 208; and child care, 198; and increased education, 241; stories passed across, 203; and wealth, 230; younger, committing crimes, 122

Generation X, 19

Ginsburg, C., 60

Gittell, M., 228, 235

God, 51, 53, 71–72, 75, 78, 152–53, 172, 245; connections to, 181; giving strength, 182–84; keeping people away from cocaine, 184

Gordon, L., 171

government, 33, 251, 255, 260; active, 256; benefits, 21, 41. *See also* Farmers Home Administration, food stamps, welfare; and drug economy, 36; interference, 256; listening, 82; selling inner city, 165

grandmothers, 210; raising grandchildren, 139, 169, 198; talking with children, 244

Gregory, S., 189

Gubrium, J. F., 276

guns, 30, 35, 43, 62, 79, 111, 118–19, 164, 174, 197, 223; registered, 124

Hall, S., 267–68

Haug, F., 203

Head Start, 201, 243, 247–50, 252, 275, 278

health: care, 202; insurance, 17, 201; national, 202. *See also* benefits, fringe benefits, Medicaid

Helton, A., 151

heritage (Puerto Rican), 89

heroin, 152

heterosexuality, 124, 147, 213; critique of, 221

Hispanic, 43, 90, 99; friends, 93

Hispanics, 20, 22–24, 94, 99, 106; crime per-

petrators, 113; as other, 41. *See also* Latinos

hitting, 144, 214; child, 215; toy, 219

Hochschild, J., 65–66, 82, 258, 261

"hombres," 87, 90, 100; rights, 105; work of, 106

home, 252; inadequate, 189; life, 156; space, 52–53, 56. *See also* living space

homeplace, 163

homesteading, 252

homework, 203, 222, 225, 241, 243

hooks, b., 163

hospital(s), 110, 150–51, 170, 173, 213, 284; state, 175; workers, 208

"hot" information, 271

household, 53, 107, 172; female-headed, 191; incomes, 240

housing, 87, 172; as expensive, 198; for profit, 75; public, 284

Howell, J., 134

Hurtado, A., 220, 281

hyphen. *See* working the hyphen

identities: gendered, 207; male, 100; new, 253; seeking, 275; white, 39

identity, 21; cultural, 91, 96, 100; formation, 21–22; Latino, 107; as white male, 61

ideology: domestic, 135, 149; of domestic life, 156; dominant, 81; of family, 89, 155, 216; family wage as, 138; gender/class/ race, 156; nuclear, 171

Ignatiev, N., 97

immigrant: anti-, policies, 206; benefits, 260; European, 208; forebears, 208

income, 26, 181; "equal," 234; gap, 40; inequality, 17; lying about, 262; mean family, 20, 40; median, 240; median, family, 17; real, 40; real, family, 21

incomes, 17; black median family, 86; combined, 209; median household, 240; Puerto Rican median family, 85; two, 40–41, 48–49

informants, 264, 267, 269–70, 280, 282

inner cities, 65, 259

inner city, 165; to black men, 60; as dangerous, 60; plight of, 168

institution(s), 74, 128; nuclear family as, 171; public, 189; welfare as, 181

Irish, 24, 97
Island, the (Puerto Rico), 86–88, 90–91, 96–97, 99
Italians, 24, 30, 41–44, 46, 93; and church, 48; and families, 51

Jaffe, P., 149
jail, 29, 34–36, 70–71, 110, 115, 121, 127, 151, 153, 198, 213, 223; black men in, 130; county, 124; men going to, 123; men in, 117; rise of, 159
Jencks, C., 18
Jersey City (NJ), 60, 71, 74–75, 89, 108, 139, 207, 252, 263; changes in, 110; and crime, 109; Criminal Index, 129; drug dealers, 165; education in, 235; and EPIC, 201, 243; Latinos in, 107, 123; mothers in, 188; police corruption in, 113; proprietary schools in, 238; Puerto Rican workers in, 88; raising children in, 245; schooling in, 233; schools, 228; shelter for battered and homeless Latinas, 153
Jews, 23, 97
Jim Crow legislation, 182
joblessness, 37, 207
job, 70, 121; availability, 64; first, as choice, 175; getting a, and proprietary schools, 239; market, 94; as men, 101; minimum wage, 181; openings, 177–78; opportunities, 228; security, 40; training, 131, 174, 239, 249
jobs, 23, 28–30, 32, 107, 139, 174, 181, 198, 210, 257; absence of, 130; blue-collar, 20–21, 138; clerical, 138, 208; and discrimination, 24; flight of, 110; focus on, 257; high tech, 29; lack of, 49; lack of, for men, 35, 60, 65, 116; and Latinas, 217; loss of, 29, 257; manufacturing, 35; masculine, 39; part-time, 175–76; privileged, 24; qualified for, 177–78; service sector, 40, 208; stable, 82, 109; training for, 31; wage, earning, 61; wage, paying, 193; well paying, to African American men, 88; white male, 28; white person getting, 92, 95; working-class, 40
Jones, A., 151
justice, 225, 263

Katz, M., 258, 282
Keith, M., 276
kids, 42–46, 66, 78, 92, 103, 177, 180, 184, 222; abused, 149; addicted to drugs, 168; in alcoholic family, 141–42; confronting, 197; and cops, 125; in the corner, 124; with degrees, 230; and domestic violence, 126; in inner city, 164; safety for, 170
killing, 30, 64, 196; feared, by father, 150; suspected, 147; threatened, 152
kin, 18, 161, 272; back home (Puerto Rico), 96; caring for, 122; children raised by, down South, 162; custody to, 202; notions of, 89; speaking to, about abuse, 150
King, Rodney, 35, 123, 261
Kurz, D., 136;

labor: costs, 256; force, 86, 207, 233, 259; force, Latinas in, 217; force, women in, 191; market, 213; market, blue-collar, 252; market, industrial, 20; market, problems of young workers, 233; market, racist, 159; market, and schooling, 229; mothering as, 188; secondary, 155; wage, 138; waged, 193; within household, 140; women's, 20
Ladner, J., 186
Lareau, A., 249
Latina women, 104, 109, 186, 198; believing police corrupt and violent, 124; calling a cop, 126; and cultural citizenship, 206; and disappointment in police and their men, 124; and domestic violence, 124–25, 170; and fear of public institutions, 189; in female-headed households, 191; and gender relationships, 213; and having a baby, 193; and home-based violence, 111; households, 27; importance of education to, 229; "living Latina," 206; and male violence, 121; mother, 248; and self, 209; and self blame, 216; socialized for subordination to men, 213; and strategic use of welfare, 223; as traditional, 217; working, 191; as young child reproducers, 221
Latino(s), 21, 40–41, 50, 85, 92, 95, 107,

ological, 198; boyfriend's, 173; close to
daughters, 169; and EPIC program, 245;
giving up children, 194; good, 189, 194,
198–99, 247; and Head Start, 247; helpful, 149; love, 104; nonviolent, 196; not
providing support to daughters, 148;
poor, 189; poor, as alone, 189; poor, as
culprits, 203; in poverty, 189; to, for protection, 188; of Puerto Ricans, 87, 209; as
role models, 78; and self-sacrifice, 104;
single, 144; taking temporary custody,
194; teenage, 277; of teenagers, 244;
white, 189; worried, and street culture,
165
mothering, 186, 189, 195; good, 186–87,
189, 197; good, alternative, 198; labors
of, 191; as natural, 187; in poverty, 188,
192; as work, 188; and working-class
women, 187
"mujeres," 89–90, 102, 104; and mamis, 90;
work of, 106
mulatto, 98
Mullings, L., 279
Munoz, V., 100, 104

NAACP, 232
National Urban League, 259
neighborhood, 32, 34, 41, 44, 79, 82, 107;
art center, 166; bad, 216; and church, 73;
as community, 168; contempt for, 165;
and drugs, 165; felt loss in, 52; filled with
violence, 62; as no longer close, 120; of
no trust, 111; now different, 163; Puerto
Rican, 95; quieter, 164; as rough, 163; as
terrifying for women and children, 122;
tough, in Buffalo, 43; watches, 45; white,
46–47; white, turned to black 34
neighbors, 156, 282
Newman, K., 39
New York (city), 84–86, 88, 96

Ogbu, J., 96
Oliver, M., 158, 159, 230
Omi, M., 61, 269
Operation Bootstrap, 87, 96
Opotow, S., 282
"other," 21, 47, 156–57, 280–81; black, 22,
41, 159; black, and brown youth as, 60;

foreign, 36; as lazy and violent, 46; neighborhood, 46; racial, 46
othered, 265
othering, 25, 265

papi, 209–10
parenting, 186, 242, 253; contemporary,
195; in poverty, 200
Pastor, J., 82
patriarchal: family, 102; household, 188;
mold of family, 261; structures, 101
patriarchy, 18, 107, 134, 213, 262; and
abuse, 88; public, of welfare, 181; Puerto
Rican, 87
pensions, 17, 29, 181, 257, 270. *See also*
fringe benefits
people of color, 18, 95
Perry, D., 37
Perry, Dolores, 245, 278
petition drives, 115–16, 132
Piven, F. F., 202, 261
Polakow, V., 188, 261
police, 31, 60, 64, 110, 127; as above the
law, 123–24; behavior, 36; black and
white, 31, 33–34; brutality, 31, 95, 110,
112–14, 117, 131; calling the, 152, 214;
as corrupt, 35, 114, 117, 123–24; as enemy, 34–35; as good guys bad for inner-
city residents, 62; harassment, 19, 28,
33–35, 65, 92, 110, 113, 116, 153, 181–
82, 219–20, 272; and Latino men, 123;
officer, 118–19, 124; protection, 115; as
protectors of community, 128; selling
inner city, 165; trust in, 112; as unresponsive to domestic abuse, 173; as
"us," 113; viewed as prejudiced, 127;
viewed by black women, 120–22;
viewed by Latina women, 124–27;
viewed by white women, 114–15
policies: economic, 57; social, 57
policy, 279, 285, 287
Polikoff, A., 198
Polish, 23–24
political: machine, 75; problems, 30
politicians, 78–80, 232; black, 86; Puerto Rican, 86
politics, 107, 208, 279; gendered, 128; racial,
124, 128

poor, 84, 107; black, 65; chronically, 18; communities, 111, 129; and education, 230; expelled from school, 69; inner city, 259; modes of existence, 138–39; mother, 187; and mothering, 187; pedagogy for, 188; people holding their own, 251; Puerto Rican, 86; Puertoriquenas, 100; punishing the, 36; undeserving, 188; urban, 168; and urban fears, 110; white men, 111; working, 88; young adults, 236; young adults, and violence, 127

positionality: gendered, 106; of white men, 61

post-structural, 265, 268–69, 280

poverty, 42, 89, 135, 158, 185, 198, 211, 243, 253; and child rearing, 186, 200; communities of, 109, 111; concentrated, 189; continued, 228; and crime, 108; cross-generational, 270; families in, 200, 202; impending, 148; on island of Puerto Rico, 86–87; and links between generations, 109; mothers living in, 196; rate, 17, 40; threatened, 149; white, 257; of white males, 20; work of mothering in, 187

Powell, L., 279

power, 217; buying, 235; economic, 134; of education, 229; gendered, 221; heterosexual, 221; male, 262; relations, 220; social, 75, 83

prayer, 72–73, 172, 182, 183–84, 252; to gods and spirits, 207

pregnant, 138, 147, 149–52, 211, 236, 245; becoming, too early, 192; Latinas, 193

prejudice, 93, 178

pride, 204; cultural, 206

prisons, 110; black men in, 130

privilege, 52; economic, 41; gender, 48; loss of, 40; male, 52, 57; white, 45, 57

privileging, 18; of white maleness, 27

public: assistance, 54, 141, 145, 201, 258, 260; services, 137; sphere, 159, 162, 174, 252, 259, 283

Puerto Rican: being, 87; culture, 90, 102, 208; descent, 157; family, 100; frog (*coqui*), 84, 90–91; parentage, 152; politicians, 86; sample of women, 206; space, 97

Puerto Rican men, 86, 94–95, 100–101, 106;

and cultural citizenship, 87, 89; expectations of women, 104 5; island-born, 88; on mainland, 90; providing for families, 106

Puerto Rican women, 86–87, 206; heading households, 217–18; in higher education, 217–18; in labor force, 217–18; as provider and mother, 100

Puerto Ricans, 32, 44, 93; as black or white, 98; citizenship, 95; and cultural citizenship, 87, 95; deteriorating relative position of, 85; identity as, 91; and labor force, 86; mainland, 99; and median family income, 85; as melting pot, 98; as minority, 96; and poverty, 86; as relatively advantaged, 96

Puerto Rico, 84, 96, 207; household in, 105; insular economy in, 87; occupying nostalgic place, 90; per capita income in 1991, 86; poverty in, 87; urban, 87

queer theory, 59, 285

quotas, 23–24; minority, 22

race, 21, 23, 99, 108, 110, 112, 186–87, 192, 231, 253, 270; as bipolar and castelike, 98; and black men, 116; of crime perpetrators, 113; and early pregnancy, 192; and fear, 109; formations, 230; and gendered violence, 136; groups, 110; in Latin America, 98; matters, 189; narrated biographies of, 38; notions of, 97; police prejudiced by, 127; positions, 57; positions, in U.S., 128; privilege, 28; Puerto Rican, 97, 99; as socially constructed, 128; as unstable aspect of biography, 267; white as, marker, 155

racial: categorization, 270; diversification, 47; status, 97; terms, 97

racism, 18–19, 28, 35–37, 64, 82, 92, 116, 189, 257; critique by African American men, 179; critique by Puerto Rican men, 94; and imprisonment, 130; and police, 30, 128; and race, 269

rape, 129, 147; at elementary school, 43

Reagan-Bush years, 191

Reagonomics, 49

reform: of schooling, 243; welfare. See welfare reform

Wade-Gayles, G., 162
wage: decent, 259; family, 17, 135, 137, 140; family, as advantageous to all family members, 138; family, as ideology, 138, 140, 148; growth and blacks, 240; labor, 177, 179; male, 155; minimum, 181, 241; white male, 158; world, 171
wages, 39, 45; declining, 17; hourly, 17; male, 18; real, 16–17, 191; of women, 18
war, 251; of maneuver, 61; of position, 61; zone, 123
Ward, J. V., 189, 221
wealth, 230; material, 189; social, 189
Weis, L., 19, 21, 70, 169, 279, 281
welfare, 26, 32, 54, 61, 110, 121, 131, 143, 158, 174, 176, 190, 202, 204, 222, 224, 257, 283; abuse, 21–22, 25–26; apply for, 180; benefits, 138, 158; "cheats," 21–22, 25, 27, 272; city, 201; corporate, 260; dismantling of, 202; and G.E.D., 236; hard living women and, 134; and job training, 239; office, 111, 188, 217; people, 25; Puerto Ricans on, 86; recipients, 27, 228; reform, 122, 135, 159, 236, 238, 241, 249, 260, 272; rolls, 181; site of, 179; state, 21; strategic use of, 223; system, 60, 177, 261. *See also* food stamps, government benefits
Whatley, M., 55, 56
White, E., 136, 250
white: elites, 86; families and wealth, 230; family forms, 159; males, 93; people, 91–92; women, 88
white males: and dominance in homes, 54; as minority, 23; working-class, and communities, 79; working-class, and women in labor force, 48
white men, 18, 58, 109; angry, 280; and assumed dominance, 133; and crime, 109; and discourses of loss, 38; and identity formation, 27; losing ground in economy, 131; as new minority, 22, 24; as privileged, 40; and racialized discourses of crime and punishment, 113; and schooling, 233; and sense of self, 39; taking no responsibility for growth of violence, 130; and trust in police, 113; working-class, 28, 159; young adult, 19, 20–28
white women, 24, 39, 57–58, 88, 109, 186;

and domestic violence, 111, 170; and early pregnancy, 192; and family silence about abuse, 154; and feminist language, 156; hard-living, 134–35, 143, 145, 148, 150–51, 153–54, 158–59; lives defined by family, 155; and male violence, 121; and nuclear family, 171; in paid labor force, 40; poor, 136; and settled living, 155; and trust of police, 114; and within-class violence, 156; working-class, 133–60; working-class, and attending church, 183; working-class, and domestic violence, 133–36
whiteness, 36, 40, 46, 159, 281; as racial identity marker, 156; and settled living, 155
whites: affluent, 157; as dominant other, 94; elite, 86; Euro-American, 97; and parochial schools, 230; urban, 257
wife: and domestic fight, 125–26; expectation of, 105; role of, 104, 138, 221
Wilson, W. J., 18, 189, 258, 259
witnessing, 215–25
wives, 48; beating of, 127; supported by men, 138
women, 22; battered immigrant, 171; being protected, 113; black, 64, 88; and college enrollment, 235; of color, 24, 39, 200, 240; diminished resources for, 159; disciplined, 214; divorced, 136; and domestic violence. *See* domestic violence; earnings of, 234; of family, 208; God with, 184; hard living, 134–35, 143, 145, 148, 150–51, 153–54, 158; keeping jobs, 29; knowing their place, 47; Latina, 88; in leadership role in family, 50; moving into labor force, 48; obedience from, 106; and prevalence of crime, 108; with resources, 189; role of, 154; as role models, 71; with settled lives, 134–35, 148, 150, 154, 158–59; subordination of, to men, 137; and support of black men, 79–81; and violence, 63; and wage growth, 17; white. *See* white women; in workforce, 18
Wong, M., 39, 279
work, 60, 153, 186; discourse on, 41; as gender role, 100; as male bastion, 100; of motherhood, 195–96; as necessity, 176; at night, 237; outside home, 105, 158; paid, 191; public sphere of, 176; public

world of, 140; in Puerto Rico, 87; as tradition, 100. *See also* jobs

workers: discouraged, 18; domestic, 208; educational, 189; employed, 18; factory, 208; and families, 16–17; lowered wages for women, 138; and nonworkers, 18; in Puerto Rico, 87; office, 208; social service, 189; unemployed, 18; urban, 96; young, and unemployment, 234–35

workforce, 254, 260

working class, 38, 107, 110, 158; abandonment of, 22; communities, 111, 129; and education, 230; high school, males, 21; male, 21; males as privileged, 40; males without steady family wage, 140; men, 60–61, 111, 159; modes of existence, 138–39; parents, 247; people holding their own, 251; Puertorriqueñas, 100; white, 18, 21, 37, 171, 257; white, and feminist language, 156; white, and living

situations, 171; white, males, and block clubs, 47; white, males, and economic loss, 40; women and domestic violence, 170; women and mothering, 187; women and working, 191; young adults, 236; young adults, and violence, 127

working the hyphen, 265, 278

Works Progress Administration (WPA), 259

young adults, 18, 231, 234, 252; death rates among, 221; poor and working-class, 236; poor and working-class, and education, 241; in U.S., 258; value of advanced degrees to, 233

youth, 30, 71, 77–78; African American, 76; African American, patrolling and armed, 82; inner-city black and brown, 60; problems associated with, 168; and urban violence, 109